TREASURES OF THE BRITISH MUSEUM

This Ticket entitles *Jn.º Chatfield* to a Sight of the **BRITISH MUSEUM,** at the Hour of *One* on *Wednesday* the *3* of *March* 179*6*. No Money is to be given to the Servants.

This Ticket had been preserved by M.ʳ Gough & was given

Treasures of the

BRITISH MUSEUM

MARJORIE CAYGILL

Colour photography by Lee Boltin

Published for the Trustees of the British Museum
by British Museum Publications Limited

Title spread illustration. South Front of the new British Museum from the corner of Great Russell Street and Bury Street, *c.*1860. William Simpson (1823–99) after E. Walker.

Half-title illustrations. The Porter at the entrance to Montagu House on the site of the present building. The Museum acquired its first home in 1754.

Admission ticket. In the 18th and early 19th centuries visitors were not permitted to wander unescorted.

Right. The great dish from the 4th c. AD treasure discovered on the edge of the Fens at Mildenhall (see Treasure). Diam. 60.5 cm (23.8 in)

Front flap. Asante lion, possibly a goldsmith's trial piece in brass. H. 6·2 cm (2.4 in)

Back flap. Gilded wooden inner coffin of Henutmehit, priestess of the god Amun, from Thebes, Egypt, 19th dynasty *c.*1290 BC. H. 1·88 m (6 ft 2 in)

Front. Bronze Egyptian cat, the living form of the goddess Bastet. Around the neck is a silver plaque bearing the sacred eye of Horus, on the chest is a winged beetle with a sun disc between its front legs. *c.*600 BC. Presented by John Gayer-Anderson (Pasha) and Mary Stout 1939. H. 29 cm (11·4 in)

Front. Decorated bronze mirror from Desborough, Northamptonshire found during digging operations for ironstone in 1908. Early 1st c. AD. H. 34·9 cm (13·7 in)

Back. Three items from the Hull Grundy gift of jewellery. Although most pieces are not individually of great importance the collection of some 1200 items is of great documentary interest and typifies the Museum's concern with history and with research.

The Trustees of the British Museum acknowledge with gratitude the support of Midland Bank International in the publication of this book.

© 1985 Trustees of the British Museum
Reprinted 1986
Published by British Museum Publications Ltd
46 Bloomsbury Street, London
WC1B 3QQ

British Library Cataloguing in Publication Data
Caygill, Marjorie L.
    Treasures of the British Museum.
    1. British Museum
    I. Title   II. British Museum.
    Trustees
    069'.09421'42   AM101.B87

ISBN 0-7141-2033-2

Designed by Roger Davies
Set in Monophoto Photina by August Filmsetting, Haydock, St Helens
and printed in Great Britain by W.S. Cowell Ltd, Ipswich

CONTENTS

Left. The staircase of the old museum in Montagu House, George Scharf the Elder, *c.*1845 with stuffed giraffes 'which looked so stiff and rigid as to have given one an idea that they had died under the influence of strychnia' (Cowtan).

Right. 'Nef' or ship-clock attributed to Hans Schlottheim of Augsburg (1547–1625) and probably made for the Holy Roman Emperor Rudolf II (*c.*1580–1600). H. 99 cm (3 ft 3 in)

PREFACE

John and Andrew van Rymsdyk, authors of one of the forerunners of this book, the first illustrated account of the British Museum, published in 1778, stated the perennial problem faced by all who produce volumes of 'Treasures of ...':

Now, in a Work of this kind, some Objects will always be found more *pleasing* than others, according to the different *Tastes*, Studies, and Geniuses of particular Men ... I leave my sensible Reader to judge whether it is possible to please every Body. Nature herself is not equally satisfactory, nor all different Dishes alike palitable. Therefore I came to a Resolution to chuse an Intermixture, which I suppose will consist of some Things fine, others middling, and a few *so so*, or perhaps but indifferent.

Today the selection in *Museum Britannicum, being an exhibition of a great variety of Antiquities and Natural Curiosities belonging to that Noble and Magnificent Cabinet the British Museum* appears a little strange. The van Rymsdyks painstakingly illustrated, *inter alia*, wasps' nests from Pennsylvania, an incrustated skull found in the Tiber, a penknife with a gold point used by a crooked alchemist, the head of a spear from Bannockburn and a brick from the Tower of Babel. They wrote of how to stuff a humming bird, of how blood-letting was invented by the Hippopotamus and on the funeral rites of the Greeks and Romans.

The Museum has some three to four million objects (more, if all the flints and sherds were to be counted separately). Any selection must still be arbitrary – no book could deal in detail with all the 'treasures' of the British Museum. However, the popular favourites are here – the mummies, the Sutton Hoo ship burial, the Rosetta Stone, the Oxus treasure, and the sculptures of the Parthenon, with some less well known items such as the Folkton Drums, the Godman collection of Islamic pottery, the Roubiliac Shakespeare, and the Bridge collection of Indian sculpture.

The intention has been to tell something of the background to the Museum's collections – who made and used these objects, how they reached the Museum – in short, to place them in a human context. In the Museum's archives there is much wonderful material, some of which has been drawn on here – the full story of the smashing of the Portland Vase in 1845, the tale of the bandits of the North-West Frontier of India related by the first European to see the Oxus treasure. A miscellany of characters appear – the Reverend Clayton Mordaunt Cracherode, an eighteenth-century semi-recluse whose entire life revolved round routine – daily walks up the Strand and a weekly watch regulation in Fleet Street – who contrasts with Captain James Cook whose aim was to venture 'not only farther than any other man has been before me, but as far as I think it possible for man to go'. There is Mrs Delany, married at seventeen to a man three times her age whom she hated, twice widowed and coming to the making of her brilliant paper mosaics only in her seventies. Artemisia sister-wife of the petty ruler of Caria, Maussollos, who built as her husband's tomb one of the seven wonders of the ancient world; the shadowy figure of 'Hindoo' Stuart who scandalised the European community of Calcutta and whose final act was to be buried in a miniature Hindu temple; Julius Classicianus, Procurator of Britain who appears briefly in Tacitus's *Annals of Imperial Rome* and his wife Julia daughter of Indus. And the unknowns – the Anglo-Saxon craftsmen who cut the four

A Maebyŏng vase, stoneware decorated in iron brown under a greyish glaze, 13th *c*. AD. H. 30·7 cm (12 in). The Museum has a fine collection of Korean ceramics and metalwork now widely appreciated by both collectors and potters.

Among the Museum's greatest treasures are the finds from the 7th c. AD Anglo-Saxon ship burial discovered at Sutton Hoo, Suffolk in 1939. The 'ghost' of the great ship, 89 ft long (27 m) is shown here being excavated.

thousand brittle Sutton Hoo garnets and embedded them in gold, the artists who produced the fearsome turquoise masks of Moctezuma, the master who carved the beautiful enigmatic scene on the Portland vase from a layer of glass one eighth of an inch thick. Many of the people associated with these objects left accounts of their discovery – who can forget Austen Henry Layard's description of the plain of Nimrud, where he was excavating, covered with so many flowers that the dogs returning from hunting were stained red, yellow or blue so heavy was the pollen through which they had passed; Charles Newton's picture of the veiled Turkish ladies of Bodrum watching, like those of Troy, the removal of part of a colossal horse from the Mausoleum; Max Mallowan's description of the 'Great Death Pit' at Ur – a golden carpet ornamented with the glittering beech leaf headdresses of the dead ladies of the court.

I hope that this selection, mostly 'fine', but perhaps some 'middling' will convey something of the fascination of the British Museum. In defence of the 'middling' I can only quote Sir John Addis, a great connoisseur and collector of Chinese porcelain who wrote of one of the lesser items in his collection 'a humble little dish like this can be more endearing than many grander pieces'. My own favourite object in the Museum, a small apple green bowl of Chinese porcelain, would never make the Museum's list of popular favourites.

I should like to express my particular thanks to Celia Clear who initiated and nurtured this project, to the book's editor Emma Myers, to their assistant Suzannah Gough, to the book's designer Roger Davies, and to Lee Boltin who enthusiastically took most of the colour photographs. To Midland Bank International are due immense thanks, for without them the book would be much less attractive.

The first illustrated book of the British Museum closed with this Apology of the Author:

In Authors Races for want of treading firm they often Slip, to publish a Picture, Book, etc. without *Errors*, is a very great Mistake; every Bean has its Black, and all things are *imperfect*. Though we look as keen as a *Hawk*, yet they will slide in unawares, nay even with open Eyes . . .

I am greatly indebted to my colleagues in the curatorial departments on whose published works I have drawn and who have patiently offered their specialist knowledge. Any errors which remain are mine.

MARJORIE CAYGILL

INTRODUCTION

by the Director,
Sir David Wilson

The British Museum (which opened its doors in Montagu House in 1759) was the first secular public museum of its kind in the world; more important, it was founded on the basis of the ideas of the French Encyclopaedists as a museum of universal knowledge, embracing within itself all human knowledge and representative of all human achievement. The Museum is today one of the handful of major museums in the world built on these principles – only the Smithsonian Institution in Washington in any way outstrips the breadth of its collections. The ideals of the founders have remained relatively intact. Although the Library and the Natural History collections have been transferred elsewhere, the British Museum still attempts to cover virtually the whole field of human endeavour within a comparative historical framework.

The Museum's functions are to collect, preserve and exhibit; but collecting is at the heart of any museum and to collect in a universal museum is the most exciting of all activities. This book aims to provide an insight into this continuing pursuit. It deals largely with the activities of our predecessors but it should be stressed that this is an activity which never stops. While the Museum tries, as it has always done, to acquire for the national heritage and to fill gaps in its existing collections it also seeks objects made in the present century, thereby continuing a long tradition. If members of the Museum staff such as Sir Augustus Wollaston Franks had not acquired, for example, early nineteenth-century porcelain within fifty years of its being made, the Museum's holdings in this area would not be as thorough or as comprehensive as they are today. The wise collecting of Franks and Henry Christy built up in the nineteenth century a worldwide collection ranging from America to China, from Africa to Norway, which played a part in bringing to the Museum its reputation for comparative antiquarian learning which persists today.

The Museum is popularly known as the home of mummies, Egyptian sculpture and the 'Elgin marbles', but there are many surprises for those who come to Bloomsbury or Burlington Gardens. In recent years, for example, the Museum has ventured more systematically into the modern

field. In the new Modern Room of the Department of Medieval and Later Antiquities alongside German tea and coffee sets of the 1930s, Russian Revolutionary plates, Tiffany glass, there is a teapot designed by Marianne Brandt of the Bauhaus. This is perhaps one of the most startling objects the Museum has bought in the last few years, but it is after all only a logical extension of our collection of European silver plate which goes back to the Roman treasure from Mildenhall by way of such material as the Huguenot silver (of which the Museum has a most remarkable collection). Oriental objects have long been collected in some quantity but among the Chinese bronzes, Mughal paintings, Islamic metalwork, etc. there is a new departure, the acquisition of a significant collection of modern Japanese prints which has established the Museum as the most important centre for this material in Europe. An expanded policy of buying modern western prints has resulted in exhibitions of American prints and of German Expressionist prints almost entirely from our own collections, many of which have been acquired over the last five years. We now have also a greatly expanded collection of modern medals. Parallel with this, ethnographic collections are being made in the field all over the world. The Museum has for example financed work in Papua New Guinea and recently bought a splendid group of traditional Guatemalan textiles at the last possible moment before modern imports take over. We are now working in Madagascar as well as in many other countries.

Enshrined in the British Museum Act of 1753 is the statement that the Museum was founded to the end that it may 'be preserved and maintained not only for the Inspection and Entertainment of the learned and curious, but for the use and benefit of the Publick'. Any part of the Museum's collections is freely available to those who can show that they have a reasonable demand on them. Artists and connoisseurs have been and are stimulated by free access to the Print Room, many students have been given the opportunity to examine in detail, with some of the world's greatest scholars, the highest products of man's achievement. The international service rendered by the Museum to the academic world through its open-handed service to scholarship and to the general public through its loans service is practically unique and we are jealous of our reputation in this respect. No museum publishes more widely or allows the scholar from outside to publish its material more freely. No museum services more international institutions with aid.

The British Museum is a great international institution, one of only a handful with vast universal collections actively curated and constantly growing. It is a living entity and in itself an important part of the world's cultural heritage. It aims to give pleasure, stimulation and instruction to all who can be tempted within its doors. This book is written in the hope that those who have visited the Museum will understand it better and that those who have not will be encouraged to use it.

Silver teapot, lightly hammered with a pierced strainer inside. German, 1924, designed by Marianne Brandt (b.1893) and made at the Bauhaus, Weimar. H. 7 cm (2·8 in)

Top. Naoko Matsubara (1937–). *Walden Pond*, cover for the portfolio which includes 11 prints illustrating the essay 'Solitude' from H.D. Thoreau's *Walden*. This print, in tones of green and white, is the most expansive and the boldest in the portfolio. 1971. 42 × 80.5 cm (16.5 × 31.7 in).

Left. *Little penthouse* (1931) by Martin Lewis (1882–1962). Born in Australia, Lewis came to America in 1900. One of the best-known American printmakers in the 1920s and 1930s his sales slumped after the War. This is one of a series of etchings of New York observed under different weather and lighting conditions. Drypoint. 25·3 × 17·7 cm (10 × 7 in)

TREASURE

I

TREASURE TROVE

Many such ancient treasures lay in the tumulus, where in times gone by an unknown man had carefully hidden the immense ancestral wealth of some great race. All had long been dead; and the chieftain who survived them, disconsolate at the loss of his kinsmen, supposed that, like them, he would possess their slowly gathered wealth for a short time only. Ready to hand upon a cliff near the sea stood a newly completed barrow ... Into this the guardian of the hoard had carried rings and beaten gold, the richest part of the treasure. He said: "Earth, hold what men could not, the wealth of princes ..."

Beowulf, transl. David Wright, Penguin, 1957, from an Early English manuscript in the British Library

Thus the Anglo-Saxon poet described the burial of a fine hoard. By the time of the Anglo-Saxons Europe was already rich in buried treasure and more was to be consigned to the earth in later centuries. Some treasure was abandoned with the pagan dead, some accidentally lost and much concealed until the owner might return – war-chests of ravaging armies, life savings of timid merchants or other rich citizens fleeing the terror of invasion or civil war, hastily concealed contents of jewellers' workshops, thieves' loot, misers' gold, the savings of prudent yeomen. Much of this treasure unclaimed by its one-time owners is now in the Museum.

The concealment of treasure and the laws governing its discovery are of great antiquity. In Job iii, 21, for example, there is a reference to those who long for death 'but it cometh not; and dig for it more than for hid treasures'. The first recorded reference in Roman law appears about 200 AD when the jurisconsult Julius Paulus laid down that:

Thensaurus est vetus quaedam depositio pecuniae, cuius non extat memoria, ut iam dominium non habeat ... (Treasure is an old deposit of money, of which the memory is no longer extant, so that it now no longer has a master ...).

Such treasure belonged to the finder. Sir George Hill, who wrote the standard work on the subject in 1936, quotes the earliest piece of medieval legislation known, an enactment of Charlemagne made about 789 which lays down that of treasure found on private land three-quarters goes to the king, one quarter to the landowner. The first known statement as to the law of treasure trove in England occurs in *Leges Henrici*, compiled about 1114–18, where it is mentioned as a right which the king has alone and above all men in his land; in the 'Laws of Edward the Confessor', written down at about the same time it states on the other hand that 'Treasures from the earth belong to the King, unless they be found in a church or a cemetery ...'

Not all treasure is therefore 'treasure trove' according to English law for in England 'treasure trove' now consists of:

Objects of gold or silver (including coins, plate and bullion) which have been hidden in the soil or in buildings, and of which the original owner cannot be traced.

This definition is qualified by the provision that there must have been on the part of the person concealing the treasure *animus revertendi*, that is an intention to return. Objects buried for eternity in a grave are not treasure trove, nor are accidental losses or votive offerings to the gods. It is for a Coroner's inquest to decide whether or not these criteria are met and on its verdict rests the claim to ownership. Except for some bodies who are allowed to claim treasure found on their land for themselves, treasure trove is the property of the Crown. For some time the Crown has at the beginning of each reign ceded its claim to the Treasury and in turn the Treasury permits the British Museum to have first refusal of such finds. In return, and to encourage complete and prompt disclosure, the Museum via the Treasury will make an *ex gratia* payment of the full market value to the finder (not the landowner if they are not the same person, nor the finder's employer or foreman) provided that the find has been properly declared and there has been no attempt at concealment. An independent Reviewing Committee, advised by the Museum, determines the value. If the Museum does not want the objects they may be offered to other museums on similar terms, eventually being returned to the finder if there are no takers.

Thus over the centuries the law has been refined and the inhabitants of England have actively sought, or more frequently stumbled across, treasure trove. Treasure seekers of the Middle Ages could follow complicated procedures with magic spells, today's treasure hunter is more likely to go out with a metal detector. The chances of a major find are however akin to a large win in a lottery. It cannot be too often repeated that treasure hunters should leave excavation to archaeologists (a properly dated find may be more valuable to the finder and certainly is to scholarship), and that they should report their finds promptly to the proper authorities (substantial rewards have been paid to those who did so, finders who concealed their discoveries received nothing or a token sum). The British national collections have been greatly enriched by the laws of treasure trove. The finds are made available to scholars and the general public not locked in a bank vault; and hoards are not arbitrarily broken up. A few of the treasure troves now in the Museum will be described here.

In May 1840, in the early evening, a group of labourers were repairing and strengthening the bank of the River Ribble in Lancashire near Cuerdale Hall in an area reputed to contain 'the richest treasure in all England'. In a hole forty yards from the river, from which they were taking earth one of them spotted what appeared to him to be small grey-white oyster shells. When he looked closer he found not shells but silver. The other workmen scrambled excitedly for a share. The steward of Cuerdale rushed to the scene and was able to extract most of the find from the workmen and take it to Cuerdale Hall, where it was laid out, entirely covering the floor of one of the sitting rooms. The workmen had discovered, buried in a disintegrated lead coffer, a Viking hoard of eighty-eight pounds of silver – even today four times bigger than any comparable find in Britain or Scandinavia. There were over seven thousand coins, $725\frac{1}{2}$ ounces of silver in ingots and $103\frac{1}{2}$ ounces of silver ornaments mostly hacked into pieces. The treasure is thought to have been hidden about 903 –

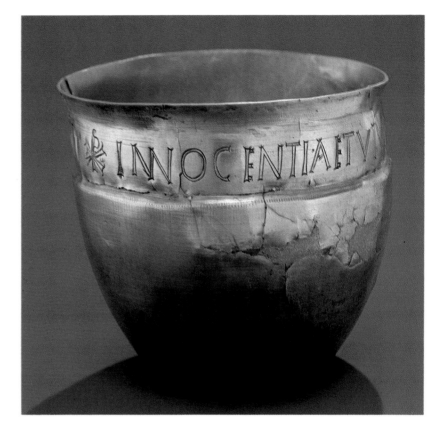

perhaps the war-chest of a Viking army which had recently fled Ireland for north-west England. For such a rich hoard to remain unclaimed suggests an army destroyed in battle. The hoard was claimed by Queen Victoria as Duke of Lancaster and divided amongst the British Museum and a number of other institutions.

Some mystery surrounds the exact circumstances of the discovery of the Mildenhall treasure which, because not promptly declared, attracted only a token reward. This treasure consists of thirty-four superb pieces of Roman silver tableware, many of brilliant craftsmanship, with a total weight of about $25\frac{1}{2}$ kilos. It was discovered at West Row, on the edge of the Fens near Mildenhall, Suffolk during winter ploughing in the early 1940s. The treasure consists of dishes, cups, bowls, spoons and ladles – a mixture of pagan and Christian elements – but pride of place must go to the pagan 'Great Dish' which weighs 8,256 grammes. In the centre is the staring face of a sea god, Neptune or Oceanus, with nereids and mythical sea-creatures dancing around him. In the outer frieze a wild revel is in progress as Bacchus celebrates his triumph over Hercules and around them maenads, satyrs and a bearded Pan whirl in an unending dance. Other dishes echo this style but five

A bowl from the Water Newton treasure discovered near the Roman town of *Durobrivae* in Huntingdonshire, the earliest known group of Christian silver yet found in the Roman empire. Some pieces are from the 3rd c. AD. This bowl is inscribed with the Christian *Chi-Rho* monogram and the words 'INNOCENTIA ET VIVENTIA . . . RVNT' (Innocentia and Viventia (gave or dedicated this)). Approx. H. 12·4 cm (4·8 in)

The Mildenhall great dish and other pieces from the treasure discovered on the edge of the Fens in the 1940s. The treasure, 34 items of 4th-c. AD Roman silver tableware, has a mixture of pagan and Christian elements. At the centre of the great dish is a seagod, around him Bacchus celebrates his triumph over Hercules, and Maenads, Satyrs and Pan whirl in unending dance. Diam. of dish 60.5 cm (23.8 in)

of the eight spoons in the hoard bear Christian inscriptions – three the *Chi-rho* symbol with alpha and omega. Whether this is the property of a pagan or Christian family we do not know, nor do we know for certain who deposited the hoard.

The style of the objects, compared with similar pieces from elsewhere gives some indication of the date of manufacture. 360, 365 and 367 AD were unsettled years when the Scots, Picts and others ravaged parts of Britain. The Greek name *Eutherios* scratched

on the underside of the two small platters suggests a connection with the earlier date. Flavius Claudius Julianus (c.331–363) a cousin of the emperor Constantius II, who himself became Emperor and won the title 'Apostate' by his attempts to reinstate paganism, had a senior official of this name. There is no evidence that Eutherios ever visited Britain but there is an intriguing theory that the plate might perhaps have belonged to one of Julian's officers, a Christian named Lupicinus, who was despatched to Britain from Gaul in 360 AD to put down a revolt. On Julian being declared emperor nothing further is heard of Lupicinus a Christian and therefore an embarrassment save that he was arrested on his return to Gaul and disappeared.

The great Snettisham torc, one of the most magnificent ever discovered, was also found by the plough in November 1950 on an estate at Ken Hill near Snettisham, Norfolk. With it were a gold bracelet and another, damaged, torc; a third torc had been found shortly before. In 1948 there had been a find in the same area which included tubular gold torcs. Damaged objects, scrap metal and British Gaulish coins on the site indicated that a metalworker had probably practised his craft in the vicinity. Torcs are ornamental neck-rings worn by the highest levels of Celtic society. The strands of metal were so twisted together that they became pliable and the ends of the torc could be forced apart and slipped round the neck. The Snettisham torc weighs 1085 grammes and is about 20 centimetres in diameter. The hoop consists of eight strands, each composed of eight twisted wires with the ends soldered into the sockets of the hollow ring terminals. It is made of an alloy of approximately 58% gold, 38% silver and 3% copper. The decoration is distinctive of Early Iron Age art of the first century BC in Britain and the discovery of a coin, an Atrebatic quarter stater of 50 BC or later in one of the terminals confirms the date of manufacture.

From the same century come the six gold torcs found at Ipswich. Five were discovered in October 1968 on the crest of a hill at Belstead on the eastern outskirts of the town by the driver of a mechanical earth-mover preparing a site for a new housing estate. Seeing something gleaming in the loose soil, he pulled out the shiny object and found it to be a gold torc with a second torc hooked into it. Three more torcs also hooked together were found. The sixth was found by a man digging the back garden of his three bedroomed semi-detached house. He lived on the new housing estate within a hundred yards of the earlier discovery and top soil from the original site had been used to make up his garden. The torcs each weigh between 858 and 1044 grammes; they are mostly about 18.7 centimetres in diameter except one of 19.6 centimetres. They too are made of an alloy of gold, silver and copper, of two rods twisted together. What is particularly interesting is that they are in varying stages of completion; one with plain terminals is highly polished and appears finished while the

Head of a seagod, Neptune or Oceanus from the Mildenhall great dish. The god's beard is of seaweed and four dolphins leap from the wild locks of his hair (detail).

Five of a group of six gold alloy torcs found at Ipswich and dating from the 1st c. BC. They are in varying stages of completion and may have been looted from a goldsmith's workshop. Diams 18·7 to 19·6 cm (7·3 to 7·7 in)

1st-c. BC torc found at Snettisham, Norfolk. The metal strands, made of an alloy of gold, silver and copper, are so constructed that they can be prized apart and the torc worn round the neck. Diam. 19·6 cm (7·7 in)

Terminal of the Snettisham torc (detail). The ornament is distinctive of Early Iron Age art of the 1st c. BC in Britain.

terminals of the others appear to have been in the process of being cleaned up with a chasing tool or chisel after having been cast from wax models. Four are in a style similar to the Snettisham torc and can be dated to the first century BC. How they came to be buried is not known – perhaps by a goldsmith, perhaps by a marauder.

The earliest known group of Christian silver from the Roman Empire was found in February 1975 in a recently ploughed field in Huntingdonshire on the site of the Roman town of *Durobrivae*. The date of deposit is difficult to establish, the pieces were probably made at different times, some in the third century AD. Experts have placed the date of concealment as not later than the fourth century AD and probably the earlier part of that century. As the two previous earliest known groups of Christian church plate, found in Italy and Turkey, dated from the sixth century AD this find is of enormous importance for the history of the early Christian church. The treasure is virtually all of silver, weighing together 3,977 grammes. There are nine silver vessels – four bowls, two jugs, a two-handled cup, a large dish and a strainer, some of which are fragmentary, and eighteen small triangular silver plaques of thin metal plus a small circular gold disc.

Nine of the plaques bear the *Chi-rho* symbol, one also has the Latin inscription 'Ancilla has fulfilled the vow which she promised'. Two bowls are engraved, one states *PUBLIANVS SANCTVM ALTARE TVVM DOMINE SVBNIXVS HONORO* (O Lord, I Publianus, relying on you, honour (or adorn) your holy sanctuary (or sacred place)). Another has a fragmentary inscription *INNOCENTIA ET VIVENTIA ... RVNT* (Innocentia and Viventia (gave or dedicated this)). It has been suggested that the treasure was being used by a Christian group, perhaps for ritual meals (*refrigeria*) for baptism or Communion. They may have worshipped in *Durobrivae* but, as the town lay on a main road between Lincoln and York to the north and Colchester and London to the south the plate could have been hidden by travellers. This may have happened during a period of persecution of the Christians as that of Diocletian in 303 and 304 AD which continued for a decade or it may have been concealed later in the mid-century for safe-keeping against theft or raiders.

If Water Newton sheds light on Early Christian worship in Britain, Thetford illuminates a pagan cult, that of a mysterious

and elusive deity Faunus, a god of the countryside whom Virgil describes as the son of Picus, grandson of Saturn and father of Latinus; a seer or foreteller who could cause dreams and nightmares. He was concerned with the woods and the fields and with the protection and fertility of flocks and herds. The treasure was found by metal detector at a place called Gallows Hill in 1979 but sadly was not declared for some time, by which time a warehouse had been built on the site and any chance of examining it for archaeological evidence and for additional items from the hoard had been lost. The Thetford treasure consists of thirty-nine items of gold jewellery, thirty-three silver spoons, and three silver strainers, all of the late fourth century AD. The jewellery is in pristine condition. This and stylistic similarities suggest that it was the stock of a jeweller's workshop. The most striking object is a rectangular gold belt buckle decorated with the figure of a dancing satyr. Thirty-one of the spoons were inscribed, twelve to the god Faunus and the inscriptions include Celtic epithets or bynames for Faunus. It is thought that the treasure was probably buried during a period of opposition to pagan cults in the late 380s and early 390s AD.

By far the most numerous treasure trove

Two-handled cup from the 4th c. AD Water Newton Christian treasure, part of a group of 9 silver vessels and 19 plaques. When found the handles had been detached. H. 12·5 cm (5 in)

Below. Three of a group of 33 silver spoons from the late 4th-c. AD treasure found at Thetford, Norfolk. The first and third contain the Latin personal names Auspicius and Agrestius, the second the name Faunus. 31 are inscribed, 12 to the mysterious and elusive deity Faunus, a god of the countryside. L. 14.5, 17.3, 18.3 cm (5.7, 6.8, 7.2 in)

Right. Part of the *Cunetio* (Wiltshire) hoard of 54,951 Roman coins, the largest such hoard found in Britain. Although some coins are earlier, it was largely gathered and buried during the years AD 260–75, a period of political and monetary crisis for the Roman Empire. It includes a representative cross-section of the coinage of Roman Britain but nearly half the hoard comes from the independent empire established in Gaul by Postumus in 260.

finds are coins – portable, negotiable, relatively easy to conceal – each year hoards of various sizes are unearthed and brought to the British Museum where they are cleaned and identified. Sometimes they provide surprises for the numismatist – for example, in 1978 only five coins of the shadowy King Beonna of East Anglia (acceded 749 AD) were known, all by the same moneyer. Between 1980 and 1982 no less than fifty-two were found at Middle Harling, Norfolk and declared treasure trove.

In October 1978 the largest hoard of Roman coins found in Britain was unearthed at another Mildenhall (in Wiltshire, not Suffolk) and is known by the town's Roman name, *Cunetio* to distinguish it from Roman finds from the Suffolk fens. The hoard consisted of about 55,000 Roman coins, mostly antoniniani of the period *c.* 200–74 AD but included also some 500 denarii – a vast amount. The nearest comparable known find in Britain, at Blackmoor, Hampshire in 1877 consisted of only 29,000 (the world record of 81,000 was discovered in Bulgaria in 1929). The coins were buried in a first-century AD storage jar and a lead container below the surface of a cobbled floor or yard, the stones having been replaced. The tremendous task of cleaning and identifying the coins was undertaken by the Museum and when the hoard was declared treasure trove it was purchased in its entirety.

In a country which had been settled and fought over for millennia there should exist much more buried treasure than has so far seen the light of day, but it is not the discovery of gold and silver alone which matters but rather what it can tell us about the past. Coin hoards may be a major addition to our understanding of kings such as Beonna of whom virtually all knowledge had been lost; the size of the Cunetio hoard provides an unrivalled opportunity for intensive study, it provides a picture of coin circulation in third century Britain and helps to establish a chronology of successive issues in a period of inflation; Water Newton pushes the tangible evidence of Christian ceremony in Britain back three centuries. There are many other historical gaps which may be filled. This can only be done by prompt disclosure and proper archaeological research.

2

THE TREASURE OF THE RIVER OXUS

In May 1880, when Captain F.C. Burton was political officer in the Tezin valley, and resident at Seh Baba three marches from Kabul, three Mohammedan merchants from Bokhara, who were known to have a quantity of gold upon their mules, were robbed on their journey from Kabul to Peshawar by men of the Khurd Kabul (Barbakkar Khels and Hisarak Ghilzais) at a spot between Seh Baba and Jagdalak: they had foolishly gone ahead of the convoy escort, and were thus themselves partially to blame for their misfortune. The robbers made off to the hills with the booty . . .

This is the first recorded appearance of the Oxus treasure. The British Museum now has some one hundred and eighty objects, mostly of gold, some of silver and copper and a few cylinder seals together with some hundred coins said to come from this hoard. They are a perplexing mixture – the objects have been given a range of dates as early as 550 BC, if not before, and as late as the third century BC. The coins attributed to the find come from the early fifth century BC to c.175 BC; they are from mints in Greece, Phoenicia, Asia Minor and Bactria. The objects are mostly from the great Achaemenid empire which spanned the years 550–330 BC and numbered amongst its rulers Cyrus the Great whose empire extended from Anatolia and Mesopotamia to the frontiers of India. Some show Greek influence, others the contorted style of the Scythians. We do not know exactly where the treasure was found, who found it and why such a collection should have come together.

To understand some of the confusion we should go back to this strange tale of the North-West Frontier of India in May 1880. Captain Burton, a British officer, later described how he was alerted late at night by the merchants' servant who had escaped. He immediately set off with two orderlies and surprised the bandits quarrelling over the treasure. According to the account published by the Museum in 1905, Burton found four bandits lying wounded and the treasure strewn over the floor of a cave. He had the initiative, and so the robbers surrendered part of the treasure and the merchants. Burton, warned of an ambush, hid out during the night and only returned to his camp the following morning. He then threatened retaliation and the robbers, deciding on discretion, surrendered what was left of the treasure, the rest having been melted down or hidden. The grateful merchants declared that three-quarters of the treasure had been recovered. They allowed Captain Burton to buy a gold

Gold model of a chariot drawn by four horses, 5th c. BC. Discovered in 1880 somewhere near the River Oxus in what is now Soviet Central Asia, this hoard is a perplexing mixture of coins and objects whose dates may range from at least 550 BC to 175 BC. L. 8·8 cm (3·5 in)

Gold plaque showing a standing man carrying a bundle of rods, perhaps the sacred *barsom* used in religious ceremonies. The presence of such plaques in the hoard supports the theory that it may come from a temple. H. 15 cm (5.9 in)

Sir Alexander Cunningham (1814–93), soldier and archaeologist, who bought much of the treasure from the merchants of Rawalpindi and wrote the first account of its discovery. Cunningham was appointed Director-General of the Archaeological Survey of India in 1870.

Gold plaque showing a crudely drawn horse. Such plaques may have been made by goldsmiths in a temple precinct for dedication to the deity. L. 12·3 cm (4·8 in)

Right. One of a pair of 5th–4th c. BC armlets from the treasure; once heavily decorated with cloisonné and champlevé enamel, now only a fragment of lazulite remains. The terminals are ornamented with winged, horned griffins with eagles' beaks and legs. Such armlets might have been presented by the great king as a mark of favour. H. 12·3 cm (4·8 in)

armlet which is now on loan to the Museum from the Victoria and Albert Museum and gave an account of the treasure's discovery three years earlier:

Most of the things were found at Khandian (Kabadian), which is submerged in the Oxus; but at certain times in the year when the river is dry, the people dig, and among the old ruins of the city of Khandian find valuable gold things …

The treasure now disappeared into the bazaars of Rawalpindi whence it gradually re-emerged. The circumstances of its reappearance are rather vague. The greater part was purchased by General Alexander Cunningham, the founder and Director-General of the Archaeological Survey of India. Some pieces made their way independently to London and into the possession of Sir Augustus Wollaston Franks of the British Museum. It is said that in some instances Franks – who had a good eye for a fake – was offered suspicious objects but bought these at a small percentage above gold value in the hopes that the genuine objects would be produced. In time these appeared from India, in silver and of unmistakably finer workmanship. Franks also purchased Cunningham's collection of objects and in 1897 bequeathed these and his own part of the treasure to the Museum.

The coins, which could provide vital evidence for dating the hoard, are an enigma. It is strongly suspected that the dealers of Rawalpindi took the opportunity to 'launder' a number of miscellaneous coins from various sources. Some accounts refer to a find of 1500 coins – the British Museum has one hundred. Cunningham reckoned that he had seen seven hundred attributed to the Oxus hoard which were sent for identification by dealers and owners. He bought a large quantity which later came to the Museum through bequest and purchase. Some ended up in the Hermitage, Leningrad. Others trickled through to the Museum from various different sources.

The objects now in the Museum are however generally thought to form part of a single hoard. Some items are known to have disappeared – Cunningham reports that the original finders quarrelled and cut up several of the larger pieces; the robbers are also said to have divided the treasure and concealed some of it. But whatever their origin, the objects form a superb collection: there are fifty-two plaques of fine beaten gold of crude workmanship depicting a variety of people and animals. Other items are masterpieces: two great omega-shaped gold armlets; a silver statuette of a Persian King perhaps Cyrus the Great; a gold model of a chariot drawn by four horses; gold clothing attachments which bring to mind Herodotus' description of the Persian army which 'glittered all over with gold'; a gold ornamental scabbard, perhaps the earliest piece in the collection, dating to *c*.600 BC and decorated with scenes of a royal lion hunt.

Where did the treasure come from? Cunningham was rather vague about the geography of the area. In 1883 he amended an earlier account and said that the treasure had been found:

On the banks of the Oxus, near a place called Kawat or Kuad, two marches from Kunduz and about midway between Khulm and Kobadian ... one of the most frequented ferries on the Oxus, and ... the chief thoroughfare on the road to Samarkand ...

as a postscript he adds that

I met a man at Simla who has several times visited the spot where these Oxus relics were found. The place is one stage to the North of the Oxus, and is called Kawadian, a large ancient town on the high road to Samarkand.

It is generally agreed that it was discovered in the territory of ancient Bactria – in whose capital Alexander the Great married his Persian queen Roxane, one of the richest regions of the ancient world. This territory now forms part of Soviet Central Asia, (Southern Tajikistan). The river Oxus is now known as Amu-Darya. The find has long fascinated Russian scholars and a recent Russian account suggest that the treasure came from the territory of the Beg of Kobadian (but not the city of that name), more specifically the ruined site of Tahkt-i Kuvad (or Kuwat – there are various spellings) which lies below the confluence of the Vakhsh and Pyandzh rivers (as Cunningham said – halfway between Khulm and Kobadian and two days from Kunduz). Here lies one of two fortresses guarding the river crossing in the strip of land below the Teshik-Tash range of mountains and the river

A silver statuette probably representing a Persian king of the Achaemenid dynasty holding a *barsom*, a ritual bundle of twigs. Early 5th c. BC H. 14.8 cm (5.8 in)

Gold armlet (detail). Composite monsters such as these griffins probably represented demonic powers and may have been intended to protect the wearer.

– a land which many invaders have swept over throughout the centuries. In a more northerly fortress, Takht-i Sangin a Russian excavation team in 1977 found a temple with corridor store-rooms and offerings reported to be of a similar range to that of the Oxus treasure.

The Oxus Treasure is and was of immense value. So how was it put together and why was it abandoned to the treasure seekers of the nineteenth century? Cunningham, with the romantic optimism of nineteenth-century scholarship, thought it might have been accumulated by a noble Bactrian family. He surmises that when Euthydemus I of Bactria and his cavalry were defeated on the River Arius at the time of Antiochus III's invasion (208 BC) one of the soldiers who joined this army did not return to his buried fortune. Another writer associates it also with the followers of gold-hungry Euthydemus but connects it with his military expedition (c. 180

BC), along the gold route from Ferghana to the borders of China, to Siberia and Mongolia. It has also been suggested that it was first amassed by one of the lower ranks of Alexander the Great's army in his victorious progress through Central Asia (334–2 BC), that it then fell into other hands and was added to in later decades. The explanation which is supported by the fifty-two gold plaques and the range of dates of the objects is that it represents offerings made to a temple over two or three centuries. A temple of the Persian goddess Anahita, a goddess of fertility and war, is known to have been situated in Bactria on the left bank of the Oxus. This might have been destroyed in Alexander the Great's invasion or shortly after at the time of his marshal Seleucus and the treasure removed or concealed (although this date is too early for many of the coins).

If we were sure which coins belonged to the hoard it would be easier to deduce its origins and the time of its concealment. Some authorities are inclined to accept that a large number do belong with the objects, others have doubts about the activities of the Rawalpindi dealers. While the earliest date from the early fifth to the mid-fourth century BC and come from the Greek mainland, there is a clustering around the time of the Greek rulers of Bactria Diodotus (*c*.245 BC) and Euthydemus (*c*.220 BC). There are later coins of other rulers of this area Pantaleon (*c*.190 BC), Agathocles (*c*.185 BC) and Antimachus (*c*.190 BC?) which may or may not have belonged to the find. The absence of coins of Demetrius (Euthydemus's successor) and Eucratides (who reigned simultaneously with or just after him) however indicates the possibility of a final date of deposit early in the second century BC and not later than *c*.175 BC. The coins are indeed a mystery. Their pattern of dates does not seem to be a simple chronological sequence of the coinage available in the Indus area. They are a hotch-potch which might well have been held by an individual interested in retaining his wealth in gold and silver, irrespective of its origin.

Probably we shall never know with certainty the origins of the treasure, although recent French and Russian excavations have expanded the comparable evidence available for placing and dating the hoard. What is unarguable is that this collection which made its strange journey from the banks of the Oxus to Victorian London a century ago is one of the finest treasures of the Museum.

Gold hair ornament ('aigrette'), 5th–2nd c. BC. A crouching winged lion-griffin with deer's hooves, its style reminiscent of the art of the Scythians. Two horizontal pins at the back were used as a fastening. L. 6·1 cm (2·4 in)

Below. The Persian army 'glittered all over with gold, vast quantities of which they wore about their persons' (Herodotus). Gold attachments from the treasure (left to right) lion griffin (diam. 4.7 cm (1.9 in)); the head of the god Bes (diam. 4.3 cm (1.7 in)); a lion's head (diam. 4.15 cm (1.6 in), 5th c, BC.

3

TURQUOISE MOSAICS FROM THE AZTEC EMPIRE

And all this happened to us.
We saw it,
We marvelled at it.
With this sad and mournful destiny
we saw ourselves afflicted ...
Gold, jade, precious raiment,
quetzal feathers,
everything once of value
has become nothing.

(Anonymous post-Conquest Aztec poet)

'In the spring of 1856, I met with Mr Christy accidentally in an omnibus at Havana' wrote the anthropologist Edward Tylor at the beginning of *Anahuac*, his delightful account of a journey to Mexico in the 1850s. 'Mr Christy' was Henry Christy (1810–65), traveller, textile manufacturer, banker, ethnographer, geologist, archaeologist, one of the Museum's major benefactors, who donated or bequeathed an enormous collection of some 10,000 objects in which pride of place must go to a group of Mixtec-Aztec turquoise mosaics. They are composed of minute fragments of turquoise and other stones, skilfully set in resin on wood (in one case on a human skull) and were almost certainly sent to Europe in the sixteenth century by the Spanish Conquistadors. The Museum now has nine (three masks, a knife, a back ornament in shield form, an animal head, a figure of a seated jaguar, a helmet and a pectoral or headdress ornament) – about one third of the authentic surviving mosaics of high quality. Three were purchased by Christy, one acquired with money he bequeathed. To study them is to be impressed by the immense skill of the craftsmen – probably Mixtec rather than Aztec – who made them with copper and flint tools four centuries ago.

Henry Christy was interested in the stages of human civilisation and thought that it would

Henry Christy (1810–65), ethnographer, traveller, textile manufacturer, banker, geologist, archaeologist and donor of three masks and an immense ethnographical and archaeological collection. When Tylor met him he had been 'descending into caves, and botanizing in tropical jungles . . . .

be possible to extrapolate from the life of contemporary non-industrial societies to that of their prehistoric forebears. Thus he collected both archaeological and ethnographical material, in travels throughout America, Northern Europe and the East. Tylor's account of their at times hair-raising journey to Mexico provides a fascinating glimpse of a now shadowy figure and of the hazards of nineteenth-century travel. They started from Havana in the American built steamer *Mejico* with a surly Spanish captain and a group of Spanish and French tradesmen, gamblers and political adventurers. The travellers eventually landed at Vera Cruz whence they journeyed on after a day's delay in a diligence, 'Mr Christy sagaciously remarking that the robbers would know of the arrival of the steamer, and would probably take the first diligence that came afterwards' (in this he was correct). On reaching the valley of Mexico and its mountains, Popocatepetl and Iztaccihuatl, Christy, anxious to make sure that they had really reached the land of Aztec civilization 'gets down from the diligence and hunting about for a few minutes by the roadside, returns in triumph with a broken arrow-head of obsidian'. The descent leading to their arrival in Mexico City was horrific, down a series of steps nearly a foot in depth at a swinging trot, the inside passengers howling for mercy as they were shot up against the roof.

Christy was not put off Mexican antiquities by this expedition and started to collect in earnest; henceforth his collections had an American bias. When he died, of a cold brought on by exploring some recently discovered caves in Belgium, he bequeathed his collection and a sum of money to four Trustees including A. W. Franks. Franks fought hard to acquire the collection for the Museum and succeeded in his battle.

Franks was himself to present three mosaics and the remaining two were bought with Museum funds. Their provenance is somewhat vague. Christy's three came from the collection of Bram Hertz which was auctioned in 1859. In a letter Hertz said that the mask and knife came originally from a celebrated collection at Florence; the skull came from Bruges. Of the Museum's later acquisitions the shield shaped ornament was said to come from Turin, the animal head from North Italy, the mask from Paris (but perhaps originally from the Medici), the jaguar from Liverpool, the helmet from Paris and the pectoral or head-

dress ornament from the Duchessa Massimo.

The clustering of the mosaics in the old Habsburg Empire lends credence to the theory that they are rare survivals of the great treasures sent from Mexico at various times at the beginning of the sixteenth century, some by Hernan Cortés himself, to the Holy Roman Emperor Charles V (1500–58) whose inheritance included the Spanish Americas as well as the Low Countries, Burgundy, Spain and Naples. Hernan Cortés was born in Castile in 1484 or 1485 and in 1504 sailed for Hispaniola. In 1511 he joined Diego Velasquez in the conquest of Cuba and was then nominated to lead an expedition to South America, Velasquez discovering too late that his subordinate had ambitions of his own in which there was little place for his patron. In March 1519 Cortés' fleet sailed to the mouth of the Tabasco River and after a brief engagement with the local inhabitants he took possession in the name of the King of Spain. As he advanced news of his arrival reached the

'A mask wrought in a mosaic of turquoise; this mask had wrought in the same stones a doubled and twisted snake . . .' (Father Bernardino de Sahagun of one of Moctezuma's gifts to Cortés). H. 17.8 cm (7 in)

The mosaics are almost certainly pre-Conquest, probably 15th century but their exact date of manufacture is not known.

Sacrificial knife with a blade of chalcedony, the handle carved in wood in the form of a crouching 'Eagle Knight' and covered with a mosaic of turquoise, malachite, white, pink, purple and orange shell and a few pieces of pearl shell. The Aztecs practised several forms of human sacrifice, the most characteristic being the removal of a pulsating heart from a living victim. L. 31·7 cm (12·5 in)

A mask thought to represent the god Quetzalcoatl, god-king of ancient Toltec times or perhaps the sun god Tonatiuh whose face was covered with boils (perhaps represented by the large irregularly shaped turquoises scattered across the mask). The eyes are of pearl shell and the teeth of white shell. H. 16·8 cm (6·6 in)

Aztec capital, Tenochtitlan (on the site of what is now Mexico City) which was then ruled by the scholarly and reserved Moctezuma. There had been a decade of strange and ominous occurrences. The Aztecs had a tradition that the god-king of their predecessors in the valley of Mexico, the Toltecs, a pale-skinned bearded man-become-god called Quetzalcoatl would return from the east to claim the land and that his return would take place in a cyclical year 'one reed'. 1519 was such a year. According to Father Bernardino de Sahagun, writing after the Conquest from eyewitness reports, Moctezuma gathered ambassadors to send to the invaders and instructed them:

Our Lord Quetzalcoatl has arrived: go and receive him and listen to what he may say to you with great attention; see to it that you do not forget anything of what he may say; see here these jewels which you are to present to him in my behalf, and which are all the priestly ornaments that belong to him ...

Among the ornaments described is one which resembles a mosaic in the Museum's collection:

A mask wrought in a mosaic of turquoise; this mask had wrought in the same stones a doubled and twisted snake, the fold of which was the beak of the nose; then the tail was parted from the head and the head with part of the body came over one eye so that it formed an eyebrow, and the tail with a part of the body went over the other eye to form the other eyebrow ...

The ambassadors took with them examples of the Aztecs' colourful featherwork, golden ornaments, white cloth edged with feathers and precious stones. When they came before Cortés they kissed the deck of his ship, placed a crown and mask on his head and around his neck put collars of precious stones and gold, and on his left arm a shield. Such a spectacle however aroused the Spaniards' passion for gold. After a series of battles Cortés and his allies advanced on the Aztec capital, then with a population estimated at 150,000 and superior in size, cleanliness and amenities to anything the Spaniards had seen in Europe. Why Moctezuma with his numerically superior forces did not attack the Spaniards we do not know. Perhaps he was influenced by the unfavourable omens and the tradition of the return of Quetzalcoatl, or perhaps he intended to deal with the invaders at leisure. At all events he allowed himself to be imprisoned. Cortés was obliged to return to the coast to deal with a force sent by the irate Velasquez. In his absence his army brutally massacred unarmed Aztec nobles and in subsequent fighting Moctezuma was killed. After Cortés' return, in July 1520, the Spaniards retreated and, on a dark, cloudy, rainy night known as la Noche Triste many died as weighed down by treasure they fought their way across the causeway from Tenochtitlan. Cortés and his army in time regrouped and nine months later returned to take a

Ornament or pectoral in the form of a double-headed serpent, carved of wood covered with a mosaic of turquoise, the gums, nostrils and a band across the nose picked out in red shell, the teeth of white shell. The mosaic continues on the reverse. H. 17·8 cm (7 in)

savage revenge during which they took and virtually razed Tenochtitlan. Bernal Diaz del Castillo left an account of these bloody battles punctuated by the terrible Aztec sacrifices:

again there was sounded the dismal drum of Huichilobos and many other shells and horns and things like trumpets . . . [we] saw that our comrades whom they had captured . . . were being carried by force up the steps . . . [they had plumes placed on their heads and were forced to dance before the god] . . . and after they had danced they immediately placed them on their backs . . . and with stone knives they sawed open their chests and drew out their palpitating hearts and offered them to the idols that were there . . . When we saw those cruelties all of us in our camp said the one to the other: "Thank God that they are not carrying me off to-day to be sacrificed".

So the great Aztec empire fell to a strange new god and a new people. Of the treasures sent to Europe relatively little remains. The gold was melted down and precious stones remounted. Most of the featherwork and textiles disintegrated (although three pieces of featherwork remain in Vienna), some of the mosaics, of less intrinsic value, survived to remind us of the richness of this vanished empire. The artist Albrecht Dürer in Brussels in 1521 saw some of this treasure perhaps amongst it some of the mosaics now in the Museum and expressed the wonder felt by the Europeans:

I also saw the things that were brought to the King from the new land of gold: a sun entirely of gold, a whole fathom wide, and a moon entirely of silver, of equal size, likewise two rooms of rare accoutrements, of all manner of their weapons, armour, bows and arrows, wonderful arms, strange gar-

ments, bed hangings and all manner of wonderful things for many uses, all much fairer to behold than any marvel. These things are all so precious that they are valued at one hundred thousand guilders. And in all the days of my life I have seen nothing that has so rejoiced my heart as these things. For I saw among them strange and exquisitely worked objects and marvelled at the subtle genius of the men in distant lands. The things I saw there I have no words to express.

Painting from the Museum's Codex Zouche Nuttall of a figure wearing a skull as part of his costume.

Right. Skulls of sacrificial victims were placed on a 'skull rack'. When decorated they might be worn, suspended by leather straps. This skull, of a 30 year old man, is inlaid with turquoise and lignite mosaic, the inside covered with soft leather. The eyes are polished discs of iron pyrites set in circles of white shell. It may represent one of the creator gods, Tezcatlipoca, 'Smoking mirror', patron of the night sky and the Great Bear and of highwaymen, sorcerers and warriors not of noble birth. H. 20·3 cm (8 in)

BURIED CIVILISATIONS

4

AMELIA EDWARDS AND THE EGYPT EXPLORATION SOCIETY

As Amelia Edwards (1831–92) wrote in her best-selling and still eminently readable book *A Thousand Miles up the Nile*, her first visit to Egypt in 1873 was to get out of the rain. Having spent a wet September in Central France:

... in simple truth we had drifted hither by accident, with no excuse of health, or business, or any serious object whatever; and just taken refuge in Egypt as one might turn aside into the Burlington Arcade or the Passage des Panoramas.

This accidental visit 'without definite plans, outfit or any kind of Oriental experience' was to change her life and to have a significant effect on the development of Egyptology.

Miss Edwards was already a well-established novelist, journalist and travel writer, 'straitened means' having compelled her to look about for a means of livelihood. She had previously had no particular interest in Egypt apart from childhood reading, but now she fell under its spell. She writes of waking at sunrise 'to see those grey-green palms outside the window solemnly bowing their plumed heads towards each other against a rose-coloured dawn' and of her first sight of the Great Pyramid – 'It shuts out the sky and the horizon. It shuts out all the other Pyramids. It shuts out everything but the sense of awe and wonder'. She travelled up the Nile by boat as far as the second cataract (actually 964½ miles but she reckoned she could see far enough from the 'Rock of Abooseer' to make up the thousand!). She visited Syria, crossing the two Lebanon ranges to Damascus and Baalbek, and returned through the Levant to Istanbul.

On her return she set about writing the book of her travels. This was to be no superficial account for 'the more one knows about the past history of the country the more one enjoys the ruins'. She was thus determined to obtain expert advice. One of her sources was Dr Samuel Birch (1813–85) Keeper of Oriental Antiquities (including the Egyptian collections) at the Museum. Birch was bombarded with queries, asked to translate hieratic inscriptions, to advise as to the best place to buy papyri, to explain the title 'Ammon Harmachis' and much more, while Miss Edwards herself laboured at hieroglyphics.

Her book completed and published in 1877 Miss Edwards had other things on her mind. She had been distressed by the neglect of ancient monuments which she had witnessed during her visit:

such is the fate of every Egyptian monument, great or small. The tourist carves it all over with names and dates, and in some instances with caricatures.

Right. Alabaster head of a cult statue of the goddess Hathor in cow form from the mortuary temple of Queen Hatshepsut at Thebes, Deir el-Bahri, 18th Dynasty, *c.* 1500 BC. The eyes and eyebrows were originally inlaid with rock-crystal and lapis lazuli and the head was surmounted by a feathered headdress and horns. H. 35.5 cm (14 in) (Presented 1905).

Left. Amelia Edwards (1831–92), novelist, journalist and Egyptologist, whose enthusiasm and determination led to the founding of the EES. Miss Edwards was horrified at the neglect of ancient monuments which she found on her first visit to Egypt in 1873 and determined to found a society devoted to Egyptian exploration but actuated by scientific interest.

The student of Egyptology, by taking wet paper "squeezes", sponges away every vestige of the original colour. The "collector" buys and carries off everything of value that he can get; and the Arab steals for him. The work of destruction, meanwhile, goes on apace. There is no one to prevent it; there is no one to discourage it. Every day, more inscriptions are mutilated – more tombs are rifled – more paintings and sculptures are defaced ...

Egypt was then, as it had been since 1517, part of the Ottoman Empire. In 1879 the Khedive Ismail was deposed in favour of his son. In a period of unrest the country came under French and British supervision, the French taking over Public Works which included the new Antiquities Department. For thirty years the archaeological scene had been dominated by Auguste Mariette Pasha, who had been appointed Director of excavations in 1858 and was later charged with forming a national museum in Bulaq. Miss Edwards sought permission from him for a small group to excavate and appears to have received a favourable reply. She began to seek financial support and press publicity. An important recruit to her campaign was Sir Erasmus Wilson, a prosperous and eminent surgeon (who had paid for the transport to London of Cleopatra's Needle). He too had been captivated by Egypt while on a sightseeing tour and he and Miss Edwards became friends. She had also enlisted the support of the Museum's Keeper of Coins & Medals, Reginald Stuart Poole (who had been brought up in Egypt), but Dr Birch remained immoveable. He was a great scholar and curator who had established the Museum's tradition of publishing important texts but had little time for 'emotional archaeology': excavation should produce museum objects (and under the strict Egyptian antiquities laws it was unlikely that these would be forthcoming). Therefore he stood aside. The first meeting of the embryo body was held in Poole's Department and a second meeting a few days later at University College London. Mariette died in January 1881; his successor was Gaston Maspero, with whom Miss Edwards had already been in contact. The eminent Swiss Egyptologist Edouard Naville, who was one of the group backing this new body, visited Maspero that winter and obtained his support. On 27 March 1882 a meeting called by Miss Edwards and Poole was held in the latter's rooms at the Museum and the Egypt Exploration Fund came into existence. Miss Edwards and Poole became joint Hon. Secretaries and Sir Erasmus Wilson their financial backer and Treasurer. Also on the Committee was the Keeper of Greek and Roman Antiquities Charles Newton. Miss

Edwards's dream had become reality. An announcement was made in several newspapers on 1 April 1882 – 'the long desired society for the Promotion of Excavation in the Delta of the Nile has at last been constituted under very favourable auspices'.

The next step was to mount an excavation. At one time Heinrich Schliemann, a friend of Miss Edwards, was suggested as director but Maspero refused point blank to accept him, and advocated a young man, preferably English, to work at first under his instruction. Ultimately the first excavator was Edouard Naville. Sir Erasmus Wilson provided £500 with a promise of £100 to follow and in January 1883, the Nile having subsided and excavation in the Delta being possible, Naville set out for Tell es–Maskhuta. This was supposedly the Biblical 'Land of Goshen' where the Hebrews spent their Egyptian exile and Naville was looking for the city of Raamses mentioned in Exodus:

Therefore they did set over them taskmasters to afflict them with their burdens. And they built for Pharaoh treasure cities, Pithom and Raamses. (1:11)

What he actually found and identified from inscriptions was Pithom. Two of the best sculptures from the site (a granite falcon and a kneeling scribe) were presented by the Khedive to Sir Erasmus Wilson and eventually came to the Museum. The Egyptian regulations for export of antiquities were subsequently modified and it was agreed that any antiquities not required by the Bulaq museum might be exported by the finders.

Naville was unable to go to Egypt the following winter and so Flinders Petrie (1853–1942) entered the scene. He was one of the few archaeologists available in Britain who had experience of work in Egypt and he had written reports on the pyramids. His early connection with the Museum as a boy was 'jackalling' for the Coin Room, picking up late Greek and Byzantine coins in suburban shops. Petrie was a marvellous find for the Fund and a complete contrast to Naville whose great interest was inscriptions. Petrie was the first excavator in Egypt to appreciate the importance of small things relating to everyday life: potsherds, bricks, beads, flints. 'The true line' he wrote 'lies as much in the careful noting and comparison of small details as in more wholesale and offhand clearances'. His first site was Tanis in the Delta but his first major discovery was that of the early Greek trading centre of Naucratis, where he ex-cavated in 1884 and 1885 and was joined by Francis Llewellyn Griffith on a Fund studentship. Petrie quarrelled with the Fund in 1886. He returned in 1895 and worked again for it for a decade but when the Fund, finances low, was faced with a choice between him and Naville they chose the latter.

Meanwhile Miss Edwards was valiantly pursuing her love affair with Egypt. Her novels were abandoned after *Lord Brackenbury* (1880) which ran to fifteen editions, and she was having to work desperately hard, raising money, keeping up correspondence, writing articles on Egypt and labelling objects. Erasmus Wilson died in 1884 without leaving provision for the Fund and finances became less secure. An American branch was founded and the poet Whittier sent a subscription, writing 'I hesitate a little about disturbing the repose of some ancient mummy, who perchance, Hobnobbed with Pharaoh glass to

The 'eminent Swiss Egyptologist', Professor Edouard Naville (1844–1926), the Fund's first excavator, supervising the excavations at Thebes in 1894.

glass . . . or dropped a halfpenny into Homer's hat'.

In the winter of 1889–90 Miss Edwards went on a highly successful five months' tour of the USA visiting New England and as far west as St Paul and Milwaukee. The tour was marred by an accident in Columbus, Ohio when she broke an arm. From this she never fully recovered. On her return she published her American lectures as *Pharaohs, Fellahs and Explorers* (1891). In 1891 she was to be found at Millwall Docks in London, trying to save money by inspecting crates of objects newly arrived from Egypt on the quayside and redirecting them to subscribers. This proved to be too much for her by now fragile health, she became ill with influenza, an illness which greatly weakened her and indirectly led to her death on 15 April 1892.

Who could have foreseen that her accidental visit in 1873 could have led to so much? Before her death her contribution to Egyptology was recognised by the award of a state pension. As part of her legacy to Egyptology she bequeathed her library and collection of antiquities to University College London together with £2415 to establish a Chair of Egyptology (the first in England) whose first occupant was Flinders Petrie.

In spite of the unenthusiastic attitude of Birch and his successors, Le Page, Renouf and Budge, to the work of the Fund, it remained the latter's policy to make regular donations of antiquities to the Museum starting with fifteen Greek coins from Naucratis in 1886. Other donations in the early years included a palmette style column, the head and lower half of a colossal statue of King Amenophis III and many temple reliefs. Relations improved in 1903 when H.R. Hall, a member of the Museum staff, joined Naville's excavation at Deir el–Bahri and the Museum received from this site some exceptional sculpture of the Middle and New Kingdoms. Throughout the twentieth century the Fund (now the Egypt Exploration Society) with its emphasis on scientific archaeology and publication has continued to enrich the Museum's collection with properly documented pieces from such sites as Saqqara, Thebes, Abydos, El-Amarna and Qasr Ibrim in Nubia. In return the Museum has provided some financial assistance and members of staff have participated in excavations. The 'EES' recently celebrated its centenary – still actively excavating and with a membership of over 2000 specialists and enthusiasts from all over the

world. One of the highlights, appropriately enough, was an exhibition held at the Museum to which came almost three hundred thousand visitors – evidence of the fascination which ancient Egypt continues to exert on those who fall under its spell.

Glass cosmetic vessel made
c. 1350 BC in the shape of a Nile
bulti-fish. Found in a private
house at el-Amarna buried
under the floor, perhaps the
concealed proceeds of a
robbery. One of many objects,
large and small, given to the
Museum by the EES since its
foundation. L. 14·5 cm (5·7 in)
(Presented 1921).

Ivory figure of an unidentified
king wearing the characteristic
short cloak of the Sed-festival
or jubilee at which the union of
Egypt under one crown was re-
enacted and the authority of
the king renewed. This usually
took place after the king had
ruled for 30 years and
thereafter at 3-yearly intervals.
It was always held at Memphis
and to it came all the gods of
the land to pay homage to the
king. From the Temple of Osiris
at Abydos. Probably 1st or 2nd
Dynasty, *c.*2800 BC. H. 8·8 cm
(3·5 in). (Presented 1903)

Bronze figure of a jackal from
Saqqara, the great cemetery at
Memphis and the site of the
Step Pyramid of Djoser. The
eyes are inlaid with shell. The
jackal was sacred to the god
Anubis. Late period after 600
BC. H. 19·2 cm (7·6 in).
(Presented 1971)

5

EXCAVATIONS AT NIMRUD

The Assyrian came down like the wolf on the fold,
And his cohorts were gleaming in purple and gold;
And the sheen of their spears was like stars on the sea,
When the blue wave rolls nightly on deep Galilee

(Lord Byron (1788–1824), *Destruction of Sennacherib*)

When Byron wrote these words virtually all trace of the warlike Assyrians of the Bible had disappeared. The names of some of their cities survived:

And Cush begat Nimrod: he began to be a mighty one in the earth.
He was a mighty hunter before the Lord . . .
Out of that land went forth Asshur and builded Nineveh, the city Rehoboth and Calah.
And Resen between Nineveh and Calah: the same is a great city.

(Genesis 10: 8, 9, 11, 12)

The Assyrian homeland lay in Upper Mesopotamia around the valleys of the Tigris and Upper and Lower Zab rivers. Strategically situated on main trade routes, Assyria was always at risk from her neighbours whom, to survive, she must dominate or neutralise. Her greatest military leaders from Adad-Nirari I (1305–1274 BC) carved out for themselves extensive empires. Westwards they came into contact with the Israelites who have left accounts of their terrible armies. We now know that the first Assyrian capital, until about 1000 BC was at Ashur (modern Qal'at Sharqat). It was moved to Kalhu (Nimrud – Biblical Calah) by Ashurnasirpal (883–859 BC) and in 721 BC transferred by Sargon II to a new city Dur–Sharrukin (Khorsabad). His successor Sennacherib (704–861 BC) transferred to the ancient city of Nineveh (Kuyunjik and Nebi Yunus). The final collapse of the Assyrian Empire came in 614 BC when the Medes and the newly independent Chaldean dynasty in Babylonia attacked Ashur. Two years later the same alliance destroyed Nineveh.

The first to undertake serious archaeological work in this area was Claudius James Rich (1786–1821). After his death the Museum bought his collection; it was placed in display in 'two glass tables' and soon forgotten. In December 1842 Paul-Emile Botta (1802–70), French consul at Mosul began to excavate at the mound now named Kuyunjik (Nineveh). Botta found little and in March 1843 tried Khorsabad (Dur Sharrukin), then a village fourteen miles to the north. Here he began to make spectacular discoveries – rooms and corridors lined with tall slabs of gypsum carved with scenes of Assyrian triumphs, although as cuneiform decipherment was still in its infancy Botta could not read the identifying inscriptions.

In 1839 the young Austen Henry Layard (1817–94) left London to travel overland to Ceylon where he hoped to find more exciting employment than that of a solicitor's office. He never reached the Far East, but fell under the spell of a long vanished civilisation. In April 1840 he arrived in Mosul where he visited the mounds of Kuyunjik and Qal'at Sharqat and had his first glimpse of the great mound on the left bank of the Tigris twenty-two miles to the south-east called by the Arabs Nimrud. Later, from a raft on the river he again saw Nimrud rising majestically from the plain:

It was evening as we approached the spot. The spring rains had clothed the mound with the richest verdure, and the fertile meadows, which stretched around it, were covered with flowers of every hue. Amidst this luxuriant vegetation were partly concealed a few fragments of bricks, pottery and alabaster, upon which might be traced the well-defined wedges of the cuneiform character.

Layard was determined to find an opportunity of thoroughly examining these remains. Early in 1842 when war between Turkey and

Sir Austen Henry Layard (1817–94) excavator of Nimrud and other Assyrian sites. Layard was en route to Ceylon when he first saw the buried remains of the Assyrian civilisation and fell under their spell.

Persia appeared imminent he was asked to brief the British Ambassador, Stratford Canning, in Constantinople. En route he visited Botta's excavations at Kuyunjik. Canning and Layard duly met and a fruitful partnership began. At first Layard was employed on unofficial political missions but he became restless as he read Botta's reports which were passing through Constantinople. Canning, unable to obtain an official appointment for his protégé, offered to finance an excavation and on 8 November 1845 Layard set off down the Tigris from Mosul bound for Nimrud.

As he tried to sleep on his first night at the site feverish dreams came to him, 'visions of palaces under-ground, of gigantic monsters, of sculptured figures and endless inscriptions'. The site had changed since his first visit. Now 'The eye wandered over a parched and barren waste, across which occasionally swept the whirlwind, dragging with it a cloud of sand . . .'. Layard at that time thought he was on the site of Nineveh – hence the title of his later book *Nineveh and its Remains*. However, this was Calah of the Bible where man had already settled well before 3000 BC. Shalmaneser I (1273–1244) occupied a city here (from about 1273–1245 BC); it fell into decay until Ashurnasirpal II (883–859 BC) began to rebuild it on a massive scale. As capital city, Nimrud functioned particularly in this period as a base for the army on its annual military campaigns. It must have been an impressive sight: its walls ran for about four and three-quarter miles and its total area was some 884 acres. It was a pleasant place with private houses, orchards, gardens, parks and other palaces and temples added over the years. Ashurnasirpal II completed the great North-West Palace in 879 BC and he and his son were also responsible for the construction of a great ziggurat, about two hundred feet in height, on the western side.

On his first day at Nimrud Layard unearthed evidence of two palaces of the Assyrian Kings. On his second day he came across fragments of ivories with traces of gilding. Since word of these discoveries was bound to come to the ears of the local Turkish Pasha, the unprepossessing one-eyed, one-eared Keritli Oglu, Layard decided to forestall interference by calling upon him. He was permitted to continue his excavations provided the Pasha's agent was there to seize any treasure. Layard expanded his workforce and employed agents to explore other mounds which he visited from time to time but his main concern was Nimrud. On 25 November Layard's team

cleared the first sculptured reliefs. Two chariots drawn by richly caparisoned galloping horses were revealed; another relief depicted the siege of a walled city. Layard was now ordered to stop work because he was disturbing Muslim graves, although local troops admitted they had been constructing false cemeteries on the mound at the order of the Pasha. Layard quietly continued his exploration and at the foot of the south east corner of the mound found the first colossal figures – lions, bulls and an immense human figure. He now knew that he had made a momentous discovery. Word was sent to Canning who was asked to obtain a firman (licence) from the authorities in Constantinople. Layard withdrew from Nimrud to Baghdad for Christmas where he met the

Human-headed winged lion from Ashurnasirpal II's palace at Nimrud *c*.865 BC. These massive gateway figures are *lamassu* or *sedu*, the horned headdress indicates divinity. 'They had awed and instructed races which flourished 3000 years ago. Through the portals which they guarded kings, priests, and warriors had borne sacrifices to their altars . . .' (Layard). H. 3 m 50 cm (11 ft 6 in)

Resident Henry Rawlinson for the first time, the beginning of a friendship which was to do much for Assyriology.

When Layard returned to Nimrud in January 1846 the Pasha had been replaced and the countryside transformed: '... the landscape was clothed in green, the black tents of the Arabs chequered the plain of Nimrud, and their numerous flocks pastured on the distant hills'. He had been joined by Hormuzd Rassam (1826–1910), brother of the British Vice-Consul, who acted as overseer and general agent. The religious authorities again forced a temporary halt by their protests about the removal of ancient treasures and the discovery of strange inscriptions but in mid-February Layard started work again, finding more reliefs and then, one morning:

I had ridden to the encampment of Sheikh Abd-ur-Rahman [a local tribal leader] and was returning to the mound when I saw two Arabs of his tribe urging their mares to the top of their speed. On approaching me they stopped. "Hasten, O Bey," exclaimed one of them – "hasten to the diggers, for they have found Nimrod himself. Wallah! it is wonderful, but it is true! we have seen him with our eyes. There is no God but God".

In a new trench was the great head of a colossal human-headed gateway figure with a calm and majestic expression. One of the workmen on catching a glimpse of the monster had thrown down his basket and fled in the direction of Mosul. Layard was supervising the removal of earth from round the head when:

Abd-ur-Rahman [arrived] followed by half his tribe ... When they beheld the head they all cried together, "There is no God but God, and Mahommed is his Prophet!" It was some time before the Sheikh could be prevailed upon to descend into the pit, and convince himself that the image he saw was of stone. "This is not the work of men's hands" exclaimed he, "but of those infidel giants of whom the Prophet, peace be with him! has said, that they were higher than the tallest date tree; this is one of the idols which Noah, peace be with him! cursed before the flood".

Twelve feet away Layard found another

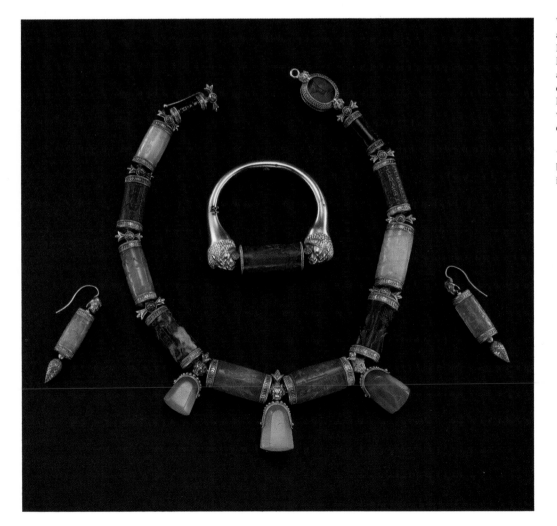

When Layard married in 1869, a selection of Assyrian and Babylonian seals acquired from his excavations was made into a necklace, bracelet and earrings as a gift for his bride. Lady Layard (1842–1912) wrote that when the couple dined with Queen Victoria in 1873 the Nineveh necklace 'was much admired and the bracelet passed round for inspection'.

Right. Foreigners from the west bringing apes to the Assyrian King. From the Palace of Ashurnasirpal II at Nimrud, *c*.865 BC. H. 2·38 m (7 ft 8 in)

figure. The following morning men, women and children from the surrounding villages came to gaze in wonder. The fleeing workman's report had caused commotion in Mosul and the religious authorities protested again, bringing work to a halt. In mid-March however, the plain of Nimrud was a delightful place.

Flowers of every hue enamelled the meadows; not thinly scattered over the grass as in northern climes, but in such thick and gathering clusters that the whole plain seemed a patchwork of many colours. The dogs, as they returned from hunting, issued from the long grass dyed red, yellow or blue, according to the flowers through which they had last forced their way...

Another governor was appointed who permitted the excavations to continue but it was now summer and Nimrud had become hot and unbearable.

Layard found more colossal human headed lions and reliefs showing the king and his attendants. The reliefs gave dramatic evidence of the fury of the Assyrian army – their great siege engines battering cities, the corpses of their victims awaiting the vultures. There were also hunting scenes – the king slaughtering lions and wild bulls.

The firman finally arrived authorising the continuation of excavations and the removal of objects. Layard had arranged for the transfer of the first sculptures which were to go to the Museum by a circuitous route: raft down the Tigris to Baghdad, boat to Basra, ship to Bombay and then to London.

The heat was so intense, as high as 117°F in the shade, that Layard decided to halt until conditions improved. When he returned in November 1846 Canning had made over his share of the discoveries to the Museum which agreed to finance the excavation. Layard regarded the Treasury contribution of £2000 as niggardly, nevertheless he set to work at the end of October: '... determined that the nation might possess as extensive and complete a collection of Assyrian antiquities as, considering the smallness of the means, it was possible to collect.' Because funds were low Layard was obliged to limit his excavations and he admits that few rooms were fully explored. He dug all over the mound, burying buildings behind him to preserve the sculptures he had recorded. More sculptures appeared and Layard uncovered a third palace, that of Tiglath-Pileser III.

One of the most important finds was the black obelisk of Shalmaneser III (858–824

Discovery of a colossal gateway figure by Layard's workmen. 'Hasten, O Bey, hasten to the diggers, for they have found Nimrod himself'.

BC), about six and a half feet in height, found lying on its side ten feet below the surface. Five rows of reliefs showed conquered peoples bringing tribute to the King. Later identified among them from a cuneiform caption was Jehu, King of Israel (or his ambassador) – a tangible link with the Bible.

Excavations resumed in the New Year. In one room were discovered small carved pieces of ivory – human heads in frames supported by low pillars, heads of lions and bulls, winged sphinxes. The country which the previous year had been so beautiful was now barren for the rains had failed and famine had come. Layard's situation at Nimrud was becoming precarious as raiding groups of hungry Bedouin became more numerous. He therefore decided to arrange for the removal of the larger sculptures to London as soon as possible. The Trustees had instructed him to leave them for future removal but Layard decided to try to move two of the smallest and best preserved of the thirteen pairs of gateway sculptures he had found: a lion and a bull from the great central hall. Layard managed to acquire sufficient wood to make a cart and reduced the weight of the figures by cutting away the uncarved back of the slabs. A trench was cut to the edge of the mound. Layard's equipment was limited – he had some ropes of poor quality, a thick hawser from Baghdad, two pairs of blocks and a pair of jack-screws acquired from a steamer. The bull was ready on 18 March 1847. It was supported by beams resting against the opposite wall. Rollers were laid on the ground parallel to it on to which it was to be lowered slowly by means of ropes passed round mounds of earth and the gradual removal of the retaining beams. Layard had invited Sheikh Abd-ur-Rahman and his tribe to watch:

The ropes held well. The mass descended gradually. It was a moment of great anxiety. The drums and shrill pipes of the Kurdish musicians increased the din and confusion caused by the war-cry of the Arabs, who were half frantic with excitement ... The women had congregated on the sides of the trenches, and by their incessant screams, and by the ear-piercing *tahlehl*, added to the enthusiasm of the men. The bull once in motion it was no longer possible to obtain a hearing. Away went the bull, steadily enough as long as supported by the props behind ... The cable and ropes stretched more and more. Dry from the climate, as they felt the strain, they creaked and threw out dust. Water was thrown over them, but in vain, for they all broke together when the sculpture was within four or five feet of the rollers ... A sudden silence succeeded to the clamor.

But the bull had landed unscathed. It was left for the night while the tribesmen celebrated. The Sheikh expressed his doubts about the practicality of digging up old stones:

In the name of the Most High, tell me, O Bey, what you are going to do with these stones. So many thousand of purses spent upon such things! Can it be, as you say, that your people learn wisdom from them; or is it ... that they are to go to the palace of your Queen, who, with the rest of the unbelievers, worships these idols?

In the morning, still singing, the Arabs started for the mound and began to drag the bull towards the river. The procession became bogged down when the cart fell into a concealed grain pit. During the night the guards were attacked by a marauding party of Arabs who were beaten off leaving behind in the bull a hole from a musket ball which is still visible today. Next morning the cart was coaxed out of the hole and reached the river to await a raft. The lion followed and on 20 April 1847 the sculptures were embarked for Basra. Layard watched them go:

As I watched the rafts, until they disappeared behind a projecting bank forming a distant reach of the river, I could not forbear musing upon the strange destiny of their burdens; which, after adorning the palaces of the Assyrian kings, the objects of the wonder and maybe the worship of thousands, had been buried unknown for centuries beneath a soil trodden by Persians under Cyrus, by Greeks under Alexander, and by Arabs under the first successors of their prophet. They were now to visit India, to cross the most distant seas of the southern hemisphere, and to be finally placed in a British Museum. Who can venture to foretell how their strange career will end?

It was becoming more dangerous to remain at Nimrud: armed parties of Arabs could be seen from the mound as they rode towards the hills in search of pillage. Layard realised the time had come to cover up the ruins as instructed by the Trustees and leave. By the middle of May 1847 Nimrud was again deserted. Layard dug next at Ashur and Kuyunjik where he located the largest of the Assyrian royal palaces, Sennacherib's 'Palace without a Rival' which contained the series of reliefs, now in the Museum, depicting the siege of Lachish. After a visit to London he returned to Mosul in October 1849 and resumed work at Kuyunjik and Nimrud. In April 1851 he finally left Mesopotamia. He had located at Nineveh the library of Ashurbanipal (668–627 BC), which with later discoveries was to provide the foundation for the reconstruction of Assyrian history and culture. At Nimrud he had found the temples of Ishtar and Ninurta. On his return home Layard turned to a distinguished career outside archaeology. He entered Parliament, held junior government posts and transferred to the Foreign Service in 1877. His book *Nineveh and its Remains* was one of the earliest examples of popular archaeology, with a massive public sale especially on railway bookshops; as Layard proudly commented in a letter, even rivalling in popularity Mrs Rundell's *Cookery*, no mean feat for an archaeological author even today.

The Nimrud Ivories

From 1949 to 1963 excavations again took place at Nimrud first under the supervision of Professor (later Sir) Max Mallowan (1904–78), then Professor D. Oates, under the auspices of the British School of Archaeology in Iraq. In April 1951 while clearing the chambers on the east side of the domestic wing of Ashurbanipal's North-West Palace the excavators found a well, its head a yard above the mud-brick floor of the room and lined with curved bricks many inscribed with the name of Ashurnasirpal. It was filled with earth thrown down in antiquity and reached a depth of eighty-three feet four inches. Excavation was unpleasant and dangerous since the well continually filled with water and threatened to collapse.

However, the effort was rewarded for the expedition found a series of superb ivories. Some came to the Museum, where they joined the collection made by Layard and Loftus (in 1854–5). Most of the ivories had been used for furniture decoration although there is some evidence that ivory was also inlaid into palace walls and made into toilet articles such as

Assyrian chariots and cavalry in battle. A vanquished enemy lies below the horses' hooves while above hovers a vulture.

spoons and combs. Some ivories had probably come to Nimrud as tribute from conquests others by loot or trade. They include the strange 'Woman at the Window' pieces: women in Egyptian-style wigs and dresses facing out of recessed windows, perhaps representing the goddess Ashtart in the role of a sacred prostitute. There are human headed winged sphinxes, crouching calves and lions, but the most outstanding are two chryselephantine plaques (one in the Museum the other in the Iraq Museum) which show a lioness mauling a negro. Only, as Mallowan wrote, 10.2 cm high it is an unforgettable piece, portraying sudden death, 'against a brilliant background, a meadow of Egyptian "lilies" and papyrus flowers with golden stems, blue and red in alternate rows, bending now one way, now the other, as if swaying before the wind'.

Lioness mauling a negro, one of a pair of ivories found in the bottom of a well in the North-West Palace in 1953, probably thrown there during the sack of Nimrud c.612 BC. Much of the surface was once overlaid with gold leaf and inlaid with carnelian and lapis lazuli. The man's hair is formed from ivory pegs inserted individually. The style is Phoenician, but the theme is Egyptian in origin, c. 8th c. BC. H. 10.2 cm (4 in)

'Woman at the Window'. A woman in Egyptian wig and dress looks out of a recessed window, perhaps an allusion to a special aspect of the worship of Ashtart the goddess of love in which the goddess or her votaress was thought of in the character of a sacred prostitute. Late 8th c. BC. H. 8.2 cm (3.2 in)

6

THE ROSETTA STONE AND THE DECIPHERMENT OF HIEROGLYPHS

Although the Rosetta Stone is by no means the most imposing object in the Egyptian Sculpture Gallery of the British Museum, the immense significance of this irregularly shaped slab of black basalt lies in the three bands of inscription in two languages carved upon it: at the top Egyptian hieroglyphic, in the middle a cursive form of this script known as demotic and at the bottom Greek. At the time of its discovery in 1799, while Greek was widely known, the knowledge of the other two scripts had been lost for many centuries. There was an increasing interest in the remains of ancient Egypt but, without the ability to read the inscriptions carved on its monuments, it was a civilisation largely hidden from the world.

The stone was found in the small village of Rashîd (known to Europeans as Rosetta) in the Nile Delta. Its discoverers were attached to Napoleon's ill-fated Egyptian expedition of 1798 which had been sent into territory then nominally ruled by Turkey with the intention of dominating the East Mediterranean and threatening the British hold on India. Although accounts of the stone's discovery in July 1799 are now rather obscure, the story most generally accepted is that it was found by accident, built into a very old wall which a company of French soldiers had been ordered to demolish so as to clear the way for the foundations of an extension to a fort. Fortunately for Egyptology, the officer in charge of the demolition squad, Pierre François Xavier Bouchard, and his fellow officers, realised the importance of the discovery, namely that the three different scripts might represent the same text and that as one of them, Greek, could be read the other versions might be deciphered from it.

The stone was despatched to Cairo and placed in the Institut National which had been founded there by Napoleon. Napoleon's expedition included a group of learned men, charged with making a study of the land and people of Egypt and these savants, naturally, fell excitedly upon the stone. Copies were made for distribution to other European scholars and the race to unlock its secrets began. The scholars' learned activities were soon to be interrupted by the British. A successful naval blockade had cut off the French Army from its home and a military force under Sir Ralph Abercromby threatened Cairo. The French scholars moved their collection of antiquities, including the stone, to Alexandria.

After the French capitulation and under the terms of the Treaty of Alexandria (1801) these became the property of the British Crown. The stone was shipped to England in the aptly named HMS *L'Égyptienne* and arrived in Portsmouth in February 1802. It was at first deposited with the Society of Antiquaries and casts or copies were sent to universities and other learned institutions of Europe. In July 1802 it was presented to the Museum by King George III together with other antiquities which included the enormous sarcophagus of Nectanebo II of the 30th dynasty (360–43 BC) which had been used as a public bath in Alexandria (the holes for letting out water are still visible today). The sculptures were placed in temporary structures in the Museum grounds since the floors of Montagu House were not strong enough to bear the weight. After a plea to Parliament for funds, the Trustees embarked on the building of a new gallery in which to house their most recent acquisitions. The stone was placed on immediate display and the public flocked to see it. Although the Greek text presented relatively

Jean François Champollion (1790–1832) who eventually solved the problem of the triple inscription. His first significant findings were published in 1822 and before his death he had laid the foundations for the study of the ancient Egyptian language.

few problems and translations were rapidly made into French, English and Latin, it was not possible to make an immediate translation of the other two texts. Pieces were missing from each section and, as was later established, the three versions were close but not exact translations of each other. It would take scholars twenty years to begin to decipher the hieroglyphic and demotic inscriptions.

Egyptian hieroglyphic script consists not of a short alphabet of the kind used by the Greeks but of a very large number of signs of different types, some of which are sense signs (ideograms) and some sound signs (phonograms). The demotic script was subject to the same complexities and, to add to the problem, looked very different since it had developed its own cursive conventions in use on papyrus, potsherds or flakes of limestone.

Although the Frenchman Jean François Champollion (1790–1832) is rightly known as the decipherer of the hieroglyphic script, he built on the work of other scholars. A Swedish diplomat, J.D. Åkerblad (1763–1819) identified several proper names in the demotic version of the Rosetta stone including Ptolemy and, through knowing their Coptic equivalents, the words 'Greeks', 'temples', 'him' and 'his'. Coptic was the language of the descendants of the Ancient Egyptians, the Copts, and although spoken Coptic had died out in the sixteenth century AD its texts – written in a script based on the Greek alphabet – were preserved and read. The next important advance was made by an Englishman, Thomas Young (1773–1829). To Young goes the credit for recognising that both hieroglyphic and demotic texts consisted of a mixture of alphabetic and non-alphabetic signs and for appreciating that these texts were closely related. Young first looked for and linked words in Greek and demotic which occurred the same number of times and built up a small vocabulary (and, king, Ptolemy, Egypt, etc). He next concentrated on the identical signs contained in the six oval 'cartouches' in the hieroglyphic section which he took to represent the name of the king – Ptolemy – which he had read in the Greek section. From his previous identification of the royal names, Berenike and another Ptolemy on a different inscription, he correctly identified the phonetic values of six hieroglyphic signs and, partly correctly, a further three.

This represented a major breakthrough but it was Champollion, with his extensive knowledge of Coptic, who finally solved the riddle of the Rosetta Stone. Young's discoveries had been communicated to him but it was not until 1821 when Champollion received a copy of the bilingual inscription in hieroglyphs and Greek on an obelisk and its base excavated by W.J. Bankes at Philae in 1815 that he appreciated the true significance of Bankes's discoveries. Bankes had rightly deduced that one of his cartouches contained the name Cleopatra. When Champollion compared this cartouche with that of Ptolemy on the Rosetta Stone he realised that they had three signs in common which occurred where the sounds P, O, L would be expected if the names were spelled alphabetically. His discovery was announced to the French Academy in September 1822. He developed his theories further, formulated a system of grammar for the Egyptian language and laid the foundations on which present knowledge is based.

The inscription is a businesslike text written in the reign of King Ptolemy V and is a copy of a decree passed by a general council of priests which assembled at Memphis on the first anniversary of Ptolemy V's coronation, that is on 27 March 196 BC. The stone lists the King's titles – the Ever-living, the beloved of Ptah, the God Epiphanes Eucharistos. The inscription sets out in some detail the honours to be bestowed upon the new king by the grateful priests of Egypt in return for services rendered by him – gifts of money and corn to the temples, etc. Amongst other promises his golden shrine is to be carried in festivals. The tone can be caught from the following detailed instructions concerning the shrine:

And in order that it may be easily distinguishable now and for all time there shall be set upon the shrine the ten gold diadems of the king, to which shall be added a uraeus but instead of the uraeus-shaped diadems which are upon the other shrines, in the centre of them shall be the crown called Pschent which he put on when he went into the temple at Memphis to perform therein the ceremonies for assuming the kingship, and there shall be placed on the square surface round about the diadems, beside the aforementioned crown, golden symbols (eight in number signifying) that it is (the shrine) of the king who makes manifest the Upper the Lower countries . . .

(Lines 43, 44, 45, 46 Greek text).

However, the fascination of stone remains as it was the key to our knowledge of Egyptian civilisation.

7

THE FOURTH-CENTURY HINTON ST MARY MOSAIC PAVEMENT

The Roman army left Britain in 410 AD and an era of darkness ensued. Much of the evidence of Roman civilisation disappeared – one such hidden remnant was a mosaic pavement, buried beneath the soil of a field in the village of Hinton St Mary, Dorset.

In an ornate roundel on this fourth-century AD pavement there is a bust of a fair-haired, clean-shaven man with dark rather penetrating eyes. He wears an inner garment (*tunica*) and outer mantle (*pallium*) shaded orange, white, black, grey and purple. Behind his head is the *Chi-Rho* symbol so-called because it is made up of the first letters of the Greek word *Christos* (Christ). His hair is combed forward and falls in curly locks. He has a slightly cleft chin. To each side is a pomegranate – the symbol of immortality. This is the earliest representation of Christ yet found in Britain and the only such portrait in a mosaic discovered in the Roman Empire.

The mosaic was found in September 1963 by a Mr W.J. White who was digging postholes for the foundation of a building in a field near his forge. At the bottom of the holes he recognised Roman *tesserae* – the small fragments used to build up a mosaic – and immediately called in professional assistance. The excavators found a pair of rooms joined by an eleven foot opening, the whole being twenty eight feet four inches by nineteen and a half feet – perhaps a *triclinium* (a room containing a dining table with couches along three sides). The pavement was between fifteen and thirty inches below modern ground level. There was a single design running from the smaller room into the larger. In the larger room the focus of the mosaic was the portrait with the *Chi-Rho* symbol; in the smaller the design was taken from pagan mythology – Bellerophon mounted on Pegasus thrusting a

The earliest representation of Christ yet found in Britain, dating from the 4th c. AD, and the only such portrait in a mosaic discovered in the Roman Empire (detail). The drapery is coloured orange, white, black, grey and purple. Diam. 95 cm (37·4 in)

Left. The mosaic at Hinton St Mary, Dorset as uncovered by the excavators in 1963. In the four corners of the larger section are portraits thought to be the four winds or the four evangelists. The half circles show hunting scenes and a great tree with grey-blue leaves. At the top is Bellerophon mounted on galloping Pegasus thrusting a spear into the lion-headed, serpent-tailed Chimaera. Total L. 8·6 m (28 ft 4 in)

spear into the fabulous chimaera.

The style of the mosaic indicated that it was laid in the fourth century, a period when we know that wealthy villas were to be found in Britain. Similar mosaics have been found in the vicinity which suggests that a firm of mosaic makers was at work.

To whom did the pavement belong? An attempt to answer this question was made by a Museum excavation team. They found traces of a substantial building complex which had flourished in the fourth century – the coins discovered date mostly between 270 and 400 AD and the lack of Samian ware pottery suggests that it is unlikely that it was occupied until after the beginning of the third century. There is no direct evidence as to the economy of the villa. The presence of the pavement suggests prosperity and we know that the neighbouring downland of Cranbourne Chase had rich flocks of sheep although in the villa area the most likely farming was arable and cattle. The main building was probably built round three sides of a courtyard, the fourth being enclosed by a ditch. The mosaic was part of the best-preserved wing. The walls on either side of the pavement had been demolished, most probably for re-use in later building. It has been suggested that the villa might have been a religious site but, apart from the Christian symbol on the pavement, there is no direct evidence to confirm or deny this.

How did it fall into decline? No evidence was found of a sudden annihilating attack as had happened elsewhere but the fourth century was a period of decline for the Roman Empire. In 367–8 AD there was a major barbarian attack as armies of Picts, Scots, Attacotti and Saxons made coordinated assaults. They were in time repulsed but throughout this period there was a general deterioration of trade and perhaps the inhabitants changed from cash crops to subsistence farming. After the departure of the Roman army Saxons and other tribes moved in. At some point the villa was abandoned, its walls torn down and the pavement became covered with a layer of soil. In an 1843 tithe map the only trace of a bustling prosperous villa was the name of the field in which the pavement was found – 'Stoney Hill'.

SCULPTURE

8

THE BUST OF RAMESSES THE GREAT AND GIOVANNI BELZONI

I met a traveller from an antique land
Who said: Two vast and trunkless legs of stone
Stand in the desert ...
And on the pedestal these words appear:
"My name is Ozymandias, king of kings:
Look on my works, ye mighty, and despair!"
Nothing beside remains. Round the decay
Of that colossal wreck, boundless and bare
The lone and level sands stretch far away.

(Percy Bysshe Shelley (1792–1822), *Ozymandias* (inspired by the imminent arrival in England of the colossal bust of Ramesses II).)

Of the many pharaohs who ruled Egypt one, Ramesses II of the Nineteenth Dynasty, now bears the title 'the Great'. He succeeded his father Sethos I *c.*1304 BC, ruled for sixty-seven years and is said to have secured the succession by fathering one hundred and fifty children. Whether Ramesses deserves his title 'the Great' is a matter of dispute, but what is not challenged is that he was able to establish this grand reputation by the erection of colossal sculptures, the appropriation of others and the carving of grandiose inscriptions. 'The King shot arrows to his right, he defended himself on his left. Two thousand five hundred chariots were overthrown' reads one such. One of his most famous monuments is the rock temple of Abu Simbel where four sixty-seven feet-high colossi survey the Nile; another is his mortuary temple at Thebes from which comes the Museum's colossal bust, of two-tone granite, now in the Egyptian Sculpture Gallery.

Ramesses' mummy is now in Cairo. He appears to have been a moderately tall man – the mummy is five feet eight inches in height – with a low and narrow forehead, long thin and arched nose, a strong jaw and thick lips. The bust in the British Museum, with its fine features and enigmatic smile is in no way a physical representation. To the ancient Egyptians such sculpture was not 'art' as we know it, nor was it usually intended to look exactly like its subject, rather it was carved according to certain conventions and intended to ensure the subject's survival after death. (Although in some periods the conventions do change and it is possible to distinguish styles and therefore appearances for different kings.)

The story of the bust's arrival in the Museum is an epic one. In 1813 Jean-Louis Burckhardt, a Swiss also known as 'Sheikh Ibrahim' because of his mastery of Arabic and sympathy and understanding of Arab life, paid his first visit to Upper Egypt where in the neighbourhood of Thebes, he saw in a ruined temple a colossal granite head of great beauty. This came to be known as 'the Younger Memnon' but was in fact part of a colossus of Ramesses II. Burckhardt conceived the intention of removing the head to England. (The peasants at the nearby village of Qurna had reported to him that members of Napoleon's earlier expedition had already made an attempt to take away the head by drilling a hole in the right breast which can be seen today). Burckhardt tried to interest a number of individuals in the project but nothing came of the matter until the involvement of one of the most colourful characters then in Cairo, Giovanni Battista Belzoni.

In his *Narrative* Belzoni gives a brief sketch of his rather chequered career: 'My native place is the city of Padua' he wrote, 'I am of Roman family, which had resided there for many years. The state and troubles of Italy in 1800 ... compelled me to leave it and from that time I have visited different parts of Europe, and suffered many vicissitudes'. Belzoni mentions that in Rome he studied hydraulics but glosses over the fact that, on reaching England in 1803 he had earned his living as a strongman appearing at Sadler's Wells and elsewhere.

With this rather unusual combination of experience, in 1814 he set off on his travels again. In Malta in May 1815 he made the acquaintance of 'Ishmael Gibraltar' an agent of Mohammed Ali Pasha, the virtual ruler of Egypt which was then, as it had been for centuries, under Turkish rule. Gibraltar, on learning of Belzoni's hydraulic knowledge intimated that bright prospects awaited him in a country so dependent on irrigation. Belzoni and his wife therefore arrived in Cairo later in the year. In 1816 came the opportunity to demonstrate his new hydraulic machine to the Pasha. Belzoni managed to raise more water than by conventional methods but the Pasha, conscious of opposition from those involved in traditional methods, managed to sabotage the demonstration and Belzoni was dismissed.

Belzoni was now becoming short of funds and desperate so he and Burckhardt became involved in a scheme to move the 'Younger Memnon'. Belzoni could provide a knowledge of hydraulics and practical experience in the moving of heavy weights. Burckhardt alone could not finance an expedition so they enlisted the assistance of Henry Salt (1780–1827) the recently arrived British Consul, who had vague instructions from Sir Joseph Banks, a Trustee, to look out for antiquities for the British Museum. Salt was happy to participate in the project and the trio came to an agreement in 1816. Belzoni was despatched to Upper Egypt to bring back the bust with lifting equipment consisting of fourteen poles, four ropes of palm leaves and four rollers. He had strict instructions that, while he should spare no expense or trouble in its removal on no account might he move it if there was any serious risk of 'injuring the head, of burying the face in the sand, or of losing it in the Nile'.

He arrived at the Ramesseum in July 1816

Giovanni Battista Belzoni (1778–1823). Born in Padua Belzoni had an extremely varied career as actor, strongman, hydraulic engineer, Egyptologist and traveller. He is described as having 'a remarkable figure, 6 ft 7 in high, and broad in proportion, with winning manners and a decidedly handsome countenance'.

and located the 'quite perfect and very beautiful' head of Ramesses II. Belzoni's immediate problem was to move it before the land between the Ramesseum and the Nile was inundated by the flood due in a month's time. He was equipped with proper authorisation from the authorities in Cairo and Asyut and he therefore addressed himself to the senior local official, the Kashief or Governor of the province of Armant, requesting an order to his subordinate the 'Caimakan of Gournou and Agalta' for eighty workmen to assist with the removal. The Kashief was polite but obstructive but Belzoni persisted and eventually assembled enough men to make a start:

The carpenter had made the car and the first operation was to endeavour to place the bust on it ... The mode I adopted to place it on the car was very simple ... By means of four levers I raised the bust, so as to leave a vacancy under it, to introduce the car; and, after it was slowly lodged on this, I had the car raised in the front with the bust on it, so as to get one of the rollers underneath. I then had the same operation performed at the back, and the colossus was ready to be pulled up ... I caused it to be well secured on the car, and the ropes so placed that the power might be divided. I stationed men with levers at each side of the car, to assist occasionally, if the colossus should be inclined to turn to either side. In this manner I kept it safe from falling. Lastly, I placed men in the front, distributing them equally at the four ropes, while others were ready to change the rollers alternately. Thus I succeeded in getting it removed the distance of several yards from its original place.

Conditions at Thebes were terrible. It was the hottest season, the air was inflamed and at night a hot wind blew, the stones of the temple were too hot to touch. On 28 July work resumed and the bust was dragged out of the Ramesseum. Slow progress was made interrupted by Belzoni's illness (Mrs Belzoni enjoyed 'tolerable health'). On 5 August the Kaimakan, choosing his moment carefully, struck. Belzoni had now dragged the head into the area which would shortly be flooded. When he went to inspect it on 6 August the workmen had disappeared. Belzoni confronted the Kaimakan who referred him to the Kashief. Belzoni headed for Armant by boat and interrupted a feast but all was well: the Kashief announced that henceforward they would be friends.

A firman was written and sealed and Belzoni immediately hurried back to Qurna, narrowly missing being drowned at Luxor en route in the strong Nile current. On 7 August men were obtained and the following day the head was out of danger from flooding. Belzoni's sickness returned – he was giddy and bleeding from nose and mouth. However, he was back at work on the 10th and 11th and on 12 August 'thank God, the young Memnon arrived on the bank of the Nile'. The workmen were paid off and Belzoni recorded his amazement at the endurance of the Fellahs who, during the month of Ramadan when they could neither eat nor drink during the day, accomplished a task which he considered to be 'more than any European could have withstood'.

The bust was left, protected by earthworks till a boat should arrive and Belzoni explored further up the Nile. In November he returned and one hundred and thirty men were engaged to construct a causeway since the river bank was fifteen feet above water level. A bridge of poles was constructed from bank to boat and the bust was slowly lowered down by ropes on to the boat, great care having to be taken not to upset the vessel. The bust reached England safely by way of Rosetta and Alexandria and was installed in the British Museum in 1818 as the gift of J.L. Burckhardt and H. Salt.

Belzoni had now found his metier and in the years following excavated and moved many other sculptures some of which eventually came to the Museum. He operated not only as an engineer but conceived an intense interest in the history of the country. As he wrote:

I had become so familiar with the sight of temples,

Right. Upper half of a colossal seated statue of Ramesses II (once thought to be 'Younger Memnon'), 19th Dynasty. *c.* 1270 BC, one of a pair from his mortuary temple at Thebes. The king wears the *nemes* head-dress surmounted by a cobra diadem. The bust is made of a single block of two-tone granite worked to distinguish the head and body H. 2.67 m (8 ft 9 in). Wt 7.25 tons.

Left. Black granite figure of Amenophis III, 18th Dynasty, *c.* 1400 BC, from Thebes. The king is represented in classic pose and dress. He wears a *nemes* headcloth, false beard and short kilt which is fitted with a ceremonial bull's tail shown between the legs. Belzoni's name is inscribed on the base. H. 2·9 m (9 ft 6 in)

Dragging the colossal bust from the Ramesseum to the Nile in 1816 from a watercolour in Belzoni's *Narrative* (1820). Belzoni's equipment consisted of 14 poles, 4 ropes of palm leaves and 4 rollers plus his own vast strength and the endurance of the Egyptian workmen during the hottest season of the year.

Right. Red granite head of a king, thought to be Amenophis III, wearing the double crown. From a standing figure, one of a pair, set up before the Temple of Khonspekhrod in the precincts of the Temple of Mut at Karnak, 18th Dynasty, c.1390 BC. One of the sculptures moved by Belzoni. H. 2·9 m (9 ft 5 in)

tombs and pyramids that I could not help forming some speculation on their origin and construction. The scholar and learned traveller will smile at my presumption, but do they always agree themselves in their opinions on matters of this sort . . . .

His work in the Valley of the Kings, was, for example, the first to be conducted with serious archaeological intent and a fair degree of care. He continued to excavate and collect for Salt but this project was soured by the Trustees' treatment of Salt who, encouraged by the enthusiasm aroused by his gift of the great bust, understood that he was collecting for the Museum. When he claimed his expenses plus a profit the Trustees considered that they were being exploited and unedifying negotiations dragged on for some years.

In 1823 a collection was purchased for £2000 (much of it made between 1817 and 1819 with Belzoni's assistance). Another large collection went elsewhere. After Salt's death the Museum had a final chance to acquire important objects from his collection and in 1835 purchased many pieces at the sale of the residue of the collection at Sothebys

(many of the 'post-Belzoni' objects had been acquired for Salt by the agency of Giovanni d'Athanasi). Belzoni left Egypt in 1819 and returned to England by way of Italy. He became the 'lion' of London society and embarked on a variety of projects including the erection of a facsimile of the Tomb of Sethos I in the Egyptian Hall, Piccadilly.

The urge to travel again overcame him and in 1823 he died of dysentry in Benin on an expedition to trace the source of the Niger. His grave soon disappeared but he has a permanent memorial. One need only, as his biographer wrote, 'sit in the Egyptian Galleries of the British Museum and look at the bland smiling face of the Young Memnon when the afternoon sun through the west windows is playing strange tricks with those mobile features . . .'. There are many other pieces in the Egyptian Sculpture Gallery which we owe to Belzoni – the colossal head and arm of a king now thought to be Amenophis III which he brought from the Temple of Mut at Karnak, two large seated statues of Amenophis III (on one of which is carved Belzoni's name) from

his mortuary temple, now destroyed, behind the Colossi of Memnon, a large bust in limestone and two colossal heads in quartzite also from this mortuary temple, three life-size wooden figures of kings from the royal tombs in the Valley of the Kings.

Belzoni removed from their ruined sites sculptures the importance of which was only just becoming evident. His methods appear crude, but not by the standards of his day. He was truly fascinated by Egypt and its antiquities and what he discovered and sent back to Europe has since done much to inspire generations of museum visitors from outside Egypt with a similar fascination with that great country.

9

NINEVEH – THE LION HUNT OF ASHURBANIPAL

After Layard's departure from Mesopotamia his assistant Hormuzd Rassam (1825–1910) continued to excavate at Nineveh and elsewhere under the direction of Henry Rawlinson. In December 1853 on the northern side of the mound of Kuyunjik he found the North Palace of Ashurbanipal built c.645 BC. There he discovered perhaps the finest animal scenes of antiquity, the bas reliefs showing the lion hunt of Ashurbanipal. Here we see Ashurbanipal with his retinue setting out for the hunting field, horses snorting and pricking their ears. Captive lions and lionesses are released from wooden cages and, enraged by the baying of hounds held on the leash, they rush out only to meet a bloody death at the hands of the king. We cannot now know what was foremost in the mind of Ashurbanipal's sculptor of undoubted genius. Was it the glorification of the king or, as one writer has suggested, 'a sympathy for the suffering beasts, so uselessly brave, roaring and defiant or twitching in agony of death.

Dying lioness – 'suffering beasts, so uselessly brave, roaring and defiant or twitching in agony of death'. (Barnett) L. 75 cm (2 ft 6 in)

Far right. Ashurbanipal, King of Assyria 668–627 BC, shooting lions from his chariot. The king wears the high Assyrian royal crown. Detail from a frieze from his palace at Nineveh, c. 645 BC.

The hunt in progress. The king shoots ahead while two guards ward off a wounded lion.
H. 1·6 m (3 ft 10 in)

THE TOWNLEY COLLECTION OF CLASSICAL SCULPTURE

The fact is, John Bull, though a person of boundless curiosity, has no great taste for the Fine Arts, and would rather spend his time and money in seeing a Calf with two heads than the finest piece of sculpture in the Towneley Collection for nothing.

(Unidentified newspaper, 1805, quoted by Richard D. Altick, *The Shows of London*, Belkhap Press, Harvard, 1978)

Although John Bull in general may not have appreciated the collection of Roman sculpture (with a few Greek originals) put together by Charles Townley (1737–1805), to connoisseurs at the turn of the eighteenth century it was one of the sights of London. Parliament was willing to spend £20,000 on its purchase and the British Museum to house it in a brand new gallery. When, however, in 1807 the 'Elgin marbles' with Pheidias's great masterpieces burst upon artists and connoisseurs Townley was eclipsed. Later acquisitions by the Museum of Greek originals from Xanthos, Ephesus and Halicarnassus reinforced in Victorian eyes the superiority of Greek sculpture and gradually the Townley collection lost esteem, it became intermixed with other classical sculptures and much of it confined to basement galleries and storage rooms, the latter visited only by a few scholarly vistors and staff.

Since 1984, however, with the aid of funds from the Wolfson Foundation it is again on show to the public in a delightfully cluttered basement gallery which reflects the taste and arrangement of the English collectors of the eighteenth century. Some of the old favourites have reappeared – Discobolus (the discus thrower) a Roman copy in marble from an original bronze by the Greek sculptor Myron (*fl.* 450 BC). There are glimpses of Discobolus throughout the nineteenth century in illustrations of the Museum; a number of copies were made in antiquity and in more recent times plaster casts. Thus to the refrain 'O God! Oh Montreal!' he provided the inspiration for

Samuel Butler's *Psalm of Montreal* which laments a plaster cast confined to a dusty basement on the other side of the Atlantic.

There is the beautiful Townley Venus 'one of the chiefest glories of his [Townley's] gallery', slightly over life-sized, draped from the hips. She was found at Ostia in the ruins of the baths of Claudius in 1775. The bust of an attractive young woman with a slightly aquiline nose, known as *Clytie* who had a place above stairs in the Museum, has now returned to join the rest of the collection in the basement. Probably recut in the eighteenth century she is now thought to be a princess of the Julio-Claudian house, perhaps Antonia (*d.*38 AD) mother of Germanicus and the Emperor Claudius, daughter of Mark Antony and Octavia the wife he left for Cleopatra. She is surrounded by marble petals and thus takes her name from the nymph who turned into a flower when spurned by Apollo. The bust was purchased from Prince Laurenzano at Naples in 1772 and was Charles Townley's favourite sculpture. It is related that when, as a Roman Catholic, he was obliged to flee from the London mob at the time of the bloody Gordon riots (1780) his priorities were such that he secured his cabinet of gems, then taking Clytie in his arms with the words 'I must take care of my wife', 'he left his house, casting one last, longing, look at the marbles which, as he feared, would never charm his eyes again'.

Charles Townley was a member of an ancient and distinguished Lancashire Catholic family. As a Catholic he was educated at Douai, returned to Lancashire after his father's

Left to Right. Figure of a young satyr, marble, 1st or early 2nd c. AD. Nymph escaping from a satyr, marble copy of a 2nd or 1st c. BC. original, 2nd c. AD. Found near Tivoli in 1772. Figure of the young Bacchus with a personification of the vine. Marble *c.* AD 150–200. Found at La Storta near Rome in 1772.

The first Townley Gallery was opened in 1808 by Queen Charlotte, accompanied by 'the Prince of Wales, the Dukes of Cumberland and Cambridge and the Princesses'.

'Clytie', 'Portrait bust of a woman of great beauty', Townley's favourite. Perhaps a portrait of Antonia (d. AD 38) daughter of Mark Antony and Octavia and mother of Germanicus and the Emperor Claudius. Marble, *c*.AD 40–50, probably recut in the 18th c. Clytie was a nymph who changed into a flower when spurned by Apollo. H. 50·8 cm (1 ft 10 in)

Right. Charles Townley (1737–1805) seated (foreground) in an idealised setting of his collection at his Park Street home: 'His learning and sagacity in explaining works of ancient art was equal to his judgment in selecting them'. Also shown are (centre) the French theorist Pierre François Hughes (Baron d'Hancarville), (rear) Townley's friends Charles Greville and Thomas Astle. The statue of 'Discobolus' was added later. Painting by Johan Zoffany (1753–1810) in the Townley Hall Art Gallery, Burnley, Lancashire. 1027 × 990 mm (3 ft 4 in × 3 ft 3 in)

death when he came of age and it is said he was by then more of a foreigner than an Englishman, more comfortable speaking French than this native tongue. In the mid-eighteenth century Rome had become the mecca for rich Englishmen on the Grand Tour. Old Roman collections were being broken up and sold by the impoverished descendants of great families – Barberini, Maccarani, Mattei. English noblemen searching for ornament for their classical-style homes became eager buyers. The Roman art market developed under the direction of such British dealers as the artist Gavin Hamilton (1730–97) who, to feed demand, began 'excavations' of nearby sites including the villa of the Roman Emperor Hadrian (76–138 AD) at Tivoli, another villa near Lanuvium (reputed to have belonged to Antoninus Pius) and the ruins of Ostia. Along-side the dealers a flourishing trade in restoration developed staffed by such sculptors as Piranesi and Bartolomeo Cavaceppi, for fragmentary statues were looked down upon. On leaving Douai, Townley first plunged into the 'gaities and temptation' of Paris then his activities took a more serious turn as he fell under the spell of Italy and classical art. In 1765 he visited Rome and Florence and travelled in southern Italy and Sicily where he made the acquaintance of Sir William Hamilton and other collectors. In about 1768 he started his own collection with a group previously known as 'the cannibal' – a boy biting a human forearm – which is in fact the remains of a statue of two youths fighting over a game of knucklebones.

Townley returned to England and purchased a house at Park Street, Westminster (now Queen Anne's Gate). He bought it as a 'shell' and here he arranged and rearranged his sculpture and library. In the Dining room were the largest statues placed symmetrically – among them the Townley Venus and the Caryatid. Thalia and Diana were in alcoves flanking the fireplace, the heads of Athena and Zeus-Serapis were at either end of the mantle-piece. Townley tried to impart an appropriately Bacchanalian atmosphere to this room; he commented that 'all ornaments are relative to the attributes of those Gods, who were supposed by the antients to preside over the festive board' even to a frieze ornamented 'with festoons of Ivy, and trophys composed of the instruments used in orgies'. Here on Sundays Townley would give dinner parties rather than orgies and entertained such guests as the artists Sir Joshua Reynolds and Johan

Zoffany and the sculptor Nollekens. Students, connoisseurs and the merely curious were liberally admitted to view the collection.

Townley has been described as 'a man of graceful person and polished address, with a kind of "Attic Irony" in his conversation'. Unlike many of his contemporaries he saw his collection as more than ornament and he developed a scholarly interest, writing several catalogues, although his only published work was a paper on the Romano-British Ribchester helmet. He continued to visit Rome, adding to the collection until about 1780 and still continued to buy. He was a Trustee of the British Museum from 1791 and it was expected that he would bequeath his collection to the Museum but in a codicil dated only twelve days before his death he changed his mind and left his sculptures to his family provided that within five years they spent at least £4500 on a gallery in Burnley or in London, failing this the collection would revert to the Museum. The family were unable to meet the terms of the will and a compromise was reached whereby the sculptures were offered to the Trustees in return for £20,000 and a seat on the Board. A Select Committee of Parliament recommended that:

It would be an object of great National Importance, for the Improvement of the Fine Arts, that a Collection of Antique Sculpture of such acknowledged and unrivalled excellence ... should be acquired and preserved for public Inspection and Use.

The Trustees had since 1802 been planning a new gallery to take Egyptian antiquities. This was now adapted to house classical sculpture as well and so the new gallery (which rapidly acquired the name of the Townley Gallery) was opened by Queen Charlotte with some ceremony in 1808. (It was demolished some forty years later to make way for Smirke's new building.) Townley's bronzes, coins, gems and drawings were purchased in 1814 for £8200. Now with the opening of the Wolfson Galleries the collection is gathered together again, not quite as it was in Park Street, but in an arrangement which provides an opportunity to appreciate the taste of this eighteenth century collector.

Left. Head from a colossal statue of Hercules. Pentelic marble, *c.*AD 120–150, restored and mounted on a bust in the 18th c. Found in 1769 in the Villa of the Emperor Hadrian at Tivoli H. 73.6 cm (2 ft 5 in)

Pair of greyhounds, a dog and a bitch, playing together. Marble, 1st or 2nd c. AD, restored in the 18th c. as were many of Townley's sculptures. Found in 1774 at Monte Cagnolo near ancient Lanuvium. A mark round the neck of the female indicates the place of a metal collar. H. 65 cm (2 ft 2 in)

'Discobolus', Townley's last major purchase. One of several Roman copies after a lost Greek original made by the sculptor Myron (*fl.* 450 BC) a contemporary of Pheidias. Found in the villa of the Emperor Hadrian at Tivoli. The head, wrongly restored by Albacini, should have been turned to watch the discus. 2nd c. AD. H. 1·7 m (5 ft 7 in)

'HINDOO' STUART AND THE BRIDGE COLLECTION OF INDIAN SCULPTURE

'He married a Hiṇḍu and she made a Hindu of him'
(*Calcutta Review* 1846)

Dotted around the main oriental gallery and on the north staircase of the Museum are a number of fine sculptures from India. From the Hindu pantheon came the great gods Brahma, Vishnu and Siva, the sinister Camunda with her necklace of skulls and cup of blood, Durga killing the buffalo demon and the portly elephant-headed Ganesa. There are Jain spirits (Yakshi) and many superb figures from the Buddhist pantheon. This is the Bridge Collection, the gift in 1872 of the three daughters of one George Bridge, after the sculptures from the great stupa at Amaravati the finest single group in the Museum's collection of Indian sculpture, with well over a hundred pieces. Its origins go back before the Indian Mutiny, to the Calcutta of 'John Company' and a gifted, unconventional individual. Major-General Charles Stuart was born in Ireland and now lies in the South Park Street Cemetery in Calcutta. He was illegitimate, reputed to be the son of one Thomas Smith elder brother of the 1st Viscount Gort. Stuart, whose career alarmed his European contemporaries continued his unconventional behaviour in death for he arranged that, although buried in a Christian graveyard, his last resting place should resemble a Hindu temple in miniature.

Today he seems less eccentric than determined to live a full and interesting life. He was far beyond his contemporaries in his tolerance and respect for the ways of a non-European people. He was also in advance in his scholarly interests; most of his contemporaries were more concerned with language, astronomy, botany, archaeology and other sciences and

Ganesa, elder son of Siva and Parvati, Lord of the Ganas, the demi-gods who attend on Siva. He is the Remover of Obstacles who helps his worshippers to attain their desires. Schist. Orissa, 13th c. AD. H. 1·2 m (3 ft 4 in)

Left. The Tomb of Major-General Charles Stuart (1758–1828) in South Park Street Cemetery, Calcutta, designed to resemble a Hindu temple in miniature.

not with the fascination of the art and beliefs of India.

In February 1777 at the age of nineteen Stuart left Ireland for India, to see his homeland but once more when on furlough in 1804–8. Stuart, like many other young men, was taking a calculated risk – a rapid death from the many diseases awaiting him in India or, if he survived, of returning with a considerable fortune. He joined the Army of the Bengal Presidency and advanced rapidly, eventually in 1819 to Major-General. His obituarist explained how he came by his nickname:

General Stuart had studied the language, manners, and customs of the natives of this country with so much enthusiasm, that his intimacy with them, and his toleration of, or rather apparent conformity to, their ideas and prejudices, obtained for him the name of *Hindoo* Stuart ... From associating and conversing much with the natives, he became, of course, well versed in their tales, legends and superstitions and possessed stores of information and experience.

During his service he put together a remarkable collection of Indian antiquities, many of them now in the Museum, which were eventually gathered together in his house which stood at the corner of Shakespeare and Wood Streets in Calcutta. There they were made available to respectable visitors. If the General were in residence he would provide a tour, politely pointing out what he thought worthy of attention. Some indication of his visitors' unenthusiastic opinion of the shadowy figures in rooms shaded against the fierce tropical sun or flickering in candlelight is indicated by the *Indian Gazette's* comment that 'the General himself set a higher value upon it (the collection) than might by others be accorded it'.

Stuart's life was colourful and it would seem that his European contemporaries found him something of an embarrassment. He is said to have married a Hindu (but there is no indication of what became of her or if there were children since his will provides only for his European relatives). He bathed daily in the Ganges and he is supposed to have erected a Hindu temple. He seems to have been a likeable individual and adopted the Indians' generous attitude to the giving of alms and was said to have fed one hundred daily at his own expense. He is described as being:

distinguished by a peculiar benignity of manners and cheerfulness of disposition, qualities which never forsook him, and which combined with his varied information and honourable character, acquired for him the esteem of those who had the pleasure of his acquaintance; although they might smile sometimes at a perceptible tinge of eccentricity . . . .

On 31 March 1828, at the age of seventy, he died suddenly after a few days' illness. It is possible that his devotion to his collection resulted in his death for he delayed his return home until arrangements could be made for it to travel with him.

Stuart was buried in India but the collection was shipped to Europe and auctioned at Christie's on 15 June 1830 for the benefit of his estate. At this point an intriguing puzzle begins to develop – exactly what was in Stuart's collection and where did it go to? There were 154 lots, some containing more than one object and it is known that some pieces had already come over in 1804. About one third of the objects in the sale were acquired by a James Bridge and someone called Reynolds got most of the remainder. Since most of the Stuart collection later turned up in the possession of the Bridge family it is possible that Reynolds was acting for Bridge. At all events the sculptures were installed or set into the walls of Wood House in Shepherd's Bush. On the death of George Bridge in 1872 a second auction was announced. A.W. Franks of the Museum who had recognised the importance of the collection was authorised by the Trustees to bid. According to a manuscript note on the sale catalogue now in the Museum Franks was the only bidder, the auctioneer objected but Franks insisted and the collection was knocked down for a nominal sum said to be five pounds. The house was about to be sold, the sculptures had to be removed quickly and Franks persuaded the family that they might at least benefit from the glory of making a presentation, which they did.

Almost certainly Stuart's Calcutta Museum had more to show than now appears in the British Museum. As a postscript we can mention the acquisition, as recently as 1983, from a private collection of a large inscription which was plausibly traced back to the 1828 catalogue of Hindoo Stuart's sale. Perhaps in due course others will emerge.

Marici, the Buddhist Dawn goddess is sometimes terrible with three grimacing faces including one in the form of a pig. Basalt. East India. 10th c. AD. H. 68.6 cm (2 ft 3.5 in)

Parvati, consort of Siva, is also called Durga, the Unapproachable. Here she is shown as Durga killing Mahisha, a fierce demon in the form of a buffalo, who had made himself tyrant of the world. Orissa. 13th c. AD. H. 1·7 m (3 ft 6 in)

Parvati sometimes displays the disturbing and sinister side of her personality and is called Kali, the Black, and Camunda. Here she is seen seated on a corpse and garlanded with skulls. Sandstone. Orissa, 9th c. AD. H. 1.19 m (3 ft 11 in)

12

THE BODHISATTVA TARA

Sir Robert Brownrigg
(1759–1833), donor of the
statue, a special protegé and
friend of the Duke of York
whose successful army career
included service in America,
the Netherlands and Ceylon.

(Detail) From the tears shed
over the miseries of this world
by Avalokitesvara, one of the
companions of Buddha, came
the Bodhisattva Tara.

From the tears shed over the miseries of this
world by Avalokitesvara, one of the companions of Buddha who remained for the
salvation of other creatures and to whom no
person in suffering appeals in vain, came the
Bodhisattva Tara. She has a double character,
both threatening and gentle.

This beautiful and sensitively modelled
bronze statue of the Bodhisattva came to the
Museum from Ceylon (now Sri Lanka) in the
nineteenth century. She is almost lifesize; a
simple and austere figure who once wore in
her hair a single jewel, now lost. Very little is
known about the statue's provenance but
there are a few documents which hint at this.
In a letter of June 1830 the donor, Sir Robert
Brownrigg (1759–1833), writes of:

one of the Hindoo goddesses which from the
manner and place it was found was supposed to be
of great antiquity and to represent the Goddess
Patina, it was found in the north-east part of Ceylon
between Trincomalee and Baticaton. [ie Baticaloa]

In a later letter, written by Lady Brownrigg to
the Museum she refers to 'the gilt female figure
which is supposed to be the Patala Deva ...
found in Ceylon and believed to be of great
antiquity'.

Sir Robert Brownrigg was a soldier who, in
spite of the fact that his 'family was not rich,
and he had only himself to depend upon for
rising in his profession' rose steadily in his
career. He joined the 14th Foot in America in
1775, but was immediately sent home. He
survived various disasters and successful
campaigns and in October 1811 he was
appointed governor and Commander-in-Chief
of the Island of Ceylon. At the time of his
appointment the British, in succession to the
Dutch, occupied only the coastal region.
Inland was the once great but now declining
Kingdom of Kandy. In 1815, with the assistance of Kandyan chiefs whose relations
with the king had deteriorated, a British-

organised military expedition led by Brownrigg marched on the capital, took the king prisoner and annexed his kingdom. Brownrigg remained in Sri Lanka until 1820 and returned home a general and a Baronet. Ten years later he donated the gilt bronze statue to the British Museum.

The statue's original identification as Pattini Devi (a goddess associated with childbirth or smallpox) has for many years been thought by Sri Lankan and other scholars, to be incorrect and she is now considered to be a Mahayanist Buddhist deity, the Bodhisattva Tara. Buddhism reached Sri Lanka from India around the third century BC. It is a religion of many strands. Within Mahayanist Buddhism the Bodhisattvas were beings resolved to become Buddhas but who used their power and even postponed their entry into Buddhahood and final release from existence to relieve the sufferings of all other beings and help them to the same goal. Although Sri Lanka's Buddhist religion and language came from the North of India, the influences which helped to direct her artistic development came from the eastern Deccan (Amaravati) and South India, as did successive waves of conquerors and settlers. The Buddhist kings of Sri Lanka were patrons of Buddhist institutions who built, maintained and endowed many shrines and monasteries. Nobles and commoners were also lavish with their support. This hauntingly beautiful statue dates from about the tenth century AD. The precise findspot of the statue was never, unfortunately, reported and it has no association with any known temple or site. There is an oral tradition in the Museum that it was 'found in a field'. This is a very likely explanation of its acquisition by Brownrigg as examination of the surface of the bronze points to burial and also as so many important Sri Lankan and South Indian bronze sculptures have been discovered in just such an accidental way.

Gilt bronze figure of the Bodhisattva Tara from Sri Lanka, c. 10th c. AD. H. 1·45 m (4 ft 9 in)

13

HOA-HAKA-NANA-IA ('BREAKING WAVES'): A Statue from Easter Island

Mynheer Jacob Roggeveen, Commander-in-Chief of an expedition despatched by the Directors of the Netherlands Chartered West India Company wrote in his ship's log on Easter Day, April 1722:

About the 10th glass in the afternoon watch the *African Galley*, which was sailing ahead of us, lay to to wait for us making the signal of land in sight; when we came up with her ... we asked what they had seen. On this we were answered that they had all very distinctly seen a low and flattish island lying away to starboard about 5½ miles to the nor'ard and west'ard.

This is the first authenticated sighting by Europeans of the remote Easter Island, 1200 miles east of Pitcairn and 2300 miles west of Chile, called by its inhabitants *Te Pito te Henua* (the navel of the world). Roggeveen also wrote the first account of the brooding mysterious statues for which the island is now famous:

we noticed only that they [the inhabitants] kindle fire in front of certain remarkably tall stone figures they set up and thereafter squatting on their heels with heads bowed down, they bring the palms of their hands together and alternately raise and lower them ....

Like later visitors the Dutch were at first amazed that a people apparently lacking heavy timber and rope could have erected such massive objects. Their visit was brief, lasting only a day, and it is possible that they never really got close to the statues for when they found a piece of clay studded with flints they jumped to the conclusion that there was no mystery and the statues were similarly made.

The Dutch were however deceived. There are some six hundred statues on the island, many reaching ten to twenty feet in height

STATUE OF
HOA-HAKA-NANA-IA.
EASTER ISLAND.
PRESENTED BY H.M. THE QUEEN, 1869.
BROUGHT HOME BY H.M.S. TOPAZE.

Hoa-Haka-Nana-Ia. Made of hard basalt from the extinct volcano of Rano Raraku, it stood originally in a stone house at Orongo, the ceremonial centre associated with the bird-god cult. The image has a unique place in religious ceremonial, for whereas other stone statues were erected to commemorate specific ancestors, this is the only one known to have been associated with this cult. H. 2·64 m (8 ft 7 in)

Left. The statue on the Museum Colonnade in the 19th c. It is unusual in its extremely careful finish and in having various symbols, some of them connected with the bird-god cult, carved on its back. When found it was coloured red and white but the pigment was washed off in transit in *HMS Topaze.*

and even one monster about thirty-two feet tall made of a single block weighing about eighty-two tons with a topknot of eleven tons. At the quarry on the extinct volcano of Rano Raraku where they were made are specimens of thirty-seven feet and a vast unfinished giant intended to be sixty-eight feet tall. The Museum has two examples, both small by Easter Island standards; the larger, Hoa-Haka-Nana-Ia (Breaking Waves) weighs about two tons and the smaller about one and a half. They were acquired by *HMS Topaze* on a voyage in 1868. The Admiralty presented the larger to Queen Victoria. The Queen seems to have concluded that her statue was more appropriate for the Museum and passed it on to the Trustees. The Admiralty reached a similar conclusion and so the two statues came to the Museum in 1869.

After Roggeveen the next Europeans to visit Easter Island were a Spanish expedition from Peru which spent four days there and recorded the presence of three thousand people of mixed appearance. Then came Captain Cook, also on a brief visit as there was no proper harbour and the drinking water was poor. He had read an account of Roggeveen's expedition and when on 13 March 1774 he anchored off the island the presence of the massive statues confirmed his position. Cook found a much reduced population, of about six or seven hundred and less than thirty women, of Polynesian appearance although he suspected, correctly, that the rest of the population was concealed in caves. He too was fascinated by the statues. He sent a party ashore and it was recorded that thirty men dined in the shade of one that was still standing. Cook noted that the statues seemed no longer to be venerated and many had been toppled over. In his log he wrote:

The Stupendous stone statues erected in different places along the Coast are certainly no representation of any Deity or places of worship; but most probable Burial Places for certain Tribes or Families. I my self saw a human Skeleton lying in the foundation of one just covered with Stones, what I call the foundation is an oblong square of about 20 or 30 feet by 10 or 12 built of and faced with hewn stones of a vast size, executed in so masterly a manner as sufficiently shews the ingenuity of the age in which they were built. They are not all of equal height, some are not raised above two or three feet, others much more ... we could not help wondering how they were set up, indeed if the Island was once inhabited by a race of Giants of 12 feet high as one of the Authors of Roggewein's Voyage tells us, then this wonder ceaseth and gives

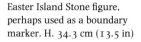

Easter Island Stone figure, perhaps used as a boundary marker. H. 34.3 cm (13.5 in)

Monuments of Easter Island, oil painting by William Hodges (1744–97), an artist on Captain James Cook's second voyage. The statues are shown with their 'top-knots' still in place.

place to another equally as extraordinary, viz. to know what is become of this race of giants . . .

Cook had posed the two questions which still intrigue anyone who sees the statues. How were they erected and by whom?

A. W. Franks pointed out in his 1869 report to the Trustees that the physiognomy of Hoa-Haka-Nana-Ia differed from the wooden figures from Easter Island already in the Museum (apart from the long earlobes) but noted that 'this may, however, also be observed on Central American sculptures, and the features have a Melanesian rather than a Polynesian cast'. Cook noted that the people he met had in colour, features and language an affinity to the rest of Polynesia. The Spaniards and Dutch however reported a people of varied physical appearance. Thor Heyerdahl who spent some time on the Island in the 1950s, recorded a tradition of two groups of inhabitants – the 'Long Ears' and 'Short Ears', the former originating in South America and the latter from Polynesia. Recent researchers however have suggested that there is no evidence, linguistic or archaeological, which can be used to support a major American settlement on the island.

Easter Island today. 'The huge standing figures look down at you with an enigmatic stare; your steps are watched from every single ledge and cave in the mountain, where giants unborn and giants dead and broken lie . . .' (Heyerdahl).

Production of the statues seems to have come to a sudden halt, leaving them distributed in various stages of completion and erection, the obsidian picks of the workmen scattered around the crater of Rano Raraku. Heyerdahl recorded a tradition of warfare between the islanders ending with the virtual extermination of one group. He did dispel the 'race of giants' theory by demonstrating that it was possible for about 180 persons to drag a statue across the island and that twelve using logs as levers and building up a ramp of stones could raise one vertically.

Some of the mysteries may have been solved, many have not, but this does not remove the fascination of this unique site. To conclude with Heyerdahl:

In Rano Raraku you feel the mystery of Easter Island at close quarters. The air is laden with it; bent on you is the silent gaze of a hundred and fifty eyeless faces. The huge standing figures look down at you with an enigmatic stare; your steps are watched from every single ledge and cave in the mountain, where giants unborn and giants dead and broken lie as in mangers and on sick-beds, lifeless and helpless because the intelligent creative force has left them. Nothing moves except the drifting clouds above you. It was so when the sculptors went, and so it will always be. The oldest figures, those who were completed, stand there proud, arrogant and tight-lipped; as though defiantly conscious that no chisel, no power will ever open their mouths and make them speak.

14

THE 'ROUBILIAC SHAKESPEARE' AND THE ACTOR DAVID GARRICK

It is said that when the famous actor-manager David Garrick saw the head of the life-size statue of Shakespeare he had commissioned being carved his loudly voiced reaction was 'What! Was Shakespeare marked with mulberries?' Unfortunately the marble was flawed and, as the sculptor's chisel chipped away, blue veins appeared. There is a story that the sculptor sawed off the offending head but nevertheless marks are still visible. In spite of the supposed mulberry juice Garrick seems to have been well pleased with the statue of the playwright whose work he did so much to popularise and rescue from neglect, especially as the price of £315 was modest. Its subject is shown in a moment of inspiration, in a pose almost certainly modelled by Garrick himself who is said to have stood declaiming 'Behold the Bard of Avon!'

The statue bears the signature of the sculptor Louis-François Roubiliac (1695–1762) and the date, 1758. Roubiliac was French by birth, emigrated to England and left many imposing monuments in his adopted country, including the statue of Handel in Poets' Corner, Westminster Abbey.

David Garrick was one of the finest actors England ever produced, and the first in a line of great Shakespearean actors. Henry Fielding, the author of *Tom Jones*, thought Garrick 'in tragedy to be the greatest genius the world hath ever produced'; Dr Johnson, the writer and lexicographer, on the other hand thought him best in comedy. He was versatile and, in contrast to many of his contemporaries, had a natural style; working on stages lit only by candles he was noted for his variety of facial expressions and his pleasant melodious voice was one of his most effective properties.

Although Garrick played many parts his greatest love was Shakespeare in whose plays

The sculptor Louis François Roubiliac (1695–1762) with a model of a statue of Shakespeare, 1762. One commentator complained of the 'frenchified head of the "Sweet Swan of Avon"'. Painting by Adrien Carpentiers.

he appeared in his most memorable roles. It is difficult now, when standard versions of Shakespeare's works are easily available, to appreciate the neglect in which Garrick found them. In the seventeenth century Shakespeare's plays were 'improved' to suit public taste and suffered for it. Garrick's great achievement was to establish Shakespeare firmly in the theatrical repertoire.

Garrick was born in 1717, son of an army officer of Huguenot extraction. He moved to London and was soon drawn into the theatrical world. In 1741 he appeared in one of his most famous roles, Richard III, and his reputation was made. In 1747 he acquired a half share in the Drury Lane theatre and two years later, after a long courtship, married Eva Maria Veigel, a dancer. It was a happy marriage and in 1753 the couple moved to Hampton House on the banks of the Thames in

Middlesex. There, in gardens laid out by 'Capability' Brown, Garrick constructed his Temple of Shakespeare, of which the centrepiece was Roubiliac's statue. The Temple was octagonal in shape, with a domed roof and a portico with eight Ionic columns and housed the actor's growing collection of Shakespearean relics. There, it is said, a dozen chairs were provided for admirers who came to pay homage and were sometimes served tea. One early visitor contributed the flattering verse:

While here to Shakespeare Garrick pays
His tributary thanks and praise,
Involves the animated stone
To make the poet's mind his own

One of the highlights of Garrick's Shakespearean career was the Stratford jubilee. In 1767 the town council of Stratford-upon-Avon, having decided that the town hall

'While here to Shakespeare Garrick pays His tributary thanks and praise'. Mr and Mrs Garrick by Garrick's temple of Shakespeare at Hampton. Roubiliac's statue can be seen through the doorway. 'A dozen chairs were provided for its admirers who were sometimes served with tea under its very shadow'. To the right is a servant with a teatray. Painting by Johan Zoffany.

The 'Garrick Casket' containing Garrick's freedom of the Borough of Stratford-upon-Avon. Mulberry wood, carved in high relief by Thomas Davies of Birmingham 1769. L. 21.8 cm (8.6 in)

Right Shakespeare by Louis François Roubiliac, commissioned by the actor David Garrick (1717–79). The statue and a collection of some 1300 plays came to the Museum under the terms of Garrick's will. Marble, life size.

specially constructed rotunda on the banks of the Avon was rather spoiled when the river rose and guests who feared to leave in the dark had to be carried over an expanse of mud when daylight came. For all its shortcomings, however, Garrick's jubilee was the forerunner of today's Shakespeare festivals and the Memorial Theatre was built almost on the site of the rotunda.

Garrick is buried in Westminster Abbey at the foot of Shakespeare's statue. In his career he played many parts, some remembered and some long forgotten – Lear and Abel Drugger, Macbeth and Benedick, Hamlet and Sir John Brute. Samuel Johnson lamented that his death had 'eclipsed the gaiety of nations and impoverished the public stock of harmless pleasure'. His fame was such that a duke and three earls were his pall bearers, the funeral procession stretched from the Adelphi in the Strand to Westminster Abbey – a fitting end for one who had always craved applause.

The Garrick Casket

A memento of the 1769 festivities was bequeathed to the Museum in 1864 by a Mr George Daniel. Little is known of Mr Daniel who was described as an 'eminent book collector and well known antiquarian and author who died in his seventy fifth year of apoplexy' and it is a mystery how the casket and other relics fell into his hands. The casket is ornately carved in high relief by Thomas Davies of Birmingham. On the back is Garrick as King Lear, on the ends Tragedy and Comedy and at the front the Three Graces. It is said to have been made of wood from the mulberry tree which stood in the grounds of Shakespeare's home at Stratford. After Shakespeare's death New Place fell into the unsympathetic hands of the Reverend Francis Castrell who, having little liking for the bard and even less for early tourists to the site, is remembered for having cut down the mulberry tree and eventually, in 1759, demolishing the house itself before leaving Stratford for ever. An enterprising tradesman, Thomas Sharp, bought logs from the tree and, until his death in 1799, a seemingly never-ending stream of Shakespearean mementoes in mulberry wood, of which this is one, appeared from his workshop.

needed redecorating and having worked out that a promising source of perhaps two portraits might be Britain's leading Shakespearean actor, agreed to 'flatter Mr Garrick into some such Handsome present' by offering the freedom of the borough, the appropriate document to be enclosed in a fine mulberry wood casket from Shakespeare's tree. Garrick accepted and, somewhat carried away by enthusiasm, planned a series of Jubilee celebrations in September 1769. Unfortunately the English weather did its worst. The large open air procession of Shakespearean characters was cancelled because of rain but Garrick's *Ode on Dedicating a Building* (the new town hall) was well received. A masked ball in a

MARBLE STATUE OF WILLIAM SHAKESPEARE
By L.F. ROUBILIAC, SIGNED AND DATED 1758
Formerly in the Temple of Shakespeare
In the garden of Garrick's Villa at Hampton
Bequeathed by David Garrick 1779

VOYAGES
OF DISCOVERY

15

CAPTAIN JAMES COOK

Pale blue jasperware medallion portrait of Captain Cook from the Museum's Wedgwood collection. Modelled *c.*1784 by John Flaxman (1755–1826). Cook wrote on his return from his first voyage 'whether I can bring my self to like ease and retirement, time will show.' H. 10.6 cm (4.5 in)

On Saturday 7 May 1774 Captain James Cook was anchored off the island of Tahiti in HMS *Resolution.* He wrote in his journal:

In the afternoon he [the King] and the whole Royal Family (Viz) his Father, Brother and three Sisters with their attendants, made me a Viset on board; His Father made me a present of a compleat Mourning dress, curiosities we most valued, in return I gave him what ever he desired and distributed red feathers to all the others and then conducted them a shore in my boat . . . .

It is almost certain that this mourner's costume, presented to Cook over two centuries ago, is the same as that now in the Museum of Mankind. The British Museum and its off-shoots, the British Library and the British Museum (Natural History) have the finest surviving collections from Cook's voyages; valuable because they portray a world unaffected by the alien culture of Europe. A member of the Museum's staff, the botanist Daniel Solander (1736–82), sailed with Cook on his first voyage as did Joseph Banks (1744–1820) who later became a Trustee. From them and others came a wealth of material – feather work from Hawaii, wooden masks from the Nootka of Vancouver Island, intricate Maori carvings, everyday objects – weapons, baskets, combs, ornaments, clothes, and much more. The artists, scientists and journal writers on the voyages filled in the background. Beaglehole, who edited Cook's journals, wrote of the Europeans' first contact with Tahiti – 'on that day the knell of Polynesia began to sound'. Cook and his companions salvaged and recorded a little. Take, for example, Cook's description of the mourning ceremonies for an old woman, ceremonies in which Joseph Banks even took part:

for several successive evenings after one of her relations dress'd himself in a very odd dress which I cannot tell how to describe or convey a better idea of it than to suppose a man dress'd with Plumes of feathers something in the same manner as those worn by Coaches, hearses, horses etc at the funerals in London, it was very neatly made up of black or brown and white cloth black and white feathers and pearl oysteres shells, it cover'd the head face

This costume from Tahiti is probably that mentioned by Cook in his journal, 1774. Made of bark cloth, it is decorated with feathers, pearl shell and coconut shell. H. 2·1 m (7 ft)

Top right. Wood kava bowl from the Hawaiian Islands, collected on Cook's last voyage. The eyes of the supporting figures are of pearl-shell and the teeth are of bone. L. 50·5 cm (1 ft 8 in)

Bottom right. 'The men on some occasions wore Masks of which they have many and various sorts . . .' (Cook's Journal, 1778, recording his visit to the Nootka Indians of Vancouver Island). H. 24 cm (9.5 in)

and body as low as the Calf of the leg or lower and not only looked grand but awfull likewise. The man thus equip'd and attended by two or three more men or women with their faces and bodies besmeared with soot and a club in their hands would about sunset take a compass of near a mile running here and there and where ever they came the people would fly from them as tho they had been so many hobgoblins not one daring to come in their way. I know not the reason for their performing this ceremony which they call Heiva a name they give to most of their divertisements.

Cook's first voyage was perhaps the eighteenth century's equivalent of a journey far out into space. No one in 1768 knew what really lay at the southern end of the globe. Ships had ventured there; islands and coastlines had been discovered and then lost until the next chance discovery. It was suspected that there might be a great undiscovered continent – *terra australis incognita* – counterbalancing the northern hemisphere, a potential source of great riches to whichever European power first found, charted and claimed it. However, the ostensible reason for Cook's voyage was scientific. Astronomers had forecast that the planet Venus would pass between the earth and the sun on 3 June 1769 (as it had done in 1761 but would not do again until 1874). Measurements made from a number of points around the globe would provide the basis for a calculation of the size of the solar system. The Royal Society, King George III and the Admiralty were enthusiastic and so a ship and funds were made available. An ideal observation point, Tahiti, had been discovered in 1767 and because of improvements in navigation its position plotted.

The Navy's choice to lead the expedition was a relatively obscure thirty-nine-year-old Lieutenant, James Cook. Cook is something of an enigma; he left detailed journals of his voyages but they include little personal comment. James Boswell described him as 'a grave steady man, and his wife a decent plump Englishwoman'. One of his few revealing remarks occurs in a journal entry of January 1774 when he was struggling through antarctic wastes at Latitude 71°10′ South:

I whose ambition leads me not only farther than any other man has been before me, but as far as I think it possible for man to go.

This determined ambition was apparent from the beginning. He was born at Marton-in-Cleveland, Yorkshire in 1728, son of a Scottish labourer. After serving in a shop he joined the merchant fleet of one John Walker sailing out

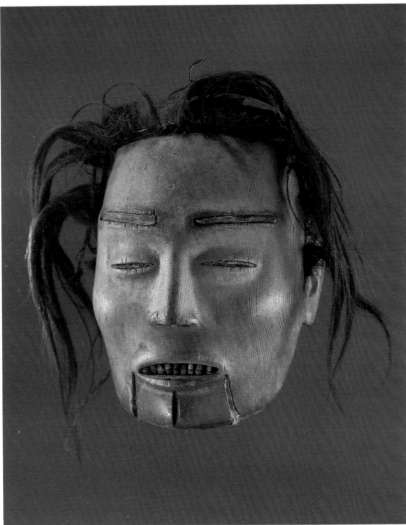

The Chief Mourner led a group of youths in procession, attacking with clubs or spears those they met. Anyone caught in the open might be killed. The group was supposed to be inspired by the spirit of the deceased to revenge any injury he might have received, or to punish those who had not shown due respect to his remains. Drawing by one of Cook's artists.

of Whitby. In 1755 occurred one of the most inexplicable actions in his career. Having been offered the comfortable and respectable position of captain of a merchantman he abruptly joined the Royal Navy as an able-seaman. One suggestion is that he gambled on obtaining preferment during the war with France, another that he was involved in smuggling and made a rapid escape into the Navy. Whatever the reason, his considerable mathematical and surveying skills marked him out for promotion.

On 26 August 1768 he made his usual methodical entry in his journal:

First part fresh breeze and Clowdy, remainder little wind and clear. At 2 PM got under sail and put to sea having on board 94 persons including officers seamen Gentlemen and their servants, near 18 months provisions, 10 Carriage guns, 12 Swivels and a good store of Ammunition and stores of all kinds.

A momentous voyage had begun which was to transform the European view of the South Pacific and to result ultimately in the European colonisation of Australia and New Zealand. Cook's vessel was a converted four-year-old Whitby collier of 366 tons, her name changed from the prosaic *Earl of Pembroke* to the more adventurous *Endeavour*. She was not

a fighting ship but she was strongly built and had the great advantage of a shallow draught and considerable storage space.

The *Endeavour* reached Rio de Janeiro in December, nearly lost the expedition's scientists in a snowstorm while they were exploring the inhospitable Tierra del Fuego, passed Cape Horn in January 1769 and entered the South Pacific. In April she reached Tahiti and dropped anchor beside the black volcanic sand beaches and coconut trees of Matavai Bay – a brilliant feat of navigation. Henceforward these islands and their peoples could no longer escape into obscurity.

For seamen accustomed to the cold and squalor of eighteenth-century England and confined for weeks aboard ship this was a paradise of plentiful food, women and sunshine. The Tahitians were friendly but it was the meeting of two very different cultures. Cook irritably commented that in stealing 'they are prodiges expert', the Tahitians viewed it as a sport. The Europeans were fascinated by what appeared to be the natives' relaxed lifestyle. In a letter sent at the end of his voyage Cook wrote of:

... the happy natives. These people may be said to be exempted from the curse of our forefathers, scarce can it be said that they earn their bread with the sweat of their brows, benevolent nature hath not only provided them with the necessarys but many of the luxuries of life.

Cook was to return a number of times to these islands and his journal entries hint at his fondness for 'these Terrestrial Paridises'.

The Europeans tried to understand the Tahitians' stratified social organisation and ceremonial and to come to terms with what appeared to them the darker side of the idyllic life. They encountered the *arioi*, whom they called 'strolling players', followers of the god of war *Oro* who toured the islands spreading the fame of the god, and were horrified at their practice of infanticide. In turn the Tahitians tried to comprehend the actions of these strange people who blundered through the islands with little concept of the dangers of infringing *tapu* – the sacred, prohibited world of the gods and the highest chiefs.

In July 1769 Cook, after recording the transit of Venus, followed the second part of his secret orders and began the search for the great southern continent. He travelled as far south as latitude 40° then turned west and in October reached the North Island of New Zealand where he made the acquaintance of the warlike Maori, 'a brave warlike people with sentiments voide of treachery'. On Monday 9 October 1769 Cook and a party went ashore, the first Europeans to do so, and were greeted by the inhabitants who 'answered us by florishing their weapons over their heads and danceing, as we supposed the war dance'. He was impressed by Maori weaponry, of which examples were brought back from this and subsequent voyages – 'they handle their arms with great Agility particularly their long Pikes or lances, against which we have no weapon that is an equal match except a loaded Musquet'. The Europeans also admired the Maoris' intricate wood carving – almost everything was decorated – weapons, tools, houses, storage boxes, canoes, musical instruments.

Cook circumnavigated New Zealand's two islands thereby disproving previous theories that the coast was part of the southern continent. On Thursday 19 April 1770 he sighted Australia, of which only the west and south coasts had previously been recorded. Cook charted the East coast, calling at 'capacious, safe and commodious' Botany Bay so named because of the large number of plants collected by Banks and Solander.

After two dangerous attempts to pass through the Great Barrier Reef Cook gave up

Cook found the Maori 'a brave warlike people with sentiments voide of treachery'. Maori man from a drawing by one of Cook's artists, Sydney Parkinson, 1770.

Wooden drum (*pahu hula*) with sharkskin membrane bound to the body with vegetable fibre bindings and base carved as five standing human figures. From the Hawaiian Islands. Acquired on Cook's last voyage but not purchased by the Museum until 1977. H. 29.2 cm (11.5 in)

and sailed up the coast. In October the expedition reached Batavia, the most unhealthy port in the east, where repairs were carried out. Seven of the crew and the two artists died of malaria and other diseases to be joined by others even after the vessel sailed for England in December. After three years, on Saturday 13 July 1771 Cook recorded in his journal 'At 3 o'Clock in the PM Anchor'd in the Downs, and soon after I landed in order to repair to London'. He and Banks were the toast of London. Cook was promoted to Commander and had an audience with the King. He wrote to his old employer John Walker.

I however have made no very great Discoveries yet I have exploar'd more of the Great South Sea, than all that have gone before me so much that little remains now to be done to have a thorough Knowledge of that part of the Globe . . . .

Not everyone was convinced of the absence of the southern continent for there were latitudes into which Cook had not ventured. A second voyage was proposed to resolve this and in June 1772 Cook set sail with two converted Whitby colliers, HMS *Resolution* (462 tons) and the 366 ton HMS *Adventure* captained by Tobias Furneaux. Serving in the *Resolution* was the 'quiet inoffensive' fifteen-year-old George Vancouver who would later make his mark as an explorer in his own right. Banks 'swore and stamp'd upon the Warfe, like a Mad Man' and retired from the expedition in a huff when he was unable to persuade the Admiralty to add an upper deck for his naturalists and artists which would have made the *Resolution* unseaworthy.

On this journey Cook sailed eastwards via the Cape of Good Hope and then down to the edge of the Antarctic ice. In January he entered the Antarctic circle, reaching Latitude 67°15' South, but his progress was blocked by icebergs and pack ice. Cook eventually retreated to Tahiti and the Tongan Islands via New Zealand for the southern winter. On his return to New Zealand he lost contact with the *Adventure* but ventured south in December 1773 in search of the great continent, reaching a point only 1,300 miles from the South Pole. He now concluded that he was pursuing a chimaera – any land was surrounded by and covered with great masses of ice and he realised that it would be a very dangerous enterprise to proceed 'one inch further South'. So as the Antarctic winter approached he struck north, making a sweep through the Pacific and visiting Easter Island which he recognised by its strange statues.

Wherever he went Cook found people of similar physical type, language and customs. He was fascinated by Polynesian settlement for he was the first to have the opportunity to record its extent – 'it is extraordinary', he remarked, 'that the same Nation should have spread themselves over all the isles in this vast Ocean'. He visited the Marquesas Islands then returned to Tahiti where he saw the magnificent sight of the great twin hulled canoes of the war fleet being prepared to sail against Moorea – 330 canoes and almost 8000 men. He then entered a different world, Melanesia, where he met with an unfriendly reception, understandable for the inhabitants saw the Europeans as a shipload of ancestral ghosts. Cook was prepared to sympathise with their attitude – 'there are few Nations who will willingly suffer you to make excursions far into their country'. In November he again called in at New Zealand where the Maori were somewhat embarrassed and evasive, having eaten an entire boat's crew of ten men from the *Adventure* which had now returned alone to Europe. Cook then also sailed for home, around Cape Horn, across the South Atlantic at Latitude 60° south, discovering the bleak islands of South Georgia and the South Sandwich Islands and back to England after three years and eighteen days. In an era plagued by scurvy, he had lost only four men; he had proved beyond doubt that a habitable antarctic continent did not exist.

Cook was now famous and could if he wished sink into comfortable semi-retirement. His security was assured by an appointment to Greenwich Naval Hospital at £200 a year. He was growing old but he was restless and wrote to John Walker in 1775:

A few months ago the whole Southern hemisphere was hardly big enough for me and now I am going to be confined within the limits of Greenwich Hospital which are far too small for an active mind like mine.

Another voyage was being planned. A Tahitian, Omai, had been brought to Europe by the *Adventure* – he must be returned and, the myth of the southern continent having been exploded, the Admiralty's attention turned again to that other chimaera, the navigable North-West passage. No one quite liked to approach Cook directly so a dinner party was arranged by Lord Sandwich at which Cook was 'so fired with the contemplation and representation of the object' that he volunteered for his last voyage.

Cook, now a Captain, again sailed in the

Maori 'tiki' worn as a neck ornament. Made of nephrite the eyes are of haliotis shell and it is similar to that shown in Parkinson's drawing. H. 21.5 cm (8.5 in)

Top left. Wood bowl from Nootka Sound carved with two handles in the form of people. The parallel knifework on the bowl indicates that the bowl belonged to a chief. L. 20 cm (7.9 in)

Left. Two wooden figures from Nootka Sound.

Interior of a House at Yuquot, Nootka Sound from a drawing by John Webber (1752–93).

Resolution, this time accompanied by the 298 ton *Discovery*. He left Plymouth for the last time in July 1776, the oldest man in the expedition and showing signs of the strain of his previous voyages. Travelling eastwards, he reached Tasmania in January 1777, and explored the Central Pacific Islands including Tonga and Tahiti before sailing for the North American coast via Christmas Island. En route, in January 1778, he unexpectedly discovered the Hawaiian Islands. He arrived at Nootka Sound on the west side of Vancouver Island in March. There he made the acquaintance of the Nootka Indians, skilled traders who obtained a large quantity of the ships' metal in return for masks and other artefacts, pelts, food, water and wood. Lacking an interpreter the Europeans had difficulty in understanding their hosts. Cook, somewhat bemused, commented on their masks, of which specimens found their way to the Museum:

The men on some occasions wore Masks of which they have many and various sorts such as the human face, the head of birds and other Animals, the most of them both well designed and executed. Whether these masks are worn as an Orament in their public entertainments, or as some thought, to guard the face against the arrows of the enimy or as

decoys in hunting, I shall not pretend to say; probably on all these occasions.

From June to July he travelled up the mountainous and heavily wooded Alaskan Coast and anchored in Prince William Sound. He sailed through misty, drizzling, rainy weather and fog along the Alaskan peninsula and the Aleutian islands, trying to find a navigable passage and in August he reached Bering Strait but was blocked by ice further north and retreated, landing at Unalaska in the Aleutians where he met Russian fur traders. He then sailed for Hawaii where his luck and usually sound judgement deserted him.

Cook anchored in Kealakekua Bay and here his journal breaks off. The ships had arrived at a significant time, the *Makahiki*, the harvest festival season of games and sports when warfare was forbidden. The god of this season was Lono; – god of rain and agriculture, forgiveness and healing whose symbol was a long pole with a cross bar and barkcloth sheet like the square sail of a ship. It had been prophesied that Lono would return and it is possible that the Hawaiians thought that he had done just that in the form of Cook. They prostrated themselves before Cook and presented him with feather gods, a helmet, feathered staff and five or six cloaks, images of wood with distorted mouths. However the behaviour of the Europeans proved them disappointingly mortal and there was great relief when the two ships set sail. Unfortunately they ran into a storm and were obliged to return for repairs and after a series of incidents relations worsened and a cutter was stolen. On 14 February 1779 in an attempt to win it back Cook landed with the intention of seizing a chief as a hostage. The islanders intervened, Cook gave up his hostage and retreated towards his boats. All might have gone well, as it had in many previous dangerous encounters, but a shot from one of the boats killed a chief. A Hawaiian threatened Cook with a dagger, he retaliated and a melee ensued. Cook fell and his men retreated to the *Resolution* leaving behind their Captain and four marines. Parts of his body were recovered and committed to the sea. Relations with the Hawaiians were restored and the Europeans left without further bloodshed.

Cook's voyages opened up a new world for the Europeans. The societies he found were, to European eyes, primitive. Although on the surface their life was idyllic and enjoyable, behind this facade sometimes lay human sacrifice, infanticide and savage warfare in which no quarter was given. But changes were not necessarily for the better; once the Europeans made contact populations were stricken by new diseases and their culture crumbled. The Museum holds a record of this vanished world.

Breast gorget, comprising a basketry base with feathers, shark teeth and dog hair. From the Society Islands. H. 61 cm (24 in)

TEMPLES AND TOMBS

16

DEATH IN EGYPT

The Egyptian mummies are probably the best-known items in the Museum and they are undoubtedly the most popular, exerting a great fascination on visitors of virtually all ages and nationalities. The Museum has about eighty complete or virtually complete human mummies and preserved human bodies together with other funerary equipment – coffins, stone sarcophagi, little *shabti* figures (who with a cry of 'Here am I' would step forward to carry out certain tasks allocated to a man in the afterworld), magical amulets, papyri bearing magic formulae to ensure entry to a pleasant life after death, jars for viscera removed from the mummified corpse, jewellery found wrapped amidst the bandages

around the body, magical bricks, model utensils and model scenes of daily life (brewing, cultivating, sailing). The collection also includes a menagerie of mummified cats, falcons, bulls and other creatures sacred to the various gods of the Egyptian pantheon.

The mummies are recognisably human. Many were young – radiographic examination has shown them mostly to have had lifespans of less than forty years. They are of short, slight build and some show evidence of health problems known to us today – osteoarthritis, arrested growth, missing or diseased teeth, spina bifida and gall stones. And yet these are people who lived between two and five thousand years ago, who might have seen the building of the pyramids or the splendour of Tutankhamun's court.

The word 'mummy' comes from the Arabic word for bitumen, *mummiya*. It was incorrectly believed, because of their appearance, that bodies had been dipped in this substance to preserve them. The process was in fact rather more complex, did not rely on bitumen and took centuries to evolve against a 'tangle of confused and contradictory ideas' relating to death. The first preserved bodies, from as early as *c*.3200 BC were in fact the product of natural processes. They were buried in simple shallow graves, sometimes covered with skin

Vignette from the Book of the Dead of the Scribe Ani showing the heart being weighed against the feather of Truth in the presence of the gods. At the far right is Ammit, part crocodile, part hippopotamus, part lion, the gobbler-down of wicked hearts. From Thebes, 19th Dynasty, *c*.1250 BC. H. 38 cm (15 in)

'... no mummy which did the things of this kind was ever in the British Museum ... The cover never went on the Titanic. It never went to America ...' (Wallis Budge, Keeper of Egyptian antiquities, writing in 1934). The 'Unlucky Mummy,' in fact the wooden coffin lid of an unnamed singer of Amen-re from Thebes, 21st Dynasty c. 1050 BC H. 1.62 m (5 ft 4 in)

or matting, in the hot sand. The sand absorbed the body's moisture, without which bacteria cannot breed and cause it to decay, leaving a dessicated preserved corpse. Towards the end of the Predynastic period (c.3100 BC) burials, at least for the elite, became more elaborate. The dead would be placed in burial chambers, surrounded by grave goods, no longer in contact with the sand and therefore they tended to decompose.

By at least the early Fourth Dynasty (c.2600 BC) it was realised that removal of the internal organs helped to prevent the body's decomposition. During the Old and Middle Kingdoms (c.2686–1786 BC) various methods of preserving the body were tried with limited success but by the New Kingdom (c.1567–1085 BC) a basic formula had been evolved, with variations according to wealth (although the poor continued to be placed in simple graves in the hot sand). Over a period of seventy days the corpse would be treated – first the removal of the brain and viscera (but not the seat of intelligence, the heart), then (it is now thought) about forty days' application of dry natron (a natural compound of sodium carbonate and sodium bicarbonate with sodium sulphate and chloride), leaving the body dehydrated but the skin supple. After further treatment with ointments, spices and resins it was wrapped in bandages into which jewellery and amulets of various kinds might be placed. Everything would be preserved – discarded swabs, temporary stuffing, etc. – and the embalmed viscera were placed in four 'canopic jars'. Burial would then take place, perhaps in a nest of wooden coffins or a stone sarcophagus placed in a tomb.

The Museum has had mummies in its collections since 1756 – three years after its foundation – when 'An Aegyptian mummy with its coffin and the hieroglyphics painted separately on canvass' was listed in the vellum donations book. This was bequeathed by Colonel William Lethieullier who said it had been 'found in its coffin among the antient catacombs about three leagues from Cairo in the year 1721'. According to his coffin this is the mummy of Iru, son of Serseru, a man who lived at the time of Twenty-Sixth Dynasty (c.664–525 BC). The bequest also included several fragments of mummies and other Egyptian antiquities and at the same time the Colonel's nephew Pitt Lethieullier donated a second mummy. The donors had belonged to the early Egyptian Society which, at a time when Egypt was still virtually closed to

travellers, met briefly from 1741 to 1743 to display and discuss Egyptian antiquities. (Another mummy in the collection (6957), an 'adult of uncertain sex' from the Ptolemaic period (c.305–30 BC) may have come to England even earlier. Presented to the Museum by the Earl of Bessborough in 1837 it is traditionally supposed to have at one time belonged to Nell Gwyn).

Probably the best-known body in the Museum is *Ginger* – a man now 5000 years old, a good example of a Late Predynastic burial before the art of artificial mummification had been developed. He is supposed to have been brought to the Museum in 1900 by the Keeper of Egyptian & Assyrian Antiquities, Sir Wallis Budge (1857–1934). On one of his many collecting trips to Egypt he was anxious to obtain 'a complete specimen of the predynastic Egyptian, whether sun-dried or mummified for there was no example of him in the British Museum'. Budge went from site to site and had almost given up hope when he was invited to visit some graves near Gebelein. These contained pottery, large flints and bodies lying on their left sides with their knees and hands up to their faces.

Ginger came from one of the largest of the graves which had been dug partly under a small projecting spur of the hill, and was nearly covered over by two or three large lumps of stone. The stones were tightly jammed together, and because of this the body in the grave had been preserved complete. To prevent the stones falling and crushing the body, they were shored up and a pit dug in front of the grave. When this was deep enough Budge dug inwards under it. Bit by bit the sandstone bed of the grave was broken away and thus the body and the contents of the grave dropped down by degrees into the pit. It was lifted out uninjured, rolled in cotton waste in a temporary box and removed to Luxor. *Ginger* was ceremonially unpacked at the Museum one Saturday in March 1900 in the presence of a Trustee, Lord Crawford, and the Principal Librarian. Budge states that when laid on a table the body was as complete as when first seen at Gebelein but when examined on the following Monday morning it was discovered that the top joint of one of the forefingers was missing and this has never been seen since.

Perhaps the mummy with the greatest popular reputation is the so-called 'unlucky mummy' actually the coffin lid of an unnamed singer of Amen-re of the Twenty-First dynasty (*c*.1050 BC) from Thebes. This object has been unjustly accused of sinking the *Titanic* and the *Empress of Ireland* but has been harmlessly on exhibition since its arrival in 1889.

Another of Budge's acquisitions was the *Book of the Dead* of the Scribe Ani – a superbly illustrated papyrus of the Nineteenth Dynasty (*c*.1250 BC) from Thebes, a written aid to Ani's future in the after-life. From the early Eighteenth Dynasty (*c*.1567 BC) onwards papyri inscribed with a selection from some two hundred spells, which were intended to help the dead pass through the perils of the underworld and reach the afterlife, were placed with the deceased – never complete but usually containing at least the important spells. The texts were based on earlier writings, some as old as 2350 BC. To the Egyptians they were known as the *Chapters of Coming-forth by Day*. Chapter 125 deals with the judgement of the deceased and the way in which he might survive his examination before the forty-two assessor gods, each of whom posed a testing question on his life on earth. In a terrifying ceremony his heart is weighed for each answer on the scales against Truth, sometimes symbolised by an ostrich feather. The weighing is supervised by Anubis the jackal god and recorded by the ibis-headed god Thoth in the presence of the deceased's *Ba*. Lurking in the vicinity is Ammit – part crocodile, part hippopotamus, part lion, waiting to gobble down a heart found wanting. As the deceased enters the Hall of Judgement he calls on his heart: 'Do not stand up as a witness against me, do not be opposed to me in the tribunal . . .'. When the weighing is completed Thoth announces the result: 'Hear this word of very truth. I have judged the heart of the deceased, and his soul stands as a witness for him. His deeds are righteous in the great balance, and no sin has been found in him . . .'. Horus then takes the dead man by the hands and leads him into the presence of Osiris to enjoy his afterlife in a country without hunger where emmer wheat, barley and flax grow as tall as a man, trees are laden with fruit and grain is stacked in heaps – in short where he can enjoy all the good things he knew in life in the beautiful land of Egypt.

It was this profound love of life and its pleasures, not a morbid obsession with death which led the Egyptians to seek immortality through the preservation of their earthly body.

'Ginger' the body of an adult man found at Gebelein, dating from *c*.3200 BC. 'One of the largest of the graves had been dug partly under a small projecting spur of a hill' (Budge). The body had been preserved by rapid drying in a shallow grave in which it was laid 5,000 years ago. Buried with it were flint knives and pots of the same date. L. unflexed 1·63 m (5 ft 4 in)

Three of a set of four limestone 'canopic' jars made for Neskhons, wife of Pinudjem, High Priest of Amun at Thebes. Although hollow, these jars were not used for the embalmed viscera which during the 21st Dynasty were replaced after treatment in the body cavity. 21st Dynasty, *c* 1000 BC. H. 38 cm (15 in).

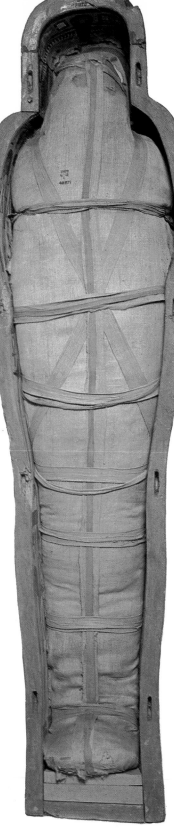

Mummy and coffin of an unnamed Priestess of Amun of the 21st Dynasty, *c.* 1050 BC, from Thebes. H. 1·64 m (6 ft 3 in)

Painted and gilded stucco mummy case with a portrait of the dead Artemidorus from Hawara, el-Faiyum, early 2nd c. AD. X-rays indicate that he died aged 19–21. The Greek inscription reads 'Artemidorus, Farewell!' H. 1·67 m (5 ft 6 in)

17

THE DISCOVERY OF THE ROYAL CEMETERY AT UR

Now these are the generations of Terah: Terah begat Abram, Nahor, and Haran; and Haran begat Lot. And Haran died before his father Terah in the land of his nativity, in Ur of the Chaldees ... And Terah took Abram his son, and Lot the son of Haran his son's son, and Sarai his daughter in law, his son Abram's wife; and they went forth with them from Ur of the Chaldees to go into the land of Canaan ...

(Genesis, 11: 27, 28, 31)

Two hundred and twenty miles south of Baghdad and a hundred and sixty miles from the head-waters of the Persian Gulf lie the remains of a once great and prosperous city. Now it is a barren, desolate place. Ten miles to the east is the great river Euphrates; once it flowed closer to the city, its waters channelled by a series of canals. In the summer the shade temperature here can reach 137°F and in the middle of winter in December/January the north-west wind is so cold that water freezes in clay drinking jars. The most prominent mound, known to the Arabs as 'Tell Muqayyar' (the mound of pitch), is made up of the remains of an ancient ziggurat, once (by the late third millennium BC) about sixty-five feet high, with a temple at its summit, a high place where generations of citizens worshipped their gods. Here lies Ur – one of the oldest cities in the world – to the Sumerians it was *Urim*, in Akkadian *Uru* and, although we have no definite proof, it is probably the Biblical '*Ur Kasdim*' (of the Chaldees), said in *Genesis* to have been the home of Abraham. Certainly it was this supposed connection which attracted nineteenth and twentieth-century excavators. No direct evidence has been found however and while the Bible tells of Abraham and Ur, this connection remains otherwise unproven.

Civilisation came early to the fertile area between the rivers Tigris and Euphrates. As early as 4000 BC men settled here who made by hand fine painted pottery, used a variety of

Delicate gold headdress and necklaces of lapis lazuli and cornelian worn by one of the attendants found in the 'Great Death Pit'. Early Sumerian c.2500 BC. H. of head 63 cm (24·1 in)

A completely excavated pit at Ur showing the great depth to which Woolley worked. The floor level dates to 2900–2800 BC and the square opening at the foot of the stairs leads into the 'Flood deposit'.

the first century BC the Euphrates had changed its course and moved eastwards. The canals ran dry and the city was abandoned – 'in the holes of the ziggurat owls made their nests and jackals found a hiding place'.

In 1849 W.K. Loftus, a member of a Turkish Boundary Commission, visited the site and others including Nippur and Uruk, and brought back to London fragments of inscribed bricks including one which Henry Rawlinson (1810–95), the decipherer of the Behistun inscription, was able to confirm bore the name of a king of Ur. The first excavations at Ur were carried out by J.G. Taylor, British Vice Consul at Basra, in 1853–4, but his finds were disappointing compared to the spectacular sculptures and reliefs which Layard was unearthing in Assyria. The excavation ceased but Taylor did manage to recover from the corners of the ruin of the ziggurat the foundation cylinders of King Nabonidus (555–539 BC) from whose inscriptions Rawlinson identified Tell Muqayyar as the Biblical Ur of the Chaldees.

The city was left to the desert for more than half a century, until interest began to develop in the early history of the Sumerian people. The University of Pennsylvania excavated briefly at the end of the nineteenth century and at the end of the First World War R. Campbell Thompson, and H.R. Hall undertook brief investigations for the Museum. In 1922 the University Museum of Pennsylvania suggested a joint expedition. The excavation started that year and was to continue for twelve seasons producing treasures which astounded the excavators. These are now divided between London, Philadelphia and Iraq.

The expedition's leader was Leonard Woolley (1880–1969). Woolley had already led expeditions to Carchemish (accompanied by T.E. Lawrence, in 1912), and to Egypt. He brought to this excavation tremendous enthusiasm, great industry, imagination and the ability to communicate with the public. Sir Max Mallowan, then Woolley's assistant, in his biography gives a lively picture of life on the site where he first met his future wife Agatha Christie. 'To follow Woolley round the site of Ur', he wrote, 'and to hear him talk about the private houses was to feel oneself among a vanished people ... While on the dig he slept little, rising with the sun and often still at work in the catalogue room until two or three o'clock in the morning'.

Woolley's excavation was an exceedingly

tools and domesticated animals. Succeeding cultures are labelled according to sites where their characteristic remains were first identified; 'Ubaid (4000–3500 BC), Uruk (3500–3000 BC), Jamdat Nasr (3000–2800 BC). Then, from about 2800 to 2370 BC came the heyday of the Sumerian theocratic city state such as Ur. Around 2370 BC Ur passed under the control of the rulers of Agade. Sumerian culture revived about 2110 BC under Ur-Nammu of the third Dynasty of Ur and his successors and survived for a century before coming to a violent end when Ur was sacked by a combined force of Elamites and Amorites. The site continued to be occupied through the Old Babylonian, Kassite, Assyrian, Neo-Babylonian and Persian periods which succeeded each other until by the end of complex one – the site was vast and time and money would permit only a fraction to be explored even with a labour force which at one time reached four hundred. He therefore concentrated largely on the sacred area within which lay the principal temples, palaces and the great ziggurat dedicated to the chief god of the city, the Moon God Nanna whose wife Ningal was known as the Great Lady. The mud brick houses had decayed over the centuries and as they did so the deposits gradually rose to some seventy or eighty feet in height. The inhabitants put down layers of rubbish, into which later generations dug graves and when the memory of the initial graves had ceased more were added with perhaps as many as twenty people being laid to rest above each other. The rulers tore down, extended and rebuilt the great public buildings.

During his twelve seasons Woolley added immeasurably to knowledge of southern Babylonia but two discoveries in particular caught the public imagination. Of the first Woolley wrote:

The shafts went deeper, and suddenly the character of the soil changed. Instead of the stratified pottery and rubbish we were in perfectly clean clay, uniform throughout, the texture of which showed that it had been laid there by water ... The clean clay continued without change ... until it had attained a thickness of a little over eight feet. Then, as suddenly as it had begun, it stopped, and we were once more in layers of rubbish full of stone implements, flint cores from which the implements had been flaked off, and pottery ...

Woolley was in little doubt that he had found the cataclysmic Flood of the Bible and of Sumerian legend. Both sources drew on a similar occurrence – in its vast collection of cuneiform tablets (discovered both by Layard and later by George Smith) the British Museum has fragments which tell of this Deluge. In the Epic of Gilgamesh it is written that Utanapishtim escaped with his family, kin and craftsmen 'Six days, a se'en night the hurricane, deluge, (and) tempest continued ...' Today the balance of opinion is that Woolley found merely an unusually high regular flood of the Euphrates. Max Mallowan did conclude later however that the Flood was an historic event, traces of which had been discovered elsewhere but not at Ur.

The flood level may be regarded with some scepticism but of the quality of the treasures of the 'Royal Cemetery' there can be no doubt. In an area partly covered by the walls of Nebuchadnezzar (604–562 BC) Woolley ex-

cavated 1840 graves mostly from the Early Dynastic period (c.2800–2370 BC). Below the simple graves of the common people lay the elite of Ur buried with magnificent treasures two and a half millennia before Christ and a thousand or more years before the presumed time of Abraham. Woolley describes how the commoners' graves emerged after four thousand years:

Often the first sign that the workmen have of a grave as they dig down into the mixed soil of the cemetery is a paper-thin wavy line of white powder or else a few small holes ... left by the decay of the wooden staves which strengthened the sides of a wooden or wickerwork coffin, the wavy white line is the edge of the reed mat which lined the grave or in which the bodies of poorer folk were wrapped. It is an astonishing thing that in soil wherein so much that seems enduring decays entirely, a fragile thing like a piece of matting, though it lose all its substance and can be blown away with a breath yet retains its appearance and its texture and can with care be exposed in such condition that a photo-

Figure of a male goat (one of a pair) standing on its hind legs with its front feet resting on the branches of a tree, a motif which appears in the late Prehistoric period and continues in Western Asia until Islamic times. The body is made of wood; gold has been hammered to the shape of the head and legs and silver over the belly. The horns, beard and locks of hair are carved in shell and lapis lazuli and attached with bitumen. Found in the 'Great Death Pit'. H. 45·7 cm (18 in)

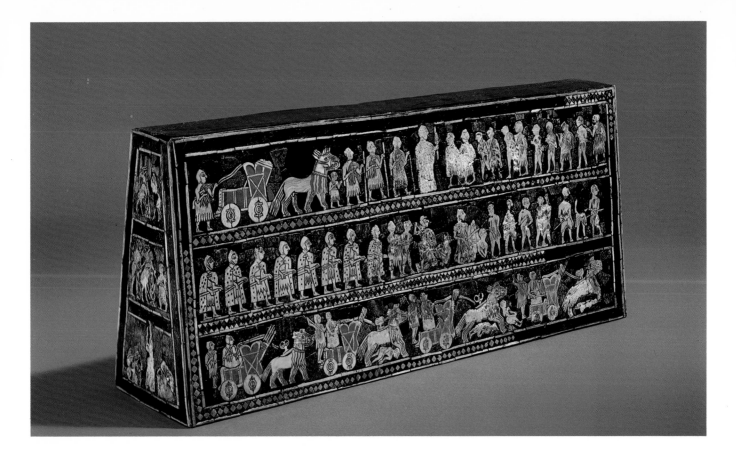

Gold feeding cup from the tomb of Pu-abi. She was found lying on a wooden bier, a gold cup near her hand, the upper part of her body entirely hidden by multi-coloured beads. H. 12·4 cm (4·9 in)

Top. The 'Standard of Ur': War. Woolley thought that this object might have been carried on a pole as a standard, but it is now considered to be the sounding box of a musical instrument. The other side depicts the Sumerian king enjoying the pleasures of peace. H. 20.3 cm (8 in)

Right. Gold head of a bull projecting from the sounding box of a lyre found in the tomb of Puabi. The Horns are modern restorations. H. of lyre approx. 106 cm (42 in)

graph of it looks like one of the real matting which perished 4,500 years ago.

In ordinary graves the dead might be wrapped in rolls of matting or laid in coffins of wood, wickerwork or terracotta. They took with them personal belongings such as beads, earrings, knives, dagger pins and sometimes their personal cylinder seal. They were found lying on their sides as if asleep.

Woolley found evidence of the richer graves early in the excavation but decided to postpone full investigation until he and his team were more experienced. On the last day of the 1926–7 season one of the most beautiful objects discovered by the excavation was found. At the bottom of an earth shaft lay a superb gold dagger (now in Baghdad), with a hilt of blue lapis lazuli decorated with gold studs, the sheath of gold worked like plaited grass. With it was a set of little toilet instruments in gold – nothing so fine had previously been unearthed in Mesopotamia and one archaeologist even asserted that the dagger could only come from Renaissance Italy. When work resumed in the autumn of 1927 more rich tombs appeared. One such was the grave of Meskalamdu, in which was found a unique hammered and chased gold helmet,

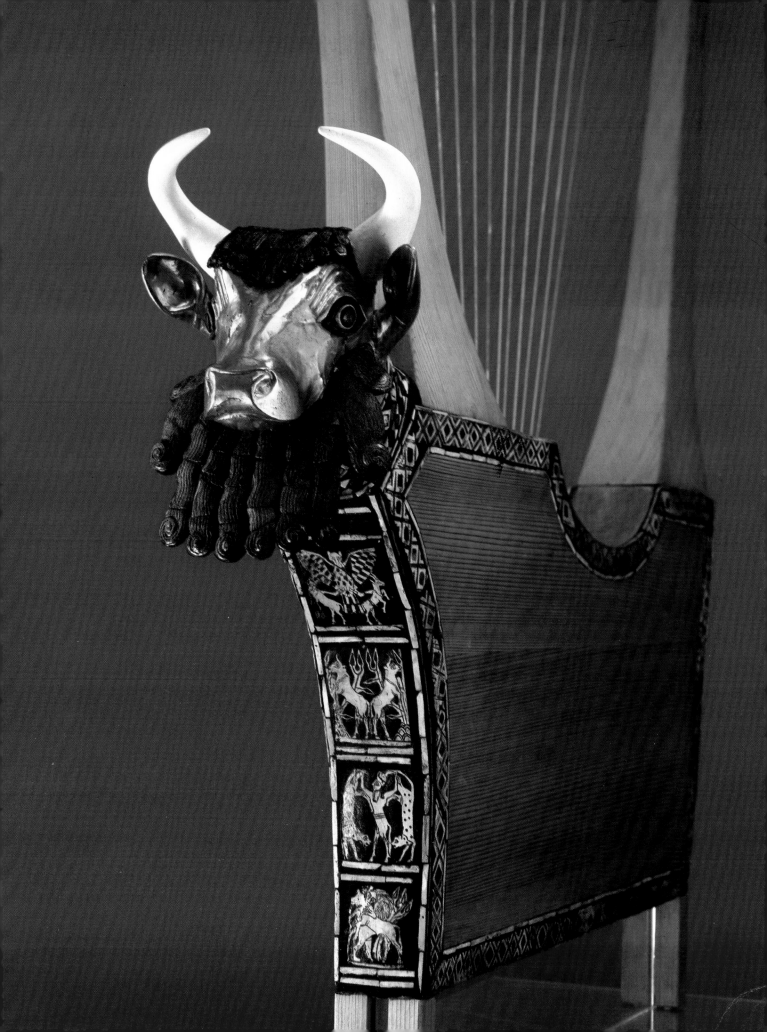

located in the shaft of what later proved to be one of the largest of the royal tombs.

In another part of the site the bodies of five men were found lying side by side in a sloping shallow trench. They had none of the objects usually left with the dead – only copper daggers at their waists and one or two small clay cups. Nearby were the bodies of ten women carefully arranged in two rows, wearing head-dresses of gold, lapis lazuli, and carnelian, and elaborate bead necklaces. At the end of the row lay the remains of a lyre. Next appeared the bones of two oxen and the remains of a wooden sledge chariot decorated with red, white and blue mosaic (one of the earliest examples of a land vehicle ever found). At the heads of the animals lay the crushed skeletons of two grooms. The grave goods included an inlaid gaming board, a set of chisels and a saw made of gold, a long tube of gold and lapis for sucking up liquid from bowls, vessels of various materials, a fluted feeding bowl and lastly the remains of a large wooden chest, six feet by three feet, decorated with lapis lazuli and shell mosaic. There appeared to be no principal occupant. However a strange discovery was made. When the wooden box was being removed it was found to be concealing a hole leading to another burial below.

The excavators explored their new find: there was another ramp leading down to the chamber, this time occupied by six soldiers in two ranks, copper spears by their sides and copper helmets crushed flat on broken skulls. Just inside were two wooden four-wheeled wagons each drawn by three oxen which had been backed down the slope, with grooms at their heads and drivers in the cars. Against the end wall were bodies of nine women also adorned with brilliant headdresses, a wooden lyre placed on them. The space between them and the wagons was crowded with other dead women and men; the passage along the side of the chamber was lined with women and with soldiers carrying daggers. At the side of the pit was a second lyre decorated with a bull's head in gold and lapis lazuli.

The main chamber, which had been plundered, lay at the far end of the open pit. Built up against it was a similar chamber where the excavators discovered the remains of a woman who had been buried with the group of attendants above – discovered in the vicinity of the hole concealed by the chest. Her name, Pu-abi, was recorded on a fine cylinder seal of lapis lazuli found in the filling of the shaft above the roof of the chamber, perhaps thrown in at the last moment. She lay on a wooden bier, a gold cup near her hand, the upper part of her body entirely hidden by multi-coloured beads. Over her crushed skull she wore an elaborate headdress, its shape such that it must have been worn over a padded wig. Two female attendants crouched at the head and foot of the bier. The tomb was strewn with gold, silver and other objects. Woolley surmised that the occupant of the empty tomb might have been the husband of Pu-abi, who died first, his wife later choosing to be buried near him. During preparations for her funeral he suggested that workmen had seized the opportunity of breaking through into her husband's chamber from the attendants' chamber above, hiding their route by placing a great clothes chest above it. The 'king' had with him sixty-five people, the 'queen' twenty-five. Even more bodies were found in another tomb known as the Great Death-Pit. The tomb chamber had been destroyed by robbers as had traces of the principal occupant but in a space measuring some twenty-seven by twenty-four feet lay the bodies of six servants, four women harpists and sixty-four other women, dressed in scarlet and adorned in gold, silver, lapis lazuli and carnelian. Max Mallowan recalled that the bottom of the shaft 'appeared, when exposed, to be a golden carpet ornamented with beech leaf head-dresses of the ladies of the court and overlaid by gold and silver harps and lyres'.

What was the explanation for the mass burials? There is no record of a general practice of human sacrifice in ancient Babylonia. Some authorities have suggested that the principal occupants of the tombs were the sacrificed priest and priestess, selected at the great New Year fertility festival, who represented the chief god and goddess of Ur in a 'Sacred Marriage Ceremony'. Against this it is argued, *inter alia*, that the principals found by Woolley were buried separately and if it were an annual festival more such graves should have been found in a cemetery spanning 600 years. Woolley thought they were the rulers of Ur (although their names do not appear on the Sumerian king list compiled in the late third millennium BC). Whatever their identity it was apparent that, although the bones were too decayed to indicate the cause of death, there were no signs of disarray as might have been caused by a struggle if the people had been dragged to their places and summarily despatched by executioners. This was supported by the lack of disturbance to the women's delicate headdresses (other than by the weight of the earth) indicating that they were dead or at least unconscious when the earth was thrown over them and the tomb sealed. The careful alignment of the bodies suggested also a deliberate arrangement before they were left for eternity. Woolley suggested that they were members of the royal household called upon to continue to serve the ruler in the next life and that they may have willingly walked into the pit and taken a drug which produced sleep or death. He mentions one haunting individual touch in the 'Great Death Pit': the excavators found only traces of the silver hair ribbons worn by the dead attendants, but on one woman a small flat disc was found which, when cleaned, proved to be one of these silver hair-ribbons probably carried in her pocket:

it was just as she had taken it from her room, done up in a tight coil with the ends brought over to prevent its coming undone ... Why the owner had not put it on one could not say; perhaps she was late for the ceremony and had not time to dress properly

Woolley has been criticised for his fertile imagination. Perhaps the following descrip-tion from his account of the excavation is fanciful; certainly there is no conclusive proof that it happened in this way, but it may have done:

Down into the open pit, with its mat-covered floor and mat-lined walls, empty and unfurnished, there comes a procession of people ... soldiers, men, servants and women, the latter in all their finery of brightly coloured garments and head-dresses of carnelian and lapis lazuli, silver and gold, officers with the insignia of their rank, musicians bearing harps or lyres, and then, driven or backed down the slope the chariots drawn by oxen, the drivers in the cars, the grooms holding the heads of the draught animals, and all take up their allotted places at the bottom of the shaft and finally a guard of soldiers forms up at the entrance. Each man and woman brought a little cup of clay or stone or metal, the only equipment needed for the rite that was to follow ... each of them drank from their cups a potion which they had brought with them or found prepared for them on the spot ... they lay down and composed themselves for death. Somebody came down and killed the animals ... and perhaps saw to it that all was decently in order ... and when that was done, earth was flung in from above, over the unconscious victims, and the filling-in of the grave-shaft was begun.

'Down into the open pit, with its mat-covered floor and mat-lined walls, ... there comes a procession of people, soldiers, men servants and women ...'. Reconstruction drawing by A. Forestier.

18

CANON GREENWELL AND THE 'FOLKTON DRUMS'

The Reverend William Greenwell (1820–1918), 'a patriarch in the field of British archaeology', who discovered the Folkton drums during one of his many barrow excavations. From the painting by Sir A.S. Cope in the Library of Durham Cathedral where Greenwell was a minor canon from 1854 to 1908.

The Folkton Drums, found in a child's grave in North Yorkshire and dating from c.1800 BC. From two of them peer faces with eyebrows, nose, eyes and mouth. The third has a similar but more abstract design. Made of solid magnesian limestone, their function is not known. Diams 14·2 cm (5·6 in), 12·1 cm (4·8 in) and 10·4 cm (4·1 in)

Towards the end of the nineteenth century Canon William Greenwell of Durham Cathedral was investigating yet another prehistoric barrow to add to his imposing total of over two hundred already excavated in the north of England. The barrow was situated in the parish of Folkton, in the East Riding of Yorkshire, about three-quarters of a mile east of a mound known as Sharp Howe. There he found an oval grave, lying in a north-south direction, 3 feet long and 1½ feet wide, sunk 14 inches below the surface. It contained the skeleton of a five year old child lying on its right side, head to the north and hands in front of its face. Behind the child's head and touching it was 'an object made of chalk' and behind and touching its hips were two other similar but larger objects, placed close together, the largest the furthest to the south.

These three objects were the unique Folkton 'drums', so called because of their shape. They are solid, made of magnesian limestone, probably from the coastal cliffs nearby bordering the North Sea. From two of them peer faces with eyebrows, nose and eyes, one with a lozenge-shaped mouth – faces which are four thousand years old. A third has a more abstract design which also resembles a human face. When they were given to the British Museum by the excavator in 1894 they were described as 'very remarkable objects, made of chalk, richly ornamented, and of unknown use'. We are still little wiser – they are probably ritual objects with a meaning we can

only guess at. Geometric designs are cut into them – circles, triangles, bands – marks similar to woodcarving. It may be therefore that they are unique survivals of a more common practice, perhaps other 'drums' existed in wood but have long since disintegrated.

Canon Greenwell describes the barrow where the child was found – 54 feet in diameter, 2½ feet high at the centre, but deeper on the sides and situated upon a natural rise in the land. At 12–15 feet from the centre was a circular trench sunk into the chalk rock and filled with earth, with a second trench nearer the centre. The child's grave touched the inner edge of the outer trench. Sharing the barrow with the child were five adults, an unidentifiable skeleton and a baby.

Who were these people? The drums give the impression of being made by three separate hands, the two faces are similar in design but exhibit differences in style to be expected from two artists. The third is rather interesting, almost as if done by an artist with abstract tendencies. The carved designs are typical of the pottery of the 'Beaker People' who emerged some generations before 2000 BC. There are still many questions unanswered about the Early Bronze Age in Britain (c.2000–1500 BC). Distinctive tall and narrow drinking beakers are found throughout Europe and the quantity which begins to appear in Britain probably reflects a movement of peoples over the North Sea or the Channel, although it has been argued that their culture could have been transmitted through trade and contact. The new inhabitants of Britain settled down. They probably lived some form of settled life, raising stock and growing crops as well as hunting, which permitted the emergence of specialist craftsmen. The settlers in the north of England buried their dead in round barrows and, in contrast to the communal burials of earlier times, provided personal goods for the dead in their separate graves; for the Folkton child these three strange ritual objects.

Their excavator, Canon Greenwell (1820–1918) is best known today for his invention of 'Greenwell's Glory' a fly still used in trout fishing (with which he was catching trout at the age of ninety-seven) and the fervour with which he, aided by a plentiful supply of estate labour, attacked barrows with methods which make today's archaeologists recoil in horror. Greenwell's favourite dictum was 'Never mind theories, collect facts' and in this he certainly succeeded. Much of the material he collected

Abstract design on the top of one of the Folkton Drums. The drums were found in one of a group of eight barrows, ¾ mile east of Sharp Howe. The barrow was 54 feet in diameter, 2½ feet high at the centre, placed on a natural rise in the land.

came to the Museum. There were a series of gifts from about 1879 to 1905 and in 1879 and 1880 he donated or sold one hundred burial urns and various odds and ends to the Museum. His flints were sold to Dr Allan Sturge in 1895 and many of them also found a home in the Museum. A collection of 2500 prehistoric bronze weapons was purchased by Pierpont Morgan in 1908 and given to the national collection. (The skulls Greenwell had excavated went to Oxford.) The money from these sales was less than the cost to the excavator and went to his family for the care of a profligate brother and the rescue of the family estate which had been sold.

Greenwell appears to have been something of a 'character' and is described as 'an admirable raconteur, with a keen sense of humour ... downright in his opinions and never hesitated to express them, when he thought right, with vigour and pungency'. His comments on reckless motor cyclists when Justice of the Peace led to questions in the House of Commons and on one occasion he threatened to throw the Mayor of Durham out of a window. He was born at Greenwell Ford, Lanchester, Co. Durham, quarrelled with his headmaster and instead of going to Oxford

took a degree at the new University of Durham. He tried London but was never quite well there, so resolutely decided that permanent residence in the south of England was not for him. He became a minor canon of Durham Cathedral in 1854 and remained there until 1908. He was a born collector, starting with Greek coins (which he later sold to Boston, USA) then in 1858 he graduated to prehistoric bronze weapons, thence to burial urns and skulls. In between collecting he was Cathedral Librarian for forty-six years.

His life spanned a greater part of the nineteenth century – his godfather fought with Wellington during the Peninsula War and he himself lived almost to the end of the First World War. When he started his excavations British archaeology and indeed scientific archaeology in general were in their infancy. Greenwell was no mere destroyer, he recorded what he found and published the results 'for the use of those interested in this important branch of our native archaeology'. He died, much honoured, at an advanced age; in his epitaph he was described as 'a patriarch in the field of British Archaeology ... a pioneer to whose enlightened researches its successful direction has been largely due.'

19

THE RILLATON GOLD CUP

The Rillaton gold cup must be one of the most unusual objects which in the course of its life became a receptacle for royal collar studs. It was fashioned from a sheet of gold, of very high purity, probably around 1600–1500 BC and was discovered in an Early Bronze Age grave in the parish of Linkinhorne, part of the Manor of Rillaton in the Duchy of Cornwall, in Spring 1837. The cup is one of only three so far found in temperate Europe and its style is similar to the pottery of the Beaker people. It was beaten from a single ingot and its handle was attached by six little rivets (three at the top and three at the bottom) passing through lozenge-shaped washers. There is little room for human fingers so the handle may be largely ornamental. The body of the cup is corrugated as is the base which as well as being decorative gives it a greater degree of strength.

It was found by labourers, searching for building stone, who decided to investigate an ancient burial mound, one of a group of four on the moor near a granite outcrop called the 'Cheesewring'. After removing some of the surface they discovered about five feet down on the outer edge of the mound, an oblong cavity, some eight feet long by three and a half feet wide and three feet high. The mound had been disturbed but the main chamber not reached. In the stone lined vault they found human remains – crumbling portions of a skull and other bones. There were two vessels lying near each other, one of earthenware, the other of gold, originally covered by a small slab of stone propped against the side of the tomb. Several other things were found, sufficient to fill four boxes, including the remains of a dagger (ten inches long when first seen but broken on removal).

The land was part of the Duchy of Cornwall so the finds being treasure trove were sent to King William IV in London. As the King died

The Rillaton Gold Cup, fashioned from a sheet of beaten gold c. 1600–1500 BC and discovered in a Bronze Age grave, in Cornwall in 1837. It is one of only three vessels of this type so far found in temperate Europe. H. 8·1 cm (3·2 in)

shortly after their arrival the cup and other objects promptly disappeared in the excitement of Queen Victoria's coronation and subsequent marriage. The Rillaton cup next emerges in Victoria's reign when the Prince Consort, Albert, discovered it in the royal collection and had it placed in the Swiss Cottage at Osborne, Isle of Wight, where the royal children collected a small museum of curiosities on their father's instructions.

In 1867 Queen Victoria and the Prince of Wales permitted the cup to be exhibited at the Royal Archaeological Institute and a detailed report was published. Then the cup disappeared again.

Archaeologists had been trying to find this elusive object for some time when, after the death of her husband King George V, Queen Mary was shown an engraving of the cup which she recognised. When King George had succeeded to the throne years before the royal couple had looked over the gold plate at Marlborough House. The King, like Albert, was attracted by the Rillaton cup and removed it to Buckingham Palace for his personal use. There it sat on his dressing table throughout his reign, holding the monarch's collar studs. Queen Mary now undertook to make it available to the public and in April 1936 it was deposited in the British Museum, on permanent loan, by King Edward VIII.

Of the four packages of objects discovered with it in 1837 very little remained. It was recalled that there were small pieces of bronze, a small bronze spear or arrow head, a dagger, a burial urn of coarse brick-like pottery, bits of ivory and greenish glass (perhaps beads of faience). Osborne was an Officers Hospital in the 1930s and the Matron was asked to help but was able to find only the dagger-blade which is today exhibited alongside the cup.

The chamber in which the cup was found, about five feet down on the outer edge of the mound, by labourers searching for building stone with which to build an engine house for a nearby tin mine. It contained human remains and several objects now lost except for a dagger-blade which is now displayed alongside the cup.

20

THE MAUSOLEUM AT HALICARNASSUS
One of the Seven Wonders of the Ancient World

Of the Seven Wonders of the Ancient World remains of two – the Mausoleum at Halicarnassus and the Temple of Diana at Ephesus – are in the Museum. Of the other five, the pyramids of Egypt remain *in situ*, the foundations of the Pharos of Alexandria are known, but the Hanging Gardens of Babylon, the Colossus of Rhodes, the Statue of Jupiter by Pheidias have long since disappeared.

The Mausoleum was truly a marvel, so much so that its name has come to describe any magnificent tomb. Its fame endured long after the building itself had disappeared and even the site was lost. Constructed of brilliantly painted white marble the Mausoleum dominated the ancient town of Halicarnassus (modern Bodrum) which lies on a remote peninsula on the south-west coast of Asia Minor in what is now Turkey. It was renowned for its superb sculptures, perhaps as many as three hundred statues, and lively friezes. The Mausoleum was erected in the fourth century BC, probably between about 367 and 350, as a memorial to Maussollos (the spelling used on his coins and inscriptions), King of Caria, who died shortly before 350 BC. The Carian dynasty, like the ancient Egyptians, favoured brother-sister marriages and, although Maussollos may have begun the tomb in his own lifetime it is his sister-wife, Artemisia, who is credited with completing much of the work before, grief-stricken, she died in 351 BC and was succeeded by another brother-sister pair, Ada and Idrieus.

The best description of the Mausoleum is that given by Pliny (23–79 AD) in his *Natural History* (although there is some argument

(Detail) From the colossal male statue which recalls Maussollos's proclamation in Lucian's *Dialogues*, 'I was a handsome man, and formidable in war'. The head of a man in his prime, his hair worn long in 4th c. BC Asiatic fashion.

Above. Reconstruction of the short side of the Mausoleum by Susan Bird, 'a work of such beauty and splendour that it was ranked by the ancients among the Seven Wonders of the World'. The Mausoleum was erected between about 367–350 BC.

Right. Head and forequarters of one of the marble chariot horses. The bronze bit is original and there are traces of red paint on the strap under the belly. The immense horses were supported by marble pillars under the belly, their tails clipped and tied up, perhaps as an indication of mourning. Reconstructed H. about 3.6 m (11 ft 9 in)

over his exact words). He names the four sculptors who worked on the Mausoleum – Scopas (east side), Bryaxis (north), Timotheos (south), Leochares (west) and relates that it:

was erected by his wife Artemisia in honour of Mausolus, a petty king of Caria, who died in the second year of the hundred and seventh Olympiad. It was through the exertions of these artists more particularly, that this work came to be reckoned one of the Seven Wonders of the World. The circumference of this building is, in all, four hundred and forty feet, and the breadth from north to south 63, the two fronts being not so wide in extent. It is 25 cubits in height, and is surrounded with 36 columns, the outer circumference being known as the "Pteron" ... before their task was completed, Queen Artemisia died. They did not

leave their work, however, until it was finished, considering that it was at once a memorial of their own fame and of the sculptor's art: and, to this day, even, it is undecided which of them has excelled. A fifth artist also took part in the work; for above the Pteron there is a pyramid erected, equal in height to the building below, and formed of 24 steps, which gradually taper upwards towards the summit; a platform, crowned with a representation of a four-horse chariot by Pythis. This addition makes the total height of the work 140 feet ...

The building is thought to have been still standing in the twelfth century when Eustathius wrote 'It was and *is* a wonder'. After years of neglect and gradual dissolution it appears eventually to have been overthrown by an earthquake. Its destruction was completed by the Knights of St John who began to fortify the town, building the Castle of St Peter in 1402. An account published in 1581 relates that in 1522 the Knights looked about for stones with which to make lime and found in the middle of a level field steps of white marble raised in the form of a terrace. This they used as a quarry.

Bodrum is accessible by sea but difficult to reach by land. Before the mid-nineteenth century few Europeans had visited it and the memory of the exact location of this Wonder of the ancient world had been lost. In 1846 Sir Stratford Canning, British Ambassador at Constantinople obtained from the Sultan permission to send to the Museum twelve slabs of frieze from the Mausoleum which had been incorporated into the Castle of St Peter. Their arrival in London aroused intense interest and in 1852 Charles Newton, lately a member of the Museum staff, was appointed Vice-Consul in Mytilene with the additional brief of collecting antiquities. On his first visit to Bodrum he strolled round the castle ramparts and then gazed in amazement at the head of a colossal white marble lion built into the walls: on looking over the battlements he saw five more – such fine beasts could only have come from the famed but long lost Mausoleum. Newton returned in November 1856 with Royal Navy support and a team of Royal Engineers. He had an approximate location from the first-century AD writer Vitruvius: in the centre of the town halfway between the harbour and the heights above. He found promising remains of the right quality and material and on 1 January 1857 he and his team began to dig in earnest. Pieces of sculpture began to emerge – legs and scraps of frieze, then a foot attached to a frieze moulding identical with that on the frieze Stratford Canning had presented to the Museum. He

Above. One of the lions from the roof of the Mausoleum at the base of the pyramid. Its tongue was originally painted red and the body yellow-brown or yellow-ochre. The lions were carved by a number of sculptors and varied in size. H. 1·5 m (4 ft 11 in)

Below right. 'Maussollos'. Because of its scale it is unlikely that this statue would have fitted into the chariot group and it probably represents one of the rulers of Caria whose statues stood between the pillars below the pyramid. The carving is so realistic that the Greek himation which he wears above an Asiatic tunic has creases below the left knee such as would have been caused by storage. H. 3 m (9 ft 8 in)

Left. 'Artemisia'. Again there is no evidence as to the identity of this figure who probably represents one of the royal ladies of Caria, her arms extended in a gesture of grief. H. 2·67 m (8 ft 9 in)

noticed in the foundations of a nearby wall a battered fragment of a marble lion. 'From that day' Newton wrote 'I had no doubt that the site of the Mausoleum was found'.

Newton now had a problem if he wished to excavate further for the site was covered with houses and plots of land. As he approached closer to one house for example which evidently stood on a great mass of debris, the owner's wife objected strongly:

One day when we were engaged in an experiment how near to the foundations we could venture to dig without undermining the house, a long gaunt arm was suddenly thrust through the shutters from within, and a discordant female voice screeched out some unpleasant Turkish imprecations on our heads.

The lady also took the opportunity of dropping hot cinders down the back of one of the party. On another occasion the team's sapper was knocked into a trench by a well-aimed blow from a chopping block hurled at his head from the same window. Eventually however the house was purchased and work continued.

Newton discovered several galleries cut out of the solid rock and Corporal Jenkins, a sapper, was despatched to follow their course. One one occasion, on probing the roof of a gallery where the rock had been replaced by masonry Jenkins' crowbar suddenly emerged through the hearthstone of a Turk quietly sitting smoking in his own home. Corporal Jenkins continued, his air shafts 'emerging sometimes in a garden and sometimes in a courtyard, much to the terror of the elder ladies and the diversion of the young ones'. Newton continued his excavations until the following year, buying land and houses wherever possible. He traced the outline of the great building and found many fragments – colossal sculptures, parts of friezes, steps and the green stone foundations. His finds were packed and despatched to London and with them the lions from the Castle. In an evocative passage Newton describes the removal of the hindquarters of a massive horse:

After being duly hauled out, he was placed on a sledge and dragged to the shore by eighty Turkish workmen. On the walls and house-tops as we went along sat the veiled ladies of Budrum. They had never seen anything so big before, and the sight overcame the reserve imposed on them by Turkish etiquette. The ladies of Troy gazing at the wooden horse as he entered at the breach could not have been more astonished.

Newton had uncovered a massive jigsaw

puzzle with most of the pieces missing. G.M.A. Bilotti excavated for the Museum between March and August 1865 and added some 130 more sculptures, mostly built into walls of later structures and therefore in poorer condition. There had been many attempts before Newton to reconstruct the famous Mausoleum – one, rather fanciful, is Hawksmoor's spire of St George's Church just over the road from the Museum which is surmounted by George I looking rather odd in a toga.

The Mausoleum consisted of a stepped lower section leading up to a 'pteron' or colonnade of thirty-six columns probably arranged eleven to the longer sides, nine to the shorter. Above this was a pyramid of twenty-four steps surmounted by a four horse chariot. Who occupied this vehicle we do not know – perhaps it was empty or more likely there were up to three passengers. Perhaps Maussollos driving to glory with Nike or perhaps Helios-Apollo. There may have been as many as three hundred and thirty other free-standing sculptures, all painted, perhaps from fifty-six to seventy-two lions at the base of the pyramid and thirty-six colossal portraits between the columns of the pteron. There was room for seventy-two portrait figures on the middle step and eighty-eight life-sized figures in Greek and Persian dress at the base. The statues included battles between Greek and Persians, a sacrificial group and a hunt.

Who planned and executed the Mausoleum? G.B. Waywell comments that it could take a skilled mason a year to carve one life-sized figure. He therefore estimated 704 man-years for the free-standing sculpture; thus if the Mausoleum were completed between about 367 and 350 BC some forty sculptors must have been involved. Pliny mentions Scopas, Bryaxis, Timotheos (Vitruvius reports that some sources name Praxiteles) and Leochares. He attributes the chariot group to 'Pytis' while Vitruvius infers that Pytheos and Satyrus were involved. It seems probable therefore that at least four masters and their workshops were brought over from mainland Greece and worked in concert, perhaps to the designs of Pytheos and Satyrus. The tradition that each master supervised one side is now regarded as dubious. However the work is divided, it is certain that for those involved even what little remains is still 'a memorial of their own fame and of the sculptor's art'.

Above. A Greek and Amazon in combat. One of the three friezes of which remains have been found. Sir Charles Newton wrote of these reliefs 'One general expression of wonder and admiration burst forth from the lips of my Turkish workmen when they beheld the "kiz" or "girl" as they called this figure. It was the first time that they had fairly recognized likeness in anything I had discovered'. H. 90.2 cm (2 ft 11.5 in)

Bodrum (ancient Halicarnassus) today. Dominating the harbour is the Castle of St Peter, built by the Knights of St John in the 15th c. AD largely from stones taken from the Mausoleum. There is a story that the Knights found a sepulchre 'strewn with fragments of cloth of gold, and spangles of the same metal' looted by pirates.

LORD ELGIN AND THE SCULPTURES OF THE PARTHENON

My spirit is too weak – mortality
Weighs heavily on me like unwilling sleep . . .

(John Keats, On seeing the Elgin Marbles, 1817)

On 3 September 1799 the frigate HMS *Phaeton* left Portsmouth carrying His Britannic Majesty's Ambassador to the Sublime Porte at Constantinople; Thomas Bruce, 7th Earl of Elgin, accompanied by his pregnant wife, secretaries, physician, a professor in search of classical manuscripts, a courier, three personal maids, other female servants and followed by a merchantman with servants, grooms, coachmen, carriages, pianos, a set of ambassadorial gold and silver plate and a

Thomas Bruce, 7th Earl of Elgin (1766–1841) who brought the collection of sculptures from the Parthenon and other classical remains to Britain. Elgin's initial intention was to improve the arts of his country by having drawings and moulds made. He revised his plans when confronted by the continued destruction of the sculptures. Drawing by G.P. Harding after Anton Graf c.1795.

great quantity of furniture. The Napoleonic Wars were in full swing; the thirty-three-year old Ambassador was, however, determined that his appointment should be remembered for more than diplomatic success. He had recently come under the influence of an architect, Thomas Harrison, a devotee of the Greek style who was working on Elgin's mansion at Broomhall. Elgin had been fired with the idea of spreading the gospel of Greek architecture in Britain and, since Greece was then part of the Turkish empire (as it had been for 450 years), his new post offered a golden opportunity. His enthusiasm did not extend to bringing back the actual remains, rather he intended to recruit a team of artists and moulders to carry out his plan.

There can be no comparison between the Athens of today or of Classical times and the 'shabby, miserable' forty-third city of the European Turkish Empire which awaited Elgin. A mixed population lived in some 1300 houses on the north and east slopes of the Acropolis. Amidst the squalor, however, were the remains of more glorious times. The finest of these was the Parthenon.

Athens is dominated by a flat topped rock on which in ancient times was located the Acropolis or 'high city' – a fortress and religious centre dedicated to the cult of the city's patron goddess Athena. By the mid-fifth century BC Athens had reached a high point in its history. Peace had been made with Persia and the city under Pericles was leader of the majority of Greek city-states who paid tribute to her. From this bounty it was decided around 448 BC to build a great temple dedicated to

Athens is dominated by a flat topped rock on which in ancient times was located the Acropolis or 'high city', a fortress and religious centre. The most important building on it was the Parthenon completed between 447 and 432 BC and dedicated to Athena. The Parthenon remained intact until the 5th c. AD when many sculptures were lost during its conversion into a Christian church. Further major damage was caused in an explosion of 1687.

Athena. The sculptor Pheidias exercised a general supervision over the scheme and was creator of the new statue of Athena. Ictinus was named as principal architect, assisted by Callicrates. The building was erected in the Doric style from shining white marble, taken from the quarries on Mount Pentelicon about ten miles from Athens. In addition to the architectural perfection of its proportions the building was remarkable for the richness of its painted sculpture. At each end was a triangular pediment, that on the east portraying the Birth of Athena and at the opposite end was the contest of Athena and Poseidon for the land of Attica. Above the columns on the outside of the building were a series of ninety-two metopes showing amongst other subjects, Lapiths (a legendary primitive mountain tribe in Thessaly) and centaurs (wild creatures, half human and half horse) engaged in drunken battle at the wedding of Hippodamia and King Pirithous. The columns of the inner porches were surmounted by a frieze which continued

along the walls of the temple showing a great jostling procession – horsemen six or seven abreast, charioteers, youths carrying water jars or conducting animals to sacrifice, girls with offering bowls, parade marshals, all travelling towards an assembly of gods and heroes. At the centre an official and his assistant held a folded cloth which is thought to represent the peplos, or sacred robe, which was taken to the cult statue of Athena.

The Temple survived relatively unscathed until the fifth century AD when it was converted into a church with an apse at the east end. Some of the frieze was then removed and many metopes were deliberately defaced. The worst damage occured in 1687 when a Turkish gunpowder magazine located in the building exploded after a direct hit by besieging Venetians. Later it suffered the attentions of souvenir hunters (to meet whose wants the local populace would hack pieces of sculpture into handy sizes) and builders (who found that burnt sculptures made fine cement).

Elgin's recording team arrived in Athens in 1800. It had been recruited with the assistance of Sir William Hamilton (husband of Nelson's Emma) and another William Hamilton, Elgin's secretary. It was a strangely assorted crew, led by a well-known Italian landscape painter Giovanni Battista Lusieri, and including Feodor Ivanovitch, known as 'Lord Elgin's Calmuck' (painter), a hunchback called Balestra and a student called Ittar (architectural draughtsman). The group initially encountered difficulties with the authorities – the Turkish military governor (the Disdar) refused to allow them to work on the Acropolis on the grounds that they would then be able to spy on Turkish women in their homes. The following year they at last managed to get on the Acropolis by the simple expedient of paying five pounds per day to the Disdar. They then started to erect scaffolding so as to make moulds but the Disdar, by then expecting a French invasion, withdrew his permission.

The only solution was to obtain authorisation from Constantinople and letters were sent to Lusieri. The terms of the proposed firman (or licence) were drafted by Philip Hunt, Elgin's chaplain, who had visited Athens and witnessed the continuing destruction of the Parthenon sculptures. It was granted on 6 July 1801 to a valued ally following the defeat of the French in Egypt by a British expeditionary force. An Italian version of this document still exists; it directed that no one should interfere with Elgin's team in their sketching and scaffolding and that they might also 'take away any pieces of stone with old inscriptions or sculptures thereon'. There has been much argument over the terms of the firman, which Elgin's team took as authority to remove sculptures from the building. Whether or not this was the initial Turkish intention the removals were subsequently specifically authorised. Elgin, Hunt and Lusieri had no doubt that they were performing a service in rescuing the sculptures from imminent destruction. As Elgin later asserted to a Parliamentary Select Committee:

Every traveller coming added to the general defacement of the statuary in his reach ... the Turks have been continually defacing the heads; and in some instances they have actually acknowledged to me that they have pounded down the statues to convert them into mortar: It was upon these suggestions and with these feelings, that I proceeded to remove as much of the sculpture as I

Top left. Horsemen from the north frieze. The friezes, which were 40 feet above the ground, show a grand procession – horsemen, charioteers, youths carrying water jars or conducting animals to sacrifice, girls with offering bowls, parade marshals and an assembly of gods and heroes.

Centre left. A figure from the east pediment reclining on an animal skin – perhaps Dionysos on a panther's skin or alternatively Herakles on a lion-skin. H. *c* 1.3 m (3 ft 8 in)

Below left. Figures from the east pediment which portrayed the birth of Athena. More than half the sculptures were lost in the 5th c. AD when the building was converted into a Christian church. The survivors are difficult to identify but these may be Demeter and her daughter Persephone and perhaps, standing, Hebe the cup-bearer of Zeus. H. (of standing figure) 1·73 m (5 ft 9 in)

Right. The head of the chariot horse of Selene (the Moon) from the east pediment. At the extreme angle of the pediment Selene's chariot drawn by exhausted animals sinks into the waters of Okeanos, contrasting with the eager beasts of Helios, the sun-god, rising at the opposite end. L. 79 cm (2 ft 7 in)

conveniently could; it was no part of my original plan to bring away any thing but my models.

And so the removals began – 247 feet of the original 524 feet of the frieze, fourteen of the ninety-two metopes, seventeen pedimental figures from the Parthenon; a caryatid and column from the Erechtheum. Fragments from the west pediment (the torso of Poseidon, the Nike, the Hermes) were found underneath the home of a Turkish soldier; a number of fragments of metopes and parts of the frieze were uncovered on the south side. The excavators were too late in many cases – after excavating beneath another Turkish home the owner laughingly told them that he had used the marble from statues found at that spot to make mortar for his house. Elgin visited the work in the Spring of 1802 – his first one of two visits to Athens – and was present for the removal from the pediment of Selene's horse. Various ships were pressed into service to transfer the marbles back to England. Elgin chartered the *Mentor* whose second voyage led to near disaster when, running before a storm, she struck a rock at the entrance to Cerigo harbour and sank. Elgin spent a considerable amount of money on local sponge divers who successfully recovered the entire cargo and sent it on its way.

Elgin tired of the East and at the beginning of 1803 departed from Constantinople, leaving instructions for Lusieri to continue his work in Athens. The timing of his return journey was unfortunate for, after a period of peace, war broke out between France and Britain while Elgin was on French territory. Elgin was arrested and detained – a most unusual procedure in an age when wars were the concern of armies and noble travellers could pass unmolested through enemy territory. Napoleon took a personal interest in the case and Lady Elgin's frantic efforts to secure her husband's release had little effect. Finally, in June 1806 Elgin was at last released on parole. His previous good fortune now deserted him. His wife had earlier returned to Britain to arrange the burial of their fourth child, his only male heir was epileptic, Lady Elgin was involved with another man and an unsavoury divorce case resulted. His public career was in ruins, no more diplomatic posts were offered and he lost his seat in the House of

Lords (his peerage was Scottish not English). He was deeply in debt and had now lost his wife's fortune; apart from his ambassadorial expenses he had spent a crippling £39,200 on his collection of antiquities, the last consignments of which because of the Napoleonic wars did not reach England until 1811.

However, Elgin rented a large house at the corner of Piccadilly and Park Lane and, in a shed in the garden began to unpack his treasures. The marbles burst upon an admiring public in 1807; the artist John Flaxman found them unsurpassed, Benjamin West (President of the Royal Academy) called them 'sublime specimens of the purest sculpture', the Swiss painter Fuseli went about declaiming 'De Greeks were godes! de Greeks were godes!'. As Elgin's financial affairs became more disastrous and as he found difficulty in providing a more permanent home than the Park Lane shed, Elgin opened negotiations with the government. His first offer of the sculptures in return for £62,440 (which he calculated as his disbursements plus interest) was rebuffed, the government offering only £30,000. In 1815 Elgin tried to sell for £73,600 and, so desperate were his affairs, that he agreed to abide by the value to be determined by a Select Committee of the House of Commons. This sat at the beginning of 1816. It found that the collection had been legitimately acquired and did not dispute Elgin's ownership. However, to his great disappointment, no doubt influenced by Richard Payne Knight and the Society of Dilettanti who had declared them inferior and Roman and by the usual government niggardliness, the Committee fixed the price at £35,000. Elgin had no option but to accept and the collection was vested in the Trustees of the British Museum.

Elgin was plagued by financial troubles for the rest of his life and bequeathed these to his heirs. He has been sadly misunderstood and his reputation blackened undeservedly: a comparison of the condition of the sculptures and casts in the Museum with those left behind should disperse any criticism. As Elgin wrote to his ex-secretary Hamilton:

No-one knows more intimately than you do, that the impulses which led me to the exertions I made in Greece were wholly for the purpose of securing to Great Britain and through it to Europe in general, the most effectual possible knowledge, and means of improving, by the excellence of Grecian art in sculpture and architecture . . .

In this Elgin succeeded admirably, the Elgin marbles which have since been seen by millions of visitors to the Museum have been most effective ambassadors for Greek culture.

The central section of the east frieze – a group of seated gods. *Left to right.* Hermes (the messenger), Dionysos (god of fertility and especially of wine), Demeter (goddess of corn) and Ares (god of war). H. *c.*1 m (3 ft 3 in)

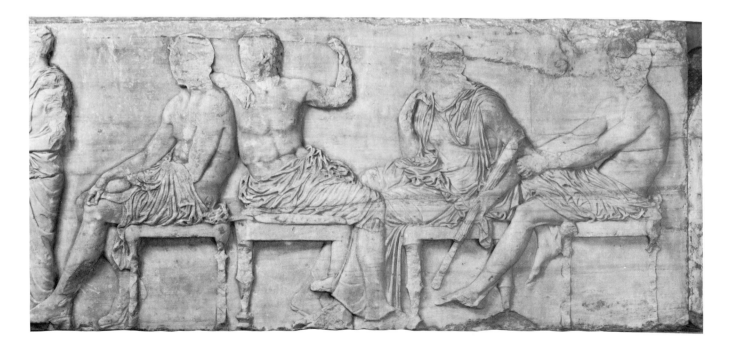

22

THE MONUMENT OF JULIUS CLASSICIANUS, PROCURATOR OF BRITAIN

... The savage British tribesmen were disinclined for peace, especially as the newly arrived imperial agent Gaius Julius Alpinus Classicianus, successor to Catus Decianus, was on bad terms with Suetonius, and allowed his personal animosities to damage the national interests. For he passed round advice to wait for a new governor who would be kind to those who surrendered, without an enemy's bitterness or a conqueror's arrogance. Classicianus also reported to Rome that there was no prospect of ending the war unless a successor was appointed to Suetonius, whose failures he attributed to perversity – and his successes to luck.

(Tacitus, *The Annals of Imperial Rome*, transl. Michael Grant, Penguin 1983)

Until this century little had been known of Julius Classicianus who appears briefly and unsympathetically in Tacitus's account of the aftermath of the bitter and bloody revolt of the Iceni of Norfolk under their Queen Boudica in 60–61 AD. The Iceni rose when, on the death of their king Prasutagus in 60 AD with no son to succeed him the Romans decided to absorb their territory and molested Queen Boudica and her two daughters. Camulodunum (Colchester) and Verulamium (near St Albans) were sacked and their inhabitants massacred. The record of the arrival of the Iceni in London can be seen today about four metres below the surface of the modern city – a red layer of burnt debris about 0.45 metres thick – ash from burning buildings. The Iceni were eventually defeated with terrible losses by a disciplined Roman army led by Gaius Suetonius Paulinus. The Romans then proceeded to take a terrible revenge.

Classicianus was appointed Procurator by the Emperor Nero to sort out the financial mess left by his fleeing predecessor, Catus Decianus. He appears, contrary to Tacitus's unfavourable description, to have been a man of good sense, concerned with the economy of the province and conscious of the futility of the vengeance which the Romans were taking upon the Iceni. His unfavourable reports back to Nero on the military governor Suetonius were confirmed by Nero's trusted freedman Polyclitus and Suetonius was replaced. Gradu-

ally under Classicianus's policy of conciliation the bitterness healed and prosperity returned to the province. Around 65 AD another Procurator was appointed and Julius Classicianus disappears from history.

The first hint of what had happened to him emerged in 1852 when excavations at Trinity Place, Trinity Square near Tower Hill unearthed a number of large stones built into one of the semi-circular bastions added in later Roman times to strengthen the city wall. Two were given to the Museum, one a massive decorated 'bolster' shaped stone, five feet long and twenty inches in diameter. The other, two and a half by five feet, was of even greater interest since it bore a partial inscription:

DIS

ANIBUS

AB. ALPINI. CLASSICIANI

DIS MANIBUS (to the spirits of the departed) was the customary formula on Roman sepulchral monuments. The stones were extremely heavy so had probably come from a cemetery nearby. The antiquary C. Roach Smith suggested that they came from a monument to Tacitus's Julius Classicianus but other scholars thought this unlikely, the odds being too high against finding the tombstone of a known prominent individual and it was suggested that the monument commemorated a sailor (*classis* = fleet).

Thirty years later, in 1885, when an underground railway was cut through the site workmen came upon several more stones. In 1935 further work revealed a large stone upside down bearing the inscription:

PROC. PROVINC. BRIT

IVLIA. INDI. FILIA. PACATA. I

UXOR

Also found were a number of stones without inscription. The style, size and spacing of the lettering matched the 1852 inscription in the Museum and the stone (buff coloured and very fine grained oolite) was of the same type. This was therefore a missing piece of this massive jigsaw. Roach Smith had been correct and it was indeed the monument to Julius Classicianus Alpinus, Imperial Procurator of the Province of Britain, who must have died in office here, his ashes being buried under the monument by his wife Julia Pacata, daughter of Indus. The fragmentary inscription has been reconstructed as follows:

( ) = abbreviations; [ ] = missing sections:

DIS [M] ANIBUS [G (AI). IUL(I). G (AI). F(ILI). F] AB (IA. TRIBU.) ALPINI.

CLASSICIANI . . . PROC(URATORIS) PROVINC(IAE). BRITA [NNIAE]. IULIA. INDI. FILIA. PACATA. I. [NDIANA] UXOR. [F(ECIT)].

The monument is thus one of the most important historical documents from Roman Britain and its presence confirms the administrative importance of London almost two millennia ago. The unrecovered gap in the middle was perhaps filled by brief details of the dead man's career. *Alpinus* indicates that he came from somewhere between the Alps and the Ardennes and from other sources we can locate the probable home of his family in the area of Trier. A Julius Indus is recorded by Tacitus – a Gaul who in 21 AD suppressed a revolt against Rome by his countrymen. If a daughter was born to him at this time she could have been of the correct marriageable age for Classicianus and might have been named *Pacata* to commemorate her father's pacification of the rebels. The monument would have been destroyed in the fourth century. Its recovery however gives us a tangible memorial to a shadowy historical figure and a link with the early days of London.

The monumental tomb of Gaius Julius Alpinus Classicianus, erected by his widow Julia Pacata some time after AD 61. The first inscribed pieces were unearthed near Tower Hill in 1852 and the others in 1935. L. 2·28 m (7 ft 6 in)

The tomb of Classicianus. Reconstruction drawing by Alan Sorrell. London was then 'a town that was not indeed dignified with the appellation of a Colony, but was very populous with its throngs of traders and (stores) of commodities' (Tacitus).

23

THE SUTTON HOO SHIP BURIAL

Then the Geats built a barrow on the headland – it was high and broad, visible from far to all seafarers . . .
They bequeathed the gleaming gold, treasure of men, to the earth . . .

(*Beowulf*, transl. by Kevin Crossley-Holland from an Early English Manuscript in the British Library)

On 27 July 1939, amidst the news from Goodwood races, and portents of war, there appeared a small paragraph in *The Times* announcing the discovery of the grave of an Anglo-Saxon chief. This find was to prove one of the richest treasures ever excavated in the British Isles.

The discovery of a great ship buried beneath the bleak sandy heathland of Suffolk brought to light the magnificence of the Anglo-Saxon kingdoms of the early years of the seventh century. The Sutton Hoo ship burial includes a stupendous treasure of gold and silver, a total of over 4000 hand cut garnets decorating some of the pieces, and sparkling blue and red millefiori glass. It brings together fine craftsmanship from England, Germany, Scandinavia, Alexandria and far Byzantium. Among the finds which amazed excavators and the Museum authorities in 1939 were a great gold buckle in pristine condition weighing 415 grammes decorated with writhing animal patterns and a pair of shoulder clasps inlaid with garnets, the blood red stones outlined in fine yellow gold. There was a beautiful purse lid, also of gold and garnet, with decoration whose meaning we can only guess at and a silver dish bearing the control stamps of

Emperor Anastasius I (491–518 AD) which had somehow made its way from Byzantium to Suffolk. Two spoons which appeared to be inscribed with the Greek names 'Saulos' and 'Paulos' were perhaps a baptismal present to a newly converted Christian. Within the barrow were the remains of a fearsome helmet, one of only two to survive in Britain from this period inlaid with silver and garnets and decorated with plaques showing battle scenes. All of these, and many other items – hanging bowls, drinking horns, a shield, a lyre, three bronze cauldrons, a sword with jewelled pommel and gold hilt – are now in the Museum.

Although this unique unrobbed grave was a revelation to scholars, at the same time it is an enigma. Who is the shadowy figure commemorated with such magnificence? Who were the craftsmen who produced such fine work? With what ceremony was the great ship dragged from the river and lowered into its final resting place? What is the significance of the grave goods, in particular the four sided stone bar, perhaps a ceremonial whetstone, or royal sceptre, carved with eight human faces? What is the strange object which has been variously described as a scalp rack, a royal standard or an elaborate torch? If these

Little Sutton Hoo farm seen from the west bank of the River Deben. The arrow marks the position of the ship burial, on the high ground behind the wood. Before sea walls were built to confine the tidal waters of the river the mound would have been about 600 yards from high water. The view of the burial field is now obscured by trees planted in the 19th c.

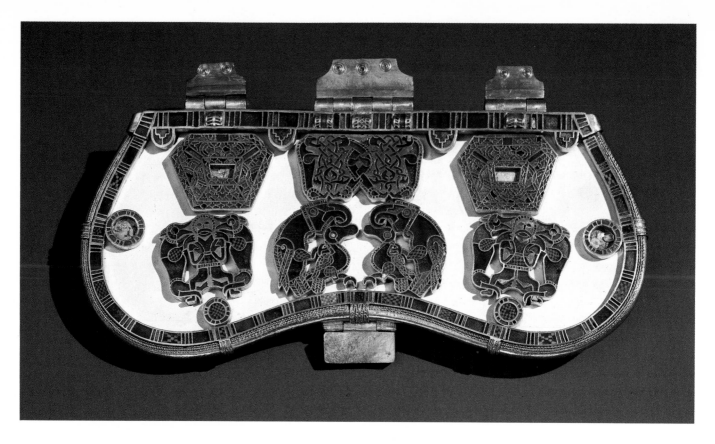

Top. The purse lid, the most original and spectacular of the pieces, once probably mounted on leather or ivory. The lid hinges at the top on three gold plates which were riveted to leather straps hanging from a belt. Inside the purse were 37 gold coins, 3 blanks and 2 ingots. The gold outer frame is decorated with bars and panels of garnet and millefiori glass and enriched with filigree bindings. There are seven decorative plaques, two of which show a man spreadeagled between two erect wolf-like animals, at his side are birds of prey swooping savagely on ducks. L. *c.* 19 cm (7.5 in)

Above. Purse lid (detail).

Right. Reconstruction incorporating original fragments on a modern base of a warrior's ceremonial helmet from the Dark Ages. The iron crest and bronze eyebrows are inlaid with silver wires and the eyebrows with square cut garnets. The nose and mouth of the mask are in gilt-bronze with cast details. Restored. H. 31.8 cm (12.5 in)

priceless objects were expendable, and could be committed to the earth, what magnificence remained above ground?

Sutton Hoo (the name is a nineteenth century derivation from Sutton How or Haugh) is situated in the ancient Kingdom of the East Angles, which in the seventh century AD was ruled over by a dynasty known as the 'Wuffingas', (the 'wolf people') who traced their descent back to the god Woden by way of Julius Caesar. Opposite the modern town of Woodbridge, on a sandy plateau overlooking the estuary of the River Deben, lies a group of around fifteen ancient burial mounds. Although the barrows are now almost half a mile inland, before sea walls were built to confine the tidal waters of the river they would have been about 600 yards from high water.

In 1938 a remarkable woman, Mrs Edith May Pretty, landowner and Justice of the Peace, decided to investigate the barrows. She is said to have been encouraged by an old man living on the estate who, perhaps from folk memory, spoke of a fabulous treasure lying under the barrows, and by her nephew, a dowser, who repeatedly forecast that there was gold buried there. The tradition of opening barrows and making off with their valuable contents goes back many centuries; the possibility of finding a burial which had not

been ransacked in the past was thus remote.

Mrs Pretty had spare labour on her estate in Spring 1938 and Mr Basil Brown, a local archaeologist, was employed by her to do the excavation, the Ipswich Museum having general oversight. The first three mounds excavated produced comparatively normal material – an interesting mixture of burial practices (cremations and a ransacked inhumed burial in a small boat) and a number of interesting but not particularly remarkable objects.

A new season of excavation began in May 1939 but this was to be very different. On this occasion the target was the tallest of the barrows – some nine feet in height. Basil Brown cut into the mound from the landward side and soon came across rusted iron rivets which he knew must belong to a boat of considerable size. Traces were found ten feet down of a late sixteenth or early seventeenth century robbers' hole with the remains of a winter's meal at the bottom, but this had been dug off centre. Brown uncovered the bows of the ship and reached the centre where a burial might be expected; encouragingly this was at a level below that reached by the robbers. As the unexpected complexity and potential importance of the find became apparent assistance was called in and Mr C.W. Phillips of Cambridge and a group of assistants took over in July. The British Museum and the Inspectorate of Ancient Monuments were also involved. In the hot summer of 1939, as Europe moved towards war, began the painstaking work of excavating the great ship which had been buried for 1300 years.

The objects were found roughly laid out in the shape of an 'H', in a specially constructed burial chamber roofed over by timber and turf.

Mrs Pretty, owner of the site, seated centre with companion, watches archaeologists at work on the ship in 1939. The shoulder clasps are being painstakingly uncovered.

This had collapsed and damaged some, but not all, of the grave goods. Jewelled trappings and weapons lay at the western end of this central chamber, kitchen utensils and more ordinary objects at the east.

The problem which mystified the excavators and which remains unsolved, even with the assistance of forensic science, is whether the excavators found a cenotaph (empty grave) or whether no trace remained of the body that had been buried in it. It is possible that a body placed in the chamber could have been dissolved by water and by the acid soil, but there was a significant absence of intimate personal objects such as rings or remains of clothing. A search by the re-excavators in the 1960s for deposits of phosphate (which indicate a body) found a high unexplained concentration in the area by the sword. But the difficulty of producing proof is indicated by other traces of bone which could represent a funeral feast and a chess set. It seems that the question will never be irrefu-

tably answered. The balance of opinion has, however, shifted from the cenotaph to an occupied grave.

Cenotaph or not, it is agreed that the great ship burial commemorated an individual of high rank; but who? The 'whetstone' is a ceremonial object – perhaps a symbol of the Saxon king in the mystic role of Wayland the Smith – the maker, giver and master of swords. The iron object might be a royal standard after the Roman model, or an elaborate torch. These objects, the location of the mound (not far from the lost royal manor at Rendlesham) and the general quality of the grave goods, point to a member of the local royal house. The main clues to the date of the burial, which at least narrow the field, are the thirty-seven small gold coins found in the purse all from different mints on the Continent of Europe in the territories controlled or occupied by the Merovingian Franks (now France, Belgium, the Rhineland and Switzerland). These at least can provide a date

Drawing by Alan Sorrell showing his interpretation of the great ship being dragged from the River Deben to its burial trench. The vessel was over 27 m (89 ft) long.

Enamelled circular plaque of Celtic workmanship from the rim of the large hanging bowl. The plaque is decorated with red enamel and inlaid millefiori glass; soldered below is a stylised bronze boar's head with garnet eyes. Diam. 6·2 cm (2·4 in)

before which the burial cannot have taken place and a possible date of assembly. It has been suggested that the probability is a date of not later than 630 AD for any coin and 625 AD as a likely date for their assembly. This narrows the field but there are still a number of candidates. The Museum's first choice is Raedwald, *Bretwalda* or High King of Anglo-Saxon England south of the Humber, the most powerful king thrown up by his dynasty, who died in 624 or 625 AD. Raedwald was a convert to Christianity, although he relapsed and set up altars to Christ and pagan gods side by side. The burial could be interpreted in this light since the whole manner of burial is unchristian but some of the grave goods are of the new religion.

The other possible Wuffingas include Sigeberht a devout Christian or his brother Ecgric who were killed in 635 or 636 fighting against King Penda of Mercia. It is perhaps unlikely that the survivors of the family, Anna a fervent Christian, and Aethelwald (d.663/4) (all of whose daughters became nuns, three of them saints) would have consented to a pagan burial for their brothers or themselves. Raedwald's son, Eorpwald (d.624 or 627/8) remains a possibility however.

Under an ancient law the treasure had to be submitted to a Coroner's Inquest to decide whether or not it was 'treasure trove'. The Inquest was held on 14 August. The Coroner stressed that, in his view, some degree of secrecy and concealment was required for the hoard to be treasure trove. Since the dragging of a ninety foot ship from the river and its interment can hardly have gone unnoticed, and since it had all the characteristics of a deliberate burial meant to lie undisturbed for eternity the Jury found that the hoard was not treasure trove and was thus the property of the landowner, Mrs Pretty.

If these unique treasures had reached the market Mrs Pretty would have been a tremendously rich woman, and the nation somewhat poorer. However, on 23 August it was announced that Mrs Pretty had decided to present the entire hoard to the nation, to be housed in the Museum. Amongst all the magnificent treasures of the Museum this was undoubtedly, as the then Keeper of British & Medieval Antiquities declared, 'the most magnificent and munificent' single gift made in the lifetime of a donor. Mrs Pretty refused to accept any honour or other recompense.

War broke out on 3 September 1939, nine days after the excavators left the site. The 'ghost' of the great ship was covered over and the treasure was transferred to the Museum, having spent some time under Mrs Pretty's bed – 'the safest place in East Anglia'. It had no sooner arrived in London than it was buried again, spending the war years deep below the capital in a disused section of the Underground railway. It was returned safe and sound after the War and is now one of the Museum's greatest treasures.

Two clasps, probably worn on the shoulders attached to a two part garment of cloth or leather. Hinged with a central pin, they are decorated with cloisonné garnets and millefiori glass. The borders which enclose a strictly geometric panel are of animal and snake interlace. The end of each clasp is filled with a design of two intertwined boars. Approx. L. 12·8 cm (5 in)

The great gold buckle. Gold inlaid with niello, its design featuring thrusting birds' heads, biting beasts and interweaving snakes. The back plate opens on a hinge and is fastened by three sliding catches. L. 13·2 cm (5·2 in)

POTTERY
AND PORCELAIN

24

THE GODMAN COLLECTION OF ISLAMIC POTTERY

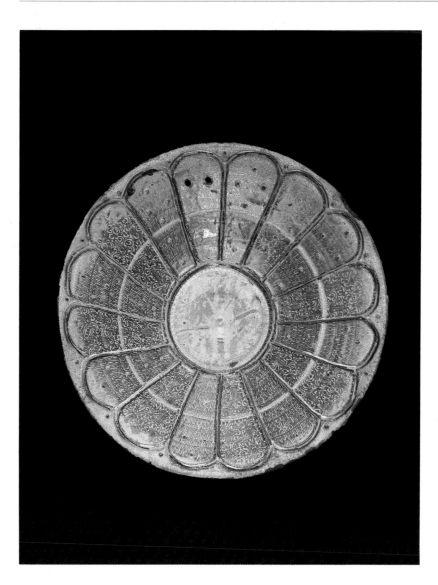

Shallow dish painted in copper lustre, with a design of bryony leaves; a central shield bears the arms of Aragon-Sicily. Valencia, c.1450. Diam. 44·7 cm (17·6 in)

Large faience jug with a serpent handle, painted in black, runny cobalt, greenish blue and bole-red with composite lotus medallions in surrounds of prunus stems and saz leaves. From the Godman collection, the most important private collection of Islamic pottery in the world. Iznik c.1560-80. H. 31·5 cm (12·4 in)

Frederick Du Cane Godman (1834–1919) appears to have been best known to *The Times* obituarist, as the author of somewhat esoteric books on petrels and the natural history of the Azores, and joint editorship of the immense sixty-three volume *Biologia Centrali-Americana*, founder of the Ornithological Union and of *Ibis* a journal devoted to ornithology. He is only known to have made one visit, while still an undergraduate, to the eastern Mediterranean and the Black Sea and yet at his death in 1919 he left behind a collection of Islamic pottery which when it came to the British Museum in 1983 was still judged to be the best in private hands in the world. Its addition to the Museum's existing collections produces what is perhaps the premier collection of Islamic pottery in any museum outside the Middle East.

Somehow, in a career dedicated to the pursuits of the 'English scientific country gentleman' Godman became a passionate collector of Islamic pottery, one of a select group of connoisseurs branching out into what was then an unknown area. With typical Victorian application Godman did not indulge himself in collecting pretty things which appealed only to the eye, rather, as he put it in a foreword to the privately printed 1901 catalogue of his collection of Oriental and Spanish Pottery and Glass:

This collection was commenced about the year 1865, and has been added to whenever desirable examples could be obtained, the principal object being to make an artistic and historical series illustrating that branch of ceramic art which comprises the works of the Moslem potters who set up their kilns wherever their armies conquered in the many countries between 'fair Seville' and 'far Kathay'.

There are still many question marks as regards

Lustre painted star and cross tiles from the Imamzade Yahya Varamin (near Teheran) Persia. Probably made at Kashan. Painted in chocolate-olive lustre on a semi-opaque white glaze some are dated 1261–2 or 1262–3 AD. Av. diam. 31 cm (12·2 in)

rougher and the designs bolder than Rayy. There are three Damascus lustre albarellos (drug-jars) sometimes known in the nineteenth century as 'Siculo-Arabic' because two early examples were found in Sicily. These date from about 1290–1300 AD and are among the finest pieces of this type in existence. This section concludes with an exceptionally large and fine group of seventeenth–eighteenth century Persian lustre wares – saucers, small dishes, ewers, basins, pomegranate-shaped sand pots for scribes and coffee cups, the most striking in brilliant cobalt, yellow or turquoise.

The second group comes from Spain – around 107 rich Hispano-Moresque dishes varying in colour from gold to pale straw, manufactured in Moorish Spain by potters adapting the lustre technique which had been perfected in Islam. Most are of the early fifteenth century, many bear the proud coats of arms of the great families of Spain and Italy (among them Castile, Gondi of Florence, Aragon, Navarre, Medici).

The pride of the collection is however a group of almost two hundred pieces of pottery from Iznik (ancient Nicaea), sixty miles south-east of Istanbul across the Marmara. There are great dishes, jugs, enormous footed bowls, plates. The dominant impression is of brilliant blues and whites with here and there sage green, red, black. Many of the pieces have hauntingly bizarre decorations – spiky tulips, strange plants like puff-balls, stylised leaves which resolve themselves into insects. There are still many mysteries about Iznik ware. Although it is firmly located, excavations in the vicinity have not yet revealed kilns and associated pottery. There is insufficient tile-work on datable buildings to provide a proper chronological account, therefore theories as to the dates of individual pieces vary. The pottery of Iznik is first recorded in inventories of the Topkapi Saray in AD 1479. Some pieces reached northern and western Europe soon after they were made; among them, for example, three jugs with Elizabethan silver gilt mounts, one in the Museum being dated 1597–98. It was widely exported in the Ottoman provinces, appearing in Cairo, Budapest, Belgrade, the Crimea and Bulgaria. By 1650 or earlier quality manufacture had ceased and it was virtually forgotten until the 1860s when for some unexplained reason a flood appeared on the European market and it caught the fancy of advanced collectors such as Godman. So obscure had it then become

the dating and location of Islamic pottery; the Godman collection, previously seen only by students of the subject, is more than an attractive exhibition, it is because of Godman's methodological approach a useful tool for art historians.

The Godman collection can conveniently be divided into three sections. The first, of about 164 items consists of Persian lustre wares including the finest specimens of grand architectural lustre tiles in any private collection in the world, among them a group of star and cross shaped wall tiles, some painted in shimmering chocolate olive lustre on opaque white glaze, from the Imamzade Yahya at Varamin, some dated 1261–2 AD or 1262–3 AD. There are also later Kashan tiles – some with delightful scenes – parakeets, cranes, pelicans, a horse and hares. There is a series of spectacular Kashan dishes (c. 1200–1250 AD), an important series of 'Rayy' pottery (a stylistic group of Kashan wares named after finds at that city, near Teheran, sacked by Genghis Khan in 1220). Another important centre sacked by the Mongols in 1259 was Raqqa (Syria) from which come a few pieces of lustre ware for comparison. The pottery is

Left. Frederick Du Cane Godman (1834–1919), naturalist and collector. His collection of Islamic pottery, began about 1865 and at his death was considered to be the finest in private hands in the world.

Below. Lustre-ware of Moorish Spain. Tall necked high-footed globular vase with wing handles, painted in cobalt and yellow lustre with stylised vine scrolls and with the arms of Piero or Lorenzo de'Medici. Datable post 1465 when Piero was granted by Louis XI the right to add the lilies of France to the Medici arms. It once belonged to Horace Walpole. Valencia *c*.1465. H. 57.4 cm (1 ft 10.5 in)

that most thought it originated in Persia and the labels applied to the three main chronological groups – which have stuck – added to the confusion: Kutahya (from the place of manufacture of some pieces), Damascus (no direct connection) and Rhodian (from a cache which turned up on the island of Rhodes).

There has long been a relationship between the pottery of Islam and that of China. The earliest group of Iznik ware is reckoned to be the so-called 'Abraham of Kutahya' ware which may be a response to unsatisfied demand for the famed Chinese blue and white. The pottery has a white body, decorated with small very detailed patterns in warm and brilliant blue, sometimes with pale turquoise too, covered with a brilliant colourless glaze. The collection contains the only dated piece of this group – a small jug with a handle in the form of a stylized dragon, on the base an Armenian inscription dated 959 of the Armenian era (AD 1510). Included also in the Godman collection is a famous cut-down pear shaped bottle of 'Golden Horn ware' which bears the Armenian date 978 (1529 AD) and an inscription which demonstrates that Kutahya was turning out pottery at that time.

The second grouping is the 'Damascus' style, perhaps manufactured around 1560–80, the last fifteen years producing some of the finest Iznik pottery ever made. The shapes and glaze are unchanged but the floral designs and colours explode, into strange shapes and a wider range of colours – blues and turquoises are joined by soft sage green, olive green, purple and greenish black. New flowers appear – stiff spiky tulips, roses, carnations, hyacinths and strange iridescent scales. The potters borrowed designs from Chinese porcelain and even Italian maiolica. There is an interesting piece, a mosque lamp in blue, turquoise and black which matches a dated piece (1549 AD) already in the Museum's collection from the Dome of the Rock in Jerusalem. The Museum now has the only three dated pieces of sixteenth century Iznik pottery.

The 'Rhodian' group comes from about 1555–1700 a period when tile manufacture came to the fore, encouraged by Suleiman's retiling of the Dome of the Rock and new mosques in Constantinople. The palette changes from the previous period, perhaps because earlier colours were difficult to mass produce as tiles. The distinctive colour is the oddly-named 'Armenian bole', at its best a bright red but on occasions deteriorating

Above. Dish painted in black, turquoise, manganese, olive green and cobalt, the centre filled with florists' flowers, sweeping saz leaves and a pair of large scaly pomegranates. Iznik, 'Damascus' Group, *c.*1540. Diam. 38·8 cm (15·3 in)

Below. Large basin on flaring foot, painted in turquoise and cobalt with a bold floral scroll on the exterior. 'Abraham of Kutahya' ware. Iznik, Turkey, early 16th c. H. 28·4 cm (11·2 in)

badly. It was produced from a thickly applied clay slip of which deposits were available in Armenia. Less care was taken of pottery vessels and from the seventeenth century the industry declined as fewer new buildings were ordered and potters found themselves more and more dependent on export markets. By 1648 it was reported that there were only nine potters' workshops in Iznik where a generation earlier there had been three hundred.

How did Godman manage to acquire his fine collection? A large number of items were bought in 1889 from the collection of a certain Monsieur Richard whom Godman describes as a 'French physician, who resided in Teheran, and having married a Persian lady adopted her religion and nationality'. Richard collected works of art of every sort over thirty years. His collection was dispersed in the 1880s. Many pieces must have come from dealers. Pieces in fine condition flooded into western Europe in the 1860s, often in groups which appear to come from complete collections. One intriguing suggestion (which however lacks supporting evidence) is that the source was the palace treasuries of Istanbul or Edirne. In the 1850s and subsequent decades the Topkapi Saray was abandoned by the Ottoman sultans for palaces on the Bosphorus; the old summer capital of Edirne had been abandoned in the eighteenth century. When the Ottoman palaces moved it was common for them to leave behind concubines who were out of favour. Perhaps the ladies who remained behind made the most of their situation by selling off Iznik pottery which had also been discarded?

During his lifetime Godman gave to the Museum a collection of sherd material from Persian medieval enamelled wares mostly excavated by Monsieur Richard at Rayy south of Teheran, useful for comparison with intact pieces since these have subsequently been widely forged. Surprisingly he did not buy intact pieces of this ware. The main collection was kept in a fine house at Horsham, the panelling of the house being virtually built around the porcelain. After Godman's death it passed to his wife then his two daughters. The youngest, Miss Edith Godman, died in 1982. She had expressed the wish that the collection go to the Museum, as had her father; it was accepted in lieu of capital transfer tax and allocated to the Museum – one of the most important collections received this century.

25

THE ADDIS GIFT OF CHINESE PORCELAIN

'I was encouraged by the example of a Chinese friend who, after a life-time of collecting, had reduced his collection to five pieces. I have not succeeded so well', wrote Sir John Addis (1914–83) of his gift to the Museum of a collection of twenty-three pieces of Chinese porcelain of superlative quality, almost wholly from the Yuan and Early Ming Dynasties (fourteenth–fifteenth centuries AD), a period which produced some of the most beautiful porcelain in the world. Each item is a masterpiece selected with discrimination and taste to illustrate all the diverse techniques used in

decoration during this period and to supplement and enhance the already magnificent holdings of the Museum which, even prior to this donation in 1975, had few rivals either in range or quality.

Sir John's preoccupation with Chinese porcelain was not merely aesthetic. He was curious about the techniques by which it had been made and how these had developed. His collection thus concentrates on a most crucial period in Chinese porcelain technology. Until recently a rather simple formula would appear in popular accounts of Chinese porcelain,

Left. Porcelain dish decorated in underglaze blue with the 'Three Friends of Winter' – pine, bamboo and prunus. Ming dynasty, Xuande mark and period. AD 1426–35. Diam. 17.6 cm (7 in). *Right*. Porcelain foliate dish decorated in underglaze blue with flower sprays. Ming dynasty, Yong'le period (AD 1403–24). Diam. 19 cm (7.5 in)

Sir John Addis (1914–83) diplomat and collector. His gift to the Museum is austere and disciplined in the Chinese manner.

namely that it was produced by a combination of china stone (petunse) ground to powder mixed with kaolin (white china clay) and fired at a very high temperature. The china stone vitrified while the kaolin ensured that the pot retained its shape. This was the method described by the Jesuit missionary Père d'Entrecolles who visited the Chinese porcelain factories at Jingdezhen and sent an account back to Europe in 1712 and 1722 and it was just such a combination of materials which European potters sought in an attempt to imitate the hard translucent pottery of China.

It has, however, recently been established that a definition of Chinese porcelain wholly allied to this formula is inadequate. Some of the credit for the adoption of a completely new approach goes to Sir John Addis and especially for his part in bringing together a Conference of Western and Asian experts in Shanghai in 1982 to discuss technical aspects of Chinese ceramics. Analyses have demonstrated that, even among the Chinese hard-fired white ware accepted by the west as 'porcelain', there was no single standard formula as implied by Père d'Entrecolles. There are, for example, unusual north Chinese porcelains (Xing wares and also the famous creamy white Ding wares made in the tenth and eleventh centuries AD whose production declined c. 1300 AD follow-ing Tartar and Mongol invasions). These were made of a variety of clay materials (not including china stone) which with the addition of other minerals were fired at very high temperatures (in excess of 1250° and even as high as 1350°C). The better known southern porcelains, including those whose production centred around the main centre of Jingdezhen in Jiangxi, had initially as their major ingredient ground up porcelain stone (a form of decomposed granite) rich in sericite (mica/quartz) but no added kaolin. This stone, of a composition different to that found in the west, is, when ground and mixed with water, very malleable and when mixed with water can be fired at over 1250°C. It is probable that the addition of kaolin was introduced at some time in the fourteenth century since the original formula holds too much water to be easily thrown in one piece and was unsuitable for the large dishes then being made to cater for Mongol taste. What Père d'Entrecolles witnessed therefore was a later method of manufacture.

The pieces in the Addis collection were largely manufactured during the rule of two dynasties – first the successors to the Song, the Mongol Yuan dynasty (1269–1368) which had swept in from the steppes of Asia, one branch of which established their capital in Beijing. For a brief period the Mongols controlled an empire reaching from the Mediterranean to the China Sea. The Yuan dynasty continued the policy of their predecessors the Southern Song whereby the Southern Chinese provinces were free to trade widely without any government restrictions.

In this period there was an upsurge in experimentation in decorative techniques for porcelain. Although underglaze decoration had been known since the Tang dynasty (AD 618–906), a new interest, and a new skill were now developed to decorate porcelain with red or blue designs. Copper oxide was used for red but this was often unsuccessful, the colour firing away to produce brownish shades, even a shade described as 'donkey liver'. More successful was the use of cobalt to produce blue (a technique which the Chinese appear to have earlier acquired from the Muslim world, since underglaze painting in blue had been popular in the Islamic world from the ninth century onwards). Sir John Addis writes with affection of:

the clear mid blue at its best ... as lovely as the deep pulsating indigo of the more admired and better-known foliated dishes ... The eye sometimes

Porcelain bowl decorated in underglaze blue with lotus and chrysanthemum 2nd half of the 14th c. AD. H. c. 16·5 cm (6·5 in)

Porcelain jar incised with a lotus and a dragon amongst waves, under a qinghai glaze. Yuan dynasty, 1st half of the 14th c. AD. H. 27 cm (10·6 in)

surfeited with the glories of blue and white can turn with special satisfaction to underglaze red, not only to the spectacular tomato and cherry-reds but also to the subtle chestnut and grey.

The finest porcelain came from a long established complex of kilns in villages round the town of Jingdezhen. Prior to the Yuan Dynasty it would appear that only white porcelain and green-glazed wares were produced here in any quantity. Much had gone for export but now the export came to be dominated by blue and white ware.

Later the Ming dynasty (1368–1644) initially reversed their predecessors' liberal trading policies. Official Chinese taste had favoured white vessels and so, for a time it is possible that with the export market dormant the manufacture of high grade blue and white ceased for a time. It would eventually resume on the accession of the Ming emperor Yong'le and it was this type which would be exported in vast quantities to meet the demands of the Near East. From such early porcelains are descended the blue and white dishes eagerly acquired in Europe in the seventeenth and eighteenth centuries.

This is the background to the Addis gift. There are larger collections in the Museum but one of the pleasures of the Addis collection is that it reflects the taste and enthusiasm of an individual. Their collector lived with the twenty-three pieces and knew them intimately. He was by profession not a scholar but a diplomat who joined the foreign service in 1938 and fell under the spell of China. Of his service there it is recalled that he delighted in bicycling round the narrow and dusty lanes of Beijing and in long sessions at the Palace Museum with the Chief Curator looking at selected pieces of porcelain. His collection is austere and disciplined in the Chinese manner. Of his legacy he wrote:

In my school-days I coined a punning Latin motto for my family name: *nisi addis, subtrahis* – unless you add, you subtract; unless you make a positive contribution, you are actually detracting; unless you continue to construct, you undo. It makes another good motto for the collector. A collection should be a living thing, always rising to higher planes. If it stops, it dies. Better than death and dispersal is the apotheosis of integration into the national collection. There can be no more gratifying consummation for the small collector.

The Addis collection now has an honoured place in the Museum alongside those of earlier collectors in this field, among them Franks, Oppenheim and Seligman.

Man's life at a hundred years
has reached its utmost length
Rarely can he hope to achieve
the fields of Immortality
But to have fragrant flowers in
spring, the moon in autumn
In summer a cooling breeze, in
winter snow
As long as no pressing business
disturbs one's mind
Then one may ascend even
among men, into a golden age.
(transl. Roderick Whitfield).
Porcelain bottle vase decorated
in underglaze red. Yuan
dynasty, 2nd quarter of the
14th c. AD. H. 23·2 cm (9·1 in)

26

THE CLEOPATRA VASES

On 15 April 1763 the Trustees of the British Museum at their fortnightly meeting received their usual collection of miscellaneous gifts, some wanted, some probably not: a new edition of Sydney's *Discourses upon Government*, a copper medal of William of Wickham, two drawings of ice alps in Switzerland, a golden ducat of Christian IV of Denmark and

Two very fine porcelain Jars of the Chelsea Manufactory, made in the year 1762, under the direction of Mr Sprimont, from a person unknown through Mr Empson.

So arrived two of the earliest 'modern' pieces in the collection, ten years after the foundation of the Museum and a year after they were made. The vases today are two fine pieces in an outstanding collection of English porcelain which includes other Chelsea pieces acquired over two centuries. The Chelsea porcelain manufactory specialised in luxury ware; the English world of fashion rated its products alone among native porcelain as comparable to the ware of Meissen or Sèvres.

The Cleopatra vases certainly merit the terms 'exuberant' and 'riotous' often applied to the rococo style in which they are modelled. Their main colour is the 'indescribably pure and brilliant mazarine blue', the delicately painted panels show the death of a voluptuous

The 'Cleopatra' Vases, decorated in 'the most rare and truly inimitable Mazarine Blue and Gold', manufactured at Chelsea in 1762 and anonymously donated to the Museum the following year. In the panels are painted scenes of the death of Cleopatra and of her discovery by Roman soldiers. From the 'gold-anchor' period. H. 50 cm (19·7 in)

A further item from the Museum's extensive collection of English porcelain. Vase for potpourri with the figure of Meleager, Chelsea c. 1755. One of a unique pair, the other shows Atalanta, after Rubens. H. 40·6 cm (16 in)

Cleopatra and her discovery by Roman soldiers and in contrast colourful exotic birds. The handles are richly gilded and polished – something of a Chelsea speciality. Compared with the delicate little figures and vessels in which the factory specialised they are of enormous size – over nineteen inches. They can be credited to no one artist or craftsman as Chelsea was a commercial concern, working virtually on assembly line techniques. At its heyday the factory, probably located in Lawrence Street, must have been a hive of activity employing 'at least one hundred hands of which is a nursery of thirty lads taken from the parishes and charity schools and bred to design and painting'. We have a possible name for the painter of the Cleopatra scenes – John Donaldson, a miniature painter from Edinburgh who worked on a piecework basis.

England was a relative late-comer to porcelain manufacture. A formula which imitated the hardness and translucency of Oriental porcelain was discovered at Meissen about 1709. The French and British however adhered to the so-called 'soft-paste' formula, which had its drawbacks – it scratched easily, absorbed dirt, was not very resistant to the sudden change in temperature required in tea, coffee and chocolate-making and was prone to collapse or lose shape in the kiln with a consequent high and expensive wastage rate. Chelsea and Bow were among the first in England to produce porcelain on a commercial scale. The Chelsea factory may well have been in operation as early as 1742 but the first tangible proof of its existence is provided by the quaint 'goat and bee' pattern jugs.

The first names associated with the factory are a French jeweller named Charles Gouyn and a Huguenot silversmith from Liège, Nicholas Sprimont (1716–71). Gouyn withdrew at an early stage and about 1750 Sprimont had assumed the factory's direction. The factory remained under his charge for most of its life. Porcelain was expensive to produce because of the many processes involved so it was a precarious existence, menaced by imports and the vagaries of fashion. The business was eventually sold to William Duesbury proprietor of the Derby porcelain concern in 1769 and closed in 1784.

The factory experimented with various pastes and glazes and with different products. The marks which denote Chelsea manufacture vary over time, not necessarily changing when there is a change in the manufacturing process. First there is the incised triangle sometimes accompanied by the date and the word *Chelsea*, then follow a trident mark in underglaze blue, a raised anchor embossed on an oval medallion sometimes painted red, a plain red anchor painted on the glaze, an underglaze blue anchor, a reddish brown enamelled anchor and finally one or two gold anchors. The marks succeed and apparently overlap in a confusing fashion; their appearance is no guarantee of Chelsea ware since they were widely copied. The Chelsea manufactory left a legacy of fine pieces now much prized by collectors, perhaps not of the overall quality of its Continental rivals, for it tended to imitate rather than lead, but nevertheless brilliant examples of the potter's art.

The identity of the anonymous donor of the Museum's pair of vases remains a mystery. One possible clue is that on 20 April 1763, five days after the gift to the Museum, a Dr George Garnier is recorded as having presented to the Foundling Hospital in Coram Street 'a fine vase of porcelain made at Chelsea'. There was an eleven days' Chelsea sale in 1763, delayed because of Sprimont's ill health, which disposed of much of the previous two years' products after which production declined. Dr Garnier might have picked up three vases at the sale and donated them to worthy causes in Bloomsbury, but it is surprising that he should have preferred anonymity in one case and not the other. Garnier came from Chelsea as did James Empson, who had for many years been curator of the Sloane collection there. Empson was one of the first members of the Museum's staff – one of three Under Librarians appointed in 1756 – and had charge of the Department which presumably housed the vases after their presentation. He retired in 1765 and died shortly after, taking with him, so far as we know, the identity of the donor of these delightful objects.

A 'goat and bee' jug, 1745. One of the first products that can be definitely ascribed to the Chelsea porcelain factory it is composed of a pair of reclining goats supporting a jug with a twig handle and a bee moulded in relief under the lip. H. 11.1 cm (4.4 in)

THE ART
OF THE
CRAFTSMAN

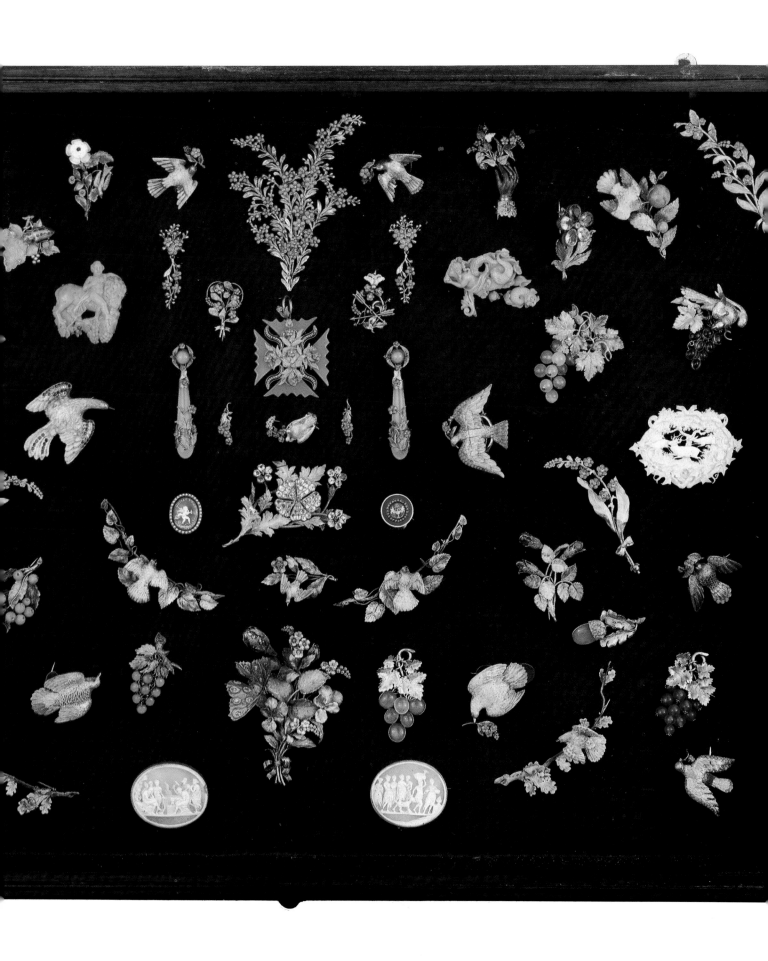

27

THE PORTLAND VASE

Sir William Hamilton (1730–1803). Diplomat, vulcanologist and antiquary. Hamilton acquired the vase in Rome and from him it passed to the Duchess of Portland. Engraving from a portrait by Sir Joshua Reynolds.

'Except the Apollo Belvedere, the Niobes, and two or three others of the first-class marbles', wrote Sir William Hamilton in 1786, 'I do not believe there are any monuments of antiquity existing that were executed by so great an artist'. The monument in question was the Portland Vase, then known as the Barberini Vase, a delicately carved Roman cameo glass

vessel of deepest cobalt blue covered with opaque milky-white glass.

The Portland Vase, an object of superb craftsmanship and great beauty, was probably made during the reign of Augustus (27 BC–14 AD) or Tiberius (14–37 AD) perhaps by an Alexandrian craftsman, in Rome or Egypt, for Alexandria was one of the most important centres of ancient glass making and this cameo technique is thought to have originated there. The blue glass body was first blown to a mere one eighth of an inch thickness then coated with a similarly thin layer of white glass up to a level just above the shoulder of the vase. After finishing and the attachment of handles fashioned from glass rods, the vase was then painstakingly engraved.

When the vase first became known in the seventeenth century the original base appeared to have been cut away and a flat disc substituted. This differs in colour, style, scale and execution and it is evident that it did not form part of the original vessel.

The interpretation of the scene portrayed on the Portland vase has taxed the imagination and knowledge of scholars for many years. Who are these seven enigmatic figures, men and women, who stand or recline, gazing at each other or into the distance? Erasmus Darwin in *The Botanic Garden* (1791) describes the scene poetically:

Here by fall'n columns and disjoin'd arcades,
On mouldering stones, beneath deciduous shades,
Sits HUMANKIND in hieroglyphic state,
Serious and pondering on their changeful state; ...

Alongside Humankind he identified Mortal Life, a Ghost, Love Divine, Immortal Life, and Pluto. Other scholars have produced long lists of names from Classical mythology. It is however now generally thought that the Vase shows the wooing by Peleus, son of Aiakos, a mortal, of Thetis, a sea-goddess, daughter of Nereus and Doris, from which union came the great hero Achilles. The other figures are thought to be Eros, Thetis' mother Doris or her grandmother Tethys; a bearded sea-god who is either Nereus, husband of Doris, or Oceanus husband of Tethys. The stately seated woman is Aphrodite, queen of love, and at Thetis' feet is Hermes, the god who brings fulfilment of lovers' desires and presides over the marriage-bed. Although the vase was at one time said to be a cinerary urn the above interpretation of the figures gives it a happier history for it is more probable that it was made as a Roman wedding-present.

The Vase first appears in the possession of Cardinal Francesco Maria del Monte (1549–1627) in the Palazzo Madama in Rome where a Provençal scholar de Peiresc (1580–1637) saw it in the winter of 1600–01. After the Cardinal's death it was bequeathed to his family who sold it to Cardinal Francesco Barberini (1597–1679). The vase was now housed in the Palazzo Barberini and its fame spread throughout Europe as visiting artists and scholars, impressed by its beauty, published accounts of it. In 1780 a Scottish painter and architect living in Rome, James Byres, purchased the vase from the impoverished Donna Cornelia Barberini-Colonna, Princess of Palestrina whose lack of skill at cards was depleting what remained of the Barberini fortune.

Now the well-known figure, Sir William Hamilton (1730–1803), appears on the scene. Hamilton, who was British Ambassador to the Court of Naples, is unfortunately best known as the complaisant husband of Lord Nelson's Emma and because of this his important role as a collector of classical antiquities tends to be ignored. His passion for antiquities however tended to outstrip his financial capabilities. Byres offered to sell the vase for £1000 and not a penny less. Hamilton with true collector's zeal, but a certain lack of business acumen immediately concluded the transaction although, as he later wrote 'God knows it was not very convenient for me at that moment'. Hamilton left Rome following the death of his first wife in 1782 bringing with him among his luggage both her body and the vase. Back in London he found himself short of funds and looked round for a purchaser for the vase. His niece Mary Hamilton was a friend of the Dowager Duchess of Portland, a noted but eccentric collector described by Horace Walpole as 'a simple woman, but perfectly sober, and intoxicated only by *empty* vases'. Mary Hamilton acted as a go-between in the secret negotiations which followed as did Mrs Delany and Hamilton parted with the vase for 1800 guineas.

The vase seems rarely to have brought its owners good fortune. The Duchess enjoyed its beauty in her museum of natural and artificial curiosities at Privy Gardens Whitehall for only a year, for she died aged seventy in July 1785. The collection she had so prized was broken up at auction but the vase remained in the Portland family, being purchased by her son, the third Duke, for £1,029. The great potter, Josiah Wedgwood, found it an inspiration and had borrowed it for twelve months in 1786 and with great skill after much experiment managed to reproduce it in Jasperware, a stoneware he had invented, hard enough to be tooled but with the translucency of porcelain.

In 1810 the Duke of Portland placed the vase on loan in the British Museum. There it was on display for many years, giving much pleasure to the public and having a significant effect on taste. The vase survived exposure to the public for thirty-five years but disaster, in the form of a drunken or disturbed Irishman, struck. Just before closing time on 7 February 1845 the vase and its case were shattered by a conveniently placed antiquity described as 'a heavy ancient brick'. There were no witnesses to the actual attack but when the attendants rushed to the scene and questioned those in the vicinity, a young man admitted that he had broken the vase. The culprit was immediately conveyed under guard to Bow Street police station, while the only Trustee on the premises, another William Hamilton, sat down anxiously to compose a letter to the Duke as the attendants carefully swept up the remains.

Frontispiece of the sale catalogue of the Duchess of Portland's collection in 1786. The vase was purchased by her son, the 3rd Duke.

153

Left. Aphrodite, goddess of love.

Below left. Thetis (detail) daughter of Nereus and Doris reclines on a rock between Aphrodite and Hermes the god of marriage. The torch slipping from her fingers shows that it is night and that she is on the point of falling asleep.

Below right. Peleus, son of Aikos (detail). After waiting at the shrine of Aphrodite he steps forward conducted by Eros and encouraged by a goddess with a sea-dragon either Doris, Thetis' mother or her grandmother Tethys.

Right. The Portland Vase, made during the reign of Augustus (27 BC–AD 14) or Tiberius (AD 14–37), one of the finest glass vessels to have survived from Roman times. The scene carved upon it is thought to portray the wooing of the sea-goddess Thetis by the mortal hero Peleus. The body is made of layers of blue and white glass each about 3 mm (⅛ in) thick. H. 24·5 cm (9·6 in)

The Portland Vase in pieces. Watercolour by the Museum's restorer John Doubleday made shortly after the near destruction of the vase in 1845.

The Duke took the news amazingly well, accepting that the Museum had done all it could to protect the vase in view of 'the indiscriminate admission of visitors which they cannot control'. The Duke concluded that it must be the work of a lunatic and rather generously commented that it was fortunate that his madness had not manifested itself in an injury to human life. Meanwhile the Trustees and the police were trying to discover the identity of the culprit for the young man had given only the name 'William Lloyd' but was 'in other respects ... entirely sullen'. There is a description of him in the Trustees' papers:

... about 22 years of age, 5 ft 7 in in height, of spare habit, dark sallow complexion, oval countenance, dark eyes and eyebrows, and hair nearly black. He calls himself William Lloyd, and states that he came away from Dublin with a servant girl, and with £800 in his pocket. His accent is Irish.

Urgent enquiries were set in train by the Trustees and these became even more urgent after the fiasco of 'William Lloyd's' appearance before the magistrate. The Trustees discovered that under the Wilful Damage Act 'Lloyd' could only be indicted for damaging an object worth £5 or less and it was only too apparent that the Portland Vase was considerably more

valuable. The only legal alternative would be for the Duke of Portland to institute a civil suit for damages but in the meantime 'Lloyd' would be at liberty. Thus Lloyd was charged with breaking the £3 glass case covering the vase and was summarily convicted, declaring to the magistrate that:

... I had been indulging in intemperance for a week before, and was then only partially recovered from the effects which that indulgence had produced upon my mind. ...

He was sentenced to a fine of £3 or two months' hard labour in default of payment. As 'Lloyd' only had nine pence on him when arrested it appeared that he would at least be disposed of for two months but a rather strange untidy letter reached the magistrate two days later together with three sovereigns in payment of the fine. 'I takes the liberty of enclosing three pounds', the unknown wrote, 'as wich is the paultry penalty in default of paying wich you have sentenced my relation through Adam and Eve poor Mister William Lloyd the Irish gintelman to two months hard labour'. 'Lloyd' was accordingly set free and, so far as can be ascertained, disappeared into obscurity. The Trustees seem to have known his real name but agreed with the Duke to protect 'Lloyd's' poor but respectable family, by not taking the matter further.

The Trustees were now faced with a valuable and beautiful antiquity in something like two hundred pieces. Offers of assistance and formulae for repairing glass came flooding in. One writer suggested an interesting mixture of isinglass and gin. However, with the Duke's agreement the pieces were handed over to the Museum's restorer, John Doubleday who assiduously worked away until in September 1845 it was again placed on display, if not restored to its former glory at least to a semblance of this. Mr Doubleday received twenty-five guineas for his work.

In 1945 the vase was at last purchased by the Museum with funds bequeathed by James Rose Vallentin. Three years later a bequest of a box of thirty-seven small chips from the 1845 breakage which had not been incorporated in the repair provided an opportune moment to take the vase to pieces to replace the old glue with modern material and to try to reincorporate the missing chips. Three pieces were included. The cracks can be seen today if the vase is examined closely but in spite of the vissicitudes of its life it remains one of the finest glass vessels to have survived from Roman times.

28

THE HULL GRUNDY GIFT OF JEWELLERY

'If you don't fall in love, don't buy it' is one of the precepts observed by Anne Hull Grundy in putting together the remarkable collection of jewellery which she and her husband donated to the British Museum in 1978 and which she continued for some years to augment. The Hull Grundy gift is a delight – almost 1200 items – elegant portrait cameos, glittering gold, intricate silver work, delicately coloured micromosaics, translucent enamels, sparkling paste and diamonds, creamy ivory, pink coral, austere iron and steel, a rich variety of precious and semi-precious stones, brooches, rings, bracelets, boxes, hair ornaments and more, much of which arrived, in a variety of parcels, by taxi from the country.

Anne Hull Grundy was born in Nuremberg and came to Britain as a child. She was brought up with antiques and, like many passionate collectors, started young. She began to build up her jewellery collection between the wars, buying with discrimination and taste at reasonable prices in a collecting area which was then unfashionable, sometimes, she relates, going without necessities to snatch a particular piece. She married artist and entomologist John Hull Grundy who brought to the partnership his interest in Martinware pottery and the sombre Berlin ironwork jewellery. For much of her collecting career Mrs Hull Grundy was confined to bed because of illness, nevertheless from her home, at the centre of a web of dealers and salerooms, a stream of postcards, telegrams and parcels would issue forth. Here she built up and distributed this excellent collection and those which have been given to other institutions.

Mrs Hull Grundy sought as wide a range as possible to illustrate the art of the jeweller and especially documentary pieces – items bearing dates, marks, signatures, inscriptions, pieces preserved by careful owners in the original cases in which they left the jeweller's shop. Her gift to the Museum is therefore an invaluable research tool for jewellery historians, its range extending from sixth-century Byzantium to the 1950s. The British Museum had a considerable collection of jewellery before the gift was made – fine examples from the ancient world and from non-European peoples but uneven in its coverage of European jewellery after 1700. The Hull Grundy gift neatly extends the collection to the mid-twentieth century, being particularly strong in the period 1700–1950. The collection is of interest in that it includes a great variety of pieces worn by levels of society below the very rich. It is thus possible to assess a variety of tastes and changing fashions. The pieces in the collection also relate to individuals – George who gave Eliza the Victorian dove carrying a heart, the

Cruciform pendant chased and enamelled gold with onyx drop-shaped pendants, compartment containing hair in the reverse, English after 1857. L. 10·7 cm (4·2 in)

Left to right. Sunflower brooch in three colour gold and silver, French *c.*1880. H. 7·1 cm (2·8 in). 18th c. English hairpin ornament, silver with petals of emeralds, diamonds, rubies, sapphires and topazes and a central emerald bordered with diamonds and sapphires, *c.*1770. Diam. 4·55 cm (1·8 in). A redcurrant spray of cornelian with leaves of bloomed and chased two colour gold, probably Austrian *c.*1840. H. 5·3 cm (2 in)

Right, left to right. French Art Nouveau pieces: Waistbuckle in gold in the form of a wreath of mistletoe in gold ombre enamel and pearls on a ground of plique-à-jour enamel, 1900–10. H. 5.9 cm (2.3 in). Waistbuckle of cast and chased gold in the form of conjoined leopards set with cornelian and green cast glass made in 1900 by Boucheron of Paris. H. 7.8 cm (3 in). Waistclasp of pierced and chased silver, parcel gilt showing a woman with flowing hair in a frame of chestnut branches designed by the Spanish sculptor, Gustave Obiols, 1900. H. 8.3 cm (3.3 in). Lalique brooch in the form of a web of pierced and chased gold with plique-à-jour and translucent enamels, set with a glass citrine, *c.*1902. Diam. 4.5 cm (1.8 in).

Pierced ivory carving of three horses with a border of oak twigs. German or Swiss c.1830–60. W. 6·3 cm (2·5 in)

worthy but plain Queens of the May at Whitelands College in the 1880s who received crosses designed under the supervision of John Ruskin (one of which is included in the gift), George IV's favourite chef John Watier to whom the grateful epicure gave a box with the royal portrait. However, the collection is primarily dedicated to the craftsman – known and unknown – and it is displayed with this in mind.

The collection is so extensive that it is only possible to dip into it here and give some indication of the areas into which it has been divided for study and display. The first group in the Catalogue, the sparkling gem set and paste set jewellery which set off the elegant fabrics of the late seventeenth to nineteenth centuries has an immediate appeal for the visitor to the Museum. The glass compound 'paste' was perfected in France by Georges Frederic Strass (1701–73). Henceforth it was no longer necessary to be very rich to cover oneself in glittering stones – paste was cheaper, easy to cut and the range of colour could be dictated by man as well as nature. The pastes were not always found on the less well off and Mrs Delany's letters are full of speculation as to the value of many of the pieces she saw worn at eighteenth-century court functions. We are accustomed to portraits showing jewellery being worn but an intriguing question, to which the answer has sometimes been lost, is how the pieces worked. A portrait of Princess Charlotte Augusta (1766–1828) daughter of George III, for example, shows her wearing an aigrette in her hair with a plume of feathers. A late eighteenth-century example in the gift in the form of a peacock's feather in silver set with pastes still has its pin attached. The description of Queen Charlotte's wedding in 1761 – she wore 'Diamond Sprigs of Flowers

in her Sleeves and to clasp back her Robe' is illuminated by an actual flower spray of silver set with diamonds and emeralds from the period.

Another deceptively sparkling material is marcasite (iron pyrites or fool's gold) which from the middle of the eighteenth century was used as a substitute for diamonds. Taste for it declined in the mid-nineteenth century but it was revived in Edwardian times and the 1930s.

A contrast to the glitter is a rather unusual sombre collection of 'Berlin ironwork'. This is mainly associated with the struggle against Napoleon in 1813 when patriotic Germans surrendered their gold jewellery to finance the fight against him and received in return a piece of iron jewellery which recorded *Gold gab ich für Eisen, 1813* or *Eingetauscht zum wohl des Vaterlands*. The fashion pre-dated the Napoleonic Wars and it was adapted for mourning jewellery after the death of the popular Queen Luisa, wife of Frederick William III of Prussia in 1810 and was even revived in the dark days of 1915. How much this jewellery was actually worn is now difficult to establish since it is practically never shown in portraits or fashion plates.

Coral is a common gift at christenings and was used in peasant communities from earliest times to ward off the evil eye. Such jewellery was fashionable in the first half of the nineteenth century; the trade was centred in Naples although there were coral workers in London. Exquisitely carved ivory also appears in this section of the gift.

Enamelling – the fusion of coloured glass – has been used since at least Mycenean times to produce a range of brilliant colours. The gift has a choice collection which demonstrates the different techniques used – cloisonné, champlevé, bassetaille, plique-à-jour, émail en ronde bosse, painted enamel and enamel miniature painting.

Coins have long been used as jewellery – the oldest coin set item in the gift is a girdle fragment with six *solidi* of Justinian I, perhaps given on the occasion of a sixth century AD marriage. A number of other examples trace this revival during the nineteenth century. There are fine pieces of medallic jewellery in the section of commemorative pieces which covers a wide range from the persecution of the Protestants in eighteenth-century Salzburg, via a miniature bugle for the Charge of the Light Brigade to Lalique's cravat pin in honour of the French *poilu* of the First World

War. Outstanding among the badges in this section is a grand enamelled specimen produced for the Anti-Gallican Society formed in 1745 to promote British manufactures.

The craftsman did not rely only upon brilliant gems and coloured enamels. A group of objects displays his virtuosity with precious metals and includes a celebrated engraving on silver by Lambert Suavius a goldsmith from Liège made to celebrate the peace of Cateau-Cambrésis in 1559, and intricate filigree work in both gold and silver used for a group of spherical containers which probably held the famed Goa or bezoar stone much used by physicians.

Jewellery was especially favoured by the Victorians to record a variety of sentiments. The dead could be remembered by incorporating their hair into jewellery, although it would appear from an 1878 manual that unscrupulous jewellers were not above substituting prepared hair for that of the dear departed, in order to save time and trouble. The sentimental Prince Albert initiated a fashion for brooches in the form of doves carrying hearts when in 1840 he gave these to the bridesmaids who attended Queen Victoria at their wedding. There are three similar examples in the collection and no less than seventeen doves carrying other messages – forget-me-not sprays, a letter, wedding rings, an envelope. One of the most delightful groups, comprising about 145 pieces, is the sentimental and naturalistic jewellery, with its complicated code of messages which appealed to the early to mid-nineteenth century Victorians – the forget-me-not for 'true love', lily of the valley 'the return of happiness', red rosebuds the direct 'you are young and beautiful', blue bells 'constancy' – a code which is sometimes rather difficult to decipher today.

Nineteenth-century jewellery also displays a taste for the playful and humorous and there is a wide selection of these novelties – frogs among bulrushes, a picture on an easel, a log split by a woodman's axe. Sporting and wildlife themes include greyhounds, an emu amidst ferns and leaves, a sculling punt, and a fishing rod and line with creel and hinged lid revealing a minute goldfish.

The cameos and intaglios of the eighteenth and nineteenth centuries complement the Museum's important holdings of ancient and post-classical gems and include many signed pieces.

One of the richest areas in the gift comprises the heavy ponderous pieces that reflect the nineteenth-century passion for archaeology. This has direct links with the Museum whose activities provided some of the inspiration – one brooch for example has a central plaque ornamented with a copy of an Assyrian relief from the throne room of Ashurnasirpal discovered at Nimrud by Sir Austen Layard. How much this jewellery was actually worn is debatable: an unflattering contemporary cartoon in Punch shows a lady with a defiant grin loading herself with yet another piece. This revivalist period also took as patterns early jewels, portraits, sculptures and ornamental motifs. A remarkable mid-nineteenth century *Agnus Dei* brooch made by the Castellani firm has an enamelled border based on a similar enamel bordering the rare Early Christian (Lombardic) brooch bought from the Castellani family of jewellers by the Museum in 1865. In the second quarter of the nineteenth century taste turned to the neo-Gothic and neo-Renaissance.

Another craze – for Japonism following the opening of Japan by Commodore Perry in 1858 – is represented by a selection from a number of manufacturers from France, America and Britain. These include examples from Tiffany & Co. whose work in the Japanese style was particularly commended by the jury at the Paris Exhibition of 1878.

The spare and elegant style of Art Nouveau which appears at the turn of the century is well represented and includes a number of pieces by the Paris firms of Boucheron and René Lalique. The collection ends with a post Second World War return to the more exotic and complex, a gold brooch in the form of a swan conjured out of a jewel encrusted baroque pearl made by an outstanding modern jeweller, the Duca di Verdura about 1950.

The jewellery collection is only part of the Hull Grundy gift to the Museum which also includes medals, silver plate and Martinware and excellent collections of Japanese ojime and netsuke. The donor expressed the philosophy behind her generosity as 'If you are lucky enough to have wonderful things you have to share them'. Mrs Hull Grundy and her husband died in 1984, within a week of each other, but this unique collection remains to give pleasure to countless thousands of visitors.

Hair ornament in the form of a peacock's feather, silver closed-back set with pastes, which set off the elegant fabrics of the late 17–19th centuries. English *c.*1770. H. 15 cm (5·9 in)

Left to right. Cameos: Profile portrait head of a man signed by Antonio Berini of Milan, sardonyx set in gold, Italian, early 19th c. The setting is probably English *c.*1830. H. 3·7 cm (1·5 in). Three cameos by Tommaso Saulini of Rome – Medusa flanked by Apollo and Diana, Italian *c.*1850, H. 3·7 cm (1·5 in). Brooch copied from two 9th c. BC Assyrian reliefs in the Museum, English, *c.*1850. W. 5·3 cm (2 in)

Right, left to right. Swan with the body of a 'baroque' pearl set with diamonds and sapphires with an enamelled beak and feet and a black pendant pearl made in the Paris workshops of the Duca di Verdura, *c.*1950. H. 3·1 cm (1·2 in). Dress clip of gold set with 14 calibre-cut rubies, English 1939. H. 3·7 cm (1·5 in). Brooch of stained chalcedony and nephrite mounted in white gold and set with diamonds in the form of a morning glory flower, perhaps German *c.*1930. H. 7·1 cm (2·8 in)

Left to right. Micromosaics: Brooch signed by Gioacchino Barberi, gold with a glass mosaic of fruit and leaves on a white opaline glass background, Italian *c.*1850. Diam. 5·2 cm (2 in). Brooch made in Italy *c.*1860 by the firm of Castellani. The border is derived from a Lombardic piece of the 7th c. AD purchased by the Museum from this firm in 1865. The centre panel depicts the Lamb of God. Diam. 5·3 cm (2 in)

29

THE TWELFTH-CENTURY LEWIS CHESSMEN

'An assemblage of elves or gnomes' was how the Lewis chessmen appeared to their superstitious discoverer. The chessmen, of walrus ivory, were probably made between 1135 and 1175 AD.

On first seeing these wide-eyed little figures it is easy to believe one of the stories told of their discovery in 1831. Of how a Scottish peasant broke into a subterranean stone building on the shore of Uig Bay on the Isle of Lewis and was 'astonished to see what he concluded to be an assemblage of elves or gnomes upon whose mysteries he had unconsciously intruded. The superstitious Highlander flung down his spade, and fled home in dismay ...'.

Although this discovery occurred in relatively recent times, no definitive account of it exists. The chessmen are supposed to have been found in a small stone structure beneath a sandbank on the seashore which was somehow uncovered – perhaps by erosion or perhaps by a wandering cow. Ninety-three pieces, all of walrus ivory, survive (eleven in the National Museum of Antiquities of Scotland and the others in the British Museum). Although the hoard included a carved belt buckle and fourteen plain counters, the focus of interest is the group of seventy-eight chessmen which have deservedly been called 'the outstanding ancient chessmen of the world'. There were in all eight kings, eight queens, sixteen bishops, fifteen knights, twelve rooks and nineteen pawns, perhaps the remains of four complete sets (with forty-five pawns, one knight and four rooks now missing), although some writers have suggested as many as eight sets. Sixty-seven are in the Museum and will be described here. One question which perplexes visitors – how could anyone have played chess with all white pieces – is answered by Sir Frederic Madden, who wrote the first detailed scholarly account of the chessmen for the Museum in 1832. Madden found traces of colouring on some of them and remarked that 'part of them were originally stained a dark red or beet-root colour'. He surmised that this dye had been largely washed away by the action of seawater. Early chess sets are known to have been red and white or red and green.

The Lewis chessmen are something of an enigma. Who made them and where were they made? How did such a large group turn up in the remote Outer Hebrides? They are too many to be the remains of an interrupted game and yet if they were the stock of a local workshop we would expect to find incomplete figures.

It is now agreed that the game of chess was invented in the east, in fifth or sixth-century India. Its early Sanskrit name – *chaturanga* – 'four divisions' refers to an Indian army (elephants, horsemen, chariots, footsoldiers) led by a king and his counsellor. The earliest Sanskrit reference to the game dates from the seventh century AD and is an evocative description of the rainy season:

The time of the rains played its game with frogs for chessmen which, yellow and green in colour, as if mottled with lac, leapt up on the garden-bed squares.

From India chess spread all over the world; as it spread so rules and pieces were changed to suit its new players. It is thought that it reached western Europe through Islam – North Africa then Muslim Spain. Although the English names used today for the pieces were introduced by the Normans, a group of tenth or eleventh-century pieces from Witchampton, Dorset and manuscript references which describe King Cnut (reigned 1016–35) as a chessplayer, indicate that the game was here before the Norman Conquest.

The chief piece on the board is the king, from whose Persian name (shāh) we derive (via French) our terms 'check' and 'checkmate' (*shāh mat* – the king is dead). The British Museum has six kings from the Lewis group who sit on ornate thrones, each holding a sword. Sir Frederic Madden likened them to King Geirraudr of the Eddaic poems, sitting with sword on knee, the blade half-drawn, listening to the words of the god Odin. The five queens replace the generals or counsellors of the eastern game. They too sit enthroned and aghast, hand clasped against face, with

Ornately carved King's and Queen's thrones. The style of carving is paralleled in other examples of 12th c. Scandinavian work.

'King Geirraudr sat with his sword on his knee, the blade half-drawn, listening to the words of Odin' (Madden).

Two rooks or warders portrayed as armed warriors, one biting his shield like a battle-mad berserker. The earliest chess game was four handed, but this was replaced by the two handed game we know today.

downturned mouth and staring eyes. The elephants have become bishops clad in traditional vestments – chasuble or cope, dalmatic, stole and tunic. All hold crosiers and some hold a book or raise a hand in benediction. Five sit and eight stand. The fourteen knights, with sword and spear, are descended from the Sanskrit *asva*, a horse soldier, although those of the Lewis group ride animals which resemble sturdy shaggy ponies rather than horses. Their helmets are not unlike those of the Bayeux tapestry; conical with noseguards and flaps protecting the neck. Their long kite-shaped shields are individually marked with designs which foreshadow the more complex and later heraldic devices. The pieces at the outer edges of the board, which we know as rooks or castles, were chariots in the Indian game. In the Lewis set they are ten armed warriors standing guard, with shield in one hand and sword in the other. Three remarkable individuals peer with distorted faces over the tops of their shields, which they bite with huge teeth like battle-mad berserks. Finally there is the lowest piece – the pawn – which is of abstract design. The eighteen in the British Museum are of various shapes and sizes, all except two plain, chiefly octagonal but some resembling tombstones.

It is to the carving on the thrones of kings, queens and bishops that scholars have turned in an attempt to date the little figures. Although two other chessmen apparently from the same workshop are known (in Florence and Stockholm) there are no other comparable pieces. However, scholars have found parallels between the interlaced animal and foliate designs on the thrones and a small group of Scandinavian carving – in wood, stone and ivory – which can be dated to the twelfth century. One of these pieces is a walrus ivory tusk, converted into a reliquary, richly carved with animals in foliage scrolls and displayed near the chessmen in the Museum. The other pieces include a fragment of walrus ivory and two ivory sword fittings in Copenhagen. There are also stone carvings at Ely Cathedral and on the wooden stave churches at Urnes, Ulvik and Hopperstad. A further clue is provided by the mitre worn by the bishops which, as today, has the points front and back instead of sideways, a style which seems not to have been adopted by the Church until at the earliest the middle years of the twelfth century. Scholarly opinion therefore places the chessmen some time between 1135 and 1175, most probably towards the end of this period. The style is Scandinavian but whether they were made there or carved in Britain by an Anglo-Norse craftsman we do not know. How they reached their resting place in the Outer Hebrides remains a mystery. The most usual explanation, which attempts to account for the number of sets, is that they belonged to an itinerant trader in walrus ivory and were hidden in the sand or brought ashore after a shipwreck. The explanation has no evidence to support it but no one has yet produced a better one.

Selection of pieces. *Left to right.* Bishop, Knight, King, Pawn, Queen. There were in all 8 kings, 8 queens, 16 bishops, 15 knights, 12 rooks and 19 pawns plus a belt buckle and 14 plain counters. The pieces range in height from 4 cm (1.6 in) (the smallest pawn) to 10.6 cm (4.2 in) (the largest king).

30

CLOCKS AND WATCHES

In the concentrated light of the Clock Room of the British Museum the clocks tick quietly away, many as they have done for hundreds of years. Occasionally (and never in concert) one of the great clocks will strike the hour or one of the quarters. A steel ball bearing in accordance with William Congreve's patent of 1808 rolls perpetually back and forth under the fascinated gaze of visitors. There are dignified 'long case' clocks with elaborate marquetry cases, brightly enamelled, jewelled and chased watches, unique examples of the most ingenious clockmaking skills, richly

Courtenay Adrian Ilbert (d.1957) with his collection, acquired by the Museum the year after his death.

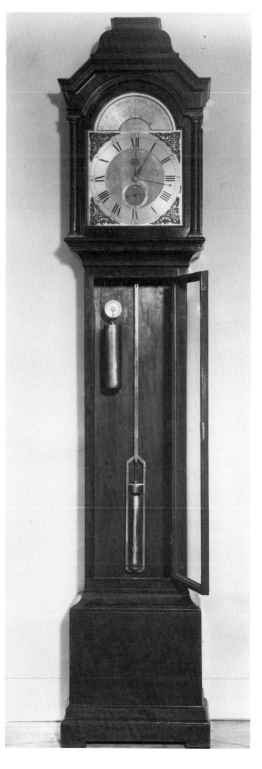

Long case clock by George Graham, London c.1740–50 from the Ilbert collection. H.2 m 34 cm (7 ft 8 in)

ornamented pieces of intricate craftsmanship which are objets d'art in their own right.

The Museum has one of the world's finest horological collections – some three thousand items. There are equally fine pieces elsewhere but for the solid business of reconstructing the detailed history of the development of time keeping the Museum collections are un-rivalled. The collection was built up from a variety of sources but, as a glance at the labels in the gallery will indicate, two – Ilbert and Morgan – have had the greatest influence.

The more recent, that of Courtenay Adrian Ilbert of Chelsea which was acquired in 1958, transformed the Museum's holdings. Ilbert collected steadily and with great knowledge and discrimination from his schooldays at Eton until his death in 1957, attempting to represent every technical improvement in the design of watch and clock movements. Over the years he managed to accumulate no less than 207 European clocks, 70 Japanese clocks, 38 chronometers, 968 antique watches, 62 modern watches, 741 watch movements, 7 Japanese watches and a num-ber of engravings, dials, hour-glasses, watch-papers, watch-keys and other miscellanea – at that time the finest concentration in existence in private hands for the systematic study of horology. Its acquisition by the Museum was a cliff-hanging affair. The clocks were rescued from auction with only a month to spare and then only by a gift of £50,000 for their purchase from Gilbert Edgar, Chairman of the H. Samuel Group and Master of the Worshipful Company of Clockmakers. The watches were the subject of a public appeal organised by M.L. Bateman, Chairman of Ingersolls' and Master of the Clockmakers Company. Edgar contributed £10,000.

Two of the most popular pieces in the gallery come from the collection of Charles Octavius Swinnerton Morgan (1803–1888) a Welsh country gentleman, Member of Parliament and one of the select group of nineteenth-century collectors who combined an appreci-

Right. A recent addition to the Museum's collection – a royal night clock made in 1689, the year of the Coronation of William and Mary, for the Royal Bedchamber in Kensington Palace by the master clockmaker Thomas Tompion (1639–1713). On the death of William III in 1702 it passed to the Earl of Romney, Gentleman of the Bedchamber. The silver figure of Britannia holds a shield bearing the combined crosses of St George and St Andrew. At the four corners are the rose of England, the thistle of Scotland and the royal lion and unicorn. H. 71 cm (28 in)

ation of beauty with intense and methodical curiosity over a wide field of interests. He was a 'delightful companion' full of information on his favourite subjects and is said to have taken up horology after buying a watch in Regensburg in 1837 similar to that in a portrait of one of his ancestors.

On the hour his five foot high carillon clock by Isaac Habrecht modelled after the great astronomical clock in Strasbourg cathedral comes alive as it has done for almost four centuries. Two small winged figures perch on the second stage, one swinging a sickle, the other turning an hour-glass. Above them on the third stage appear a great collection of figures – four floors in all. At the bottom level, in shining silver relief against a blue star-spangled ground are the classical gods of the days of the week each driving a splendid chariot, above are a seated Madonna and Child in silver who accept the homage of bowing angels to a musical accompaniment, provided by a ten bell carillon, then comes an old man, the last of the Four Ages of Man who appear in succession each quarter hour. At the top the silver figure of Death strikes the hour whilst through a doorway the Resurrected Christ appears and reappears to reassure mankind. At the summit a silver cock, perhaps

Far left. Carillon Clock said to have been made for Pope Sixtus V (1585–90) in 1589 by Isaac Habrecht (1544–1620) and modelled on the great astronomical clock of Strasbourg Cathedral. From the collection of Octavius Morgan. H. 1·57 m (5 ft 2 in)

Left. 'Nef' or Ship-clock (detail) attributed to Hans Schlottheim of Augsburg (1547–1625) and probably made for the Holy Roman Emperor Rudolf II *c.*1580–1600. Nefs were used to mark the place of the host in the same manner as the English salt. This specimen was designed to bear down on guests, pitching, rolling and firing its cannon. See also page 7. H. 99 cm (3 ft 3 in)

Right. 3 watches with painted enamelled cases. *Bottom left.* Signed *Paul Viet, Blois,* case attributed to Henry Toutin, *c.*1640. Diam. 5·2 cm (2 in). *Right.* Signed *Blaise Foucher, Blois,* gold enamelled case with scenes of the Amazons. *Top left.* Watch with balance spring signed *Philippus van Ceulen, Hage* and case signed *I.L. Durant,* a painter in Geneva *c.*1680–90.

St Peter's, flaps its wings and emits a small noise now produced by pipe and bellows. It was probably made in 1589 and is one of a small number of immensely elaborate and grandiose clocks designed for the princely courts of Renaissance Europe. It may have graced the apartments of the reforming Pope Sixtus V (1521–90). It probably left Italy during the Napoleonic Wars and subsequently re-emerged in the collection of William I King of the Netherlands (who died in 1844) whence it came to London in 1848.

Another piece from Morgan's collection, described when he gave it in 1866 as 'a towering ship of the sixteenth century', must in its heyday have been a welcome relief at boring banquets as, pitching and rolling over the table on its wheeled carriage, it bore down on the guests, cannon firing, lookouts revolving, trumpets blowing, courtiers turning, seven electors processing, before the Holy Roman Emperor. The least item on the great ship is the clock dial – only two and three eighths inches in diameter below a Habsburg double eagle. The fanfare would have been provided by organ pipes playing a different tune each quarter, and although the pipes are now missing experts were able some years ago to reconstruct their sequence and to record the music which enlivened imperial banquets. There is no maker's mark or signature on the nef but it is known that an Augsburg clockmaker, Hans Schlottheim (1547–1625) finished a nef in 1581 ordered by Emperor Rudolf II (1552–1612). Morgan also bequeathed to the Museum in 1888 '46 clocks of great quality and interest, 238 watches and 84 watch movements' together with a rather esoteric series of papal rings of investiture and gilt keys of office worn by chamberlains.

These are only two of the collectors represented in the Clock Room and associated students' room. The horological collection continues to grow; there can be few such contrasts as two 1980s acquisitions: an Ingersoll watch with hands showing the comic-strip cartoon character Dan Dare and the magnificent royal night clock made in 1689, the year of the Coronation of William and Mary, by the master clock-maker Thomas Tompion, designed to go and to strike without rewinding for an entire year.

171

31

THE MARLBOROUGH GOLD ICE PAILS

(Detail) Hinged handle with a lion mask, skilfully designed to sustain the weight of the pail and its contents. The fluted spiral ornamentation was an idiom popular on English silver in the period c.1680–90.

'She had a weakness for his brother John, to whom she left all her disposable property, in spite of his dissolute and extravagant life' comments the *Dictionary of National Biography* on the bequest by Sarah Churchill, 1st Duchess of Marlborough in 1744 to her grandson the Hon. John Spencer. Direct ancestor of the present Princess of Wales, John Spencer was also younger brother of Charles, who inherited the Marlborough title and amongst whose famous descendants is to be found Sir Winston Churchill.

Included in Sarah's 'disposable property' were two magnificent solid gold ice pails of high purity, 22 carat, which together weigh approximately twenty-five pounds. These are now in the Museum, having been acquired from Earl Spencer in 1982. They are unique; no other gold ice pails from the late seventeenth or early eighteenth century are now recorded either in England or abroad.

The introduction of ice pails as an alternative for the large wine cooler or cistern is thought to have taken place at the French Court towards the end of the seventeenth century and been rapidly copied in London by leading wealthy families. The spiral fluting on the Marlborough pails was an idiom popular on English silver in the period 1680–90. They cannot be attributed with certainty to a particular craftsman, but much plate was produced by Huguenot craftsmen driven out of France by the Revocation of the Edict of Nantes in 1686. One such, David Willaume, was in London at the appropriate time and made the earliest known pair of ice pails, in silver, for the first Duke of Devonshire in 1698. These were also cylindrical in shape and with lion masks. Willaume produced a pair of silver gilt covered cups in 1711 (which came to the

Museum with the Wilding Bequest) and which have certain similarities in workmanship and ornamentation to the Marlborough pails.

Another intriguing question is the date and circumstances by which such magnificent pieces came into the possession of the Churchills. The meteoric career of John Churchill is described by Sir Winston Churchill who wrote proudly of his ancestor:

He commanded the armies of Europe against France for ten campaigns. He fought four great battles and many important actions. It is the common boast of his champions that he never fought a battle that he did not win, nor besieged a fortress he did not take.

John Churchill was already a promising young soldier when he met Sarah Jennings, a seventeen-year-old lady-in-waiting in the household of Mary of Modena, second wife of King Charles II's brother and heir presumptive James, Duke of York. Although not as beautiful as her elder sister Sarah was considered to be one of the most striking women of her time with 'fair flaxen hair, blue eyes sparkling with vivacity, a clear rosy complexion, firm engaging lips, and a nose well chiselled, but with a slightly audacious upward tilt' and the temper of the devil. Churchill pursued Sarah for two and a half years until their secret marriage, against the wishes of his family, some time in the winter of 1677/78.

John Churchill fought for France at the time of Charles II and then served James II who succeeded his brother in 1685. Three years later the Churchills, staunch Protestants, went over to William and Mary (James's daughter) when they arrived in England to take the throne, but it was to Mary's sister Anne, now next in succession, that their fortunes were tied. Five years younger than Sarah, she had been captivated by Sarah's sparkling personality and in 1683 when she married the stolid, boring but good natured Prince George of Denmark, she appointed Sarah one of the ladies of her bedchamber. A close friendship developed with Sarah as the dominant partner. John Churchill was created Earl of Marlborough in 1689 and after the death of Mary in 1694 and of William III in 1702 his star was in the ascendant. He was made Captain General of the forces and his wife became groom of the stole, mistress of the robes, keeper of the privy purse and had the rangership of Windsor Park. Hostilities with France had been taking place intermittently for some years and during the next decade Marlborough's victorious armies crossed and recrossed Europe in a series of complicated and often bloody campaigns.

Marlborough's battles abroad were carried out against a backcloth of bitter political infighting at home, complicated by Sarah's violent temperament. In time she went too far in her bullying of the Queen who had had enough of the oft-repeated 'Lord, Ma'am it must be so!'. Sarah was supplanted by her cousin Abigail Hill (Mrs Masham) and handed in her golden key of office in 1711. Marlborough was dismissed later that year.

Sarah Churchill (née Jennings), 1st Duchess of Marlborough (1660–1744). Of her marriage Winston Churchill wrote 'this was the only surrender to which the Duke of Marlborough was ever forced . . . the only occasion . . . when he was ever frightened'. Sarah bequeathed the pails to her grandson John Spencer in whose family they remained until their acquisition by the Museum in 1982.

Two ice pails made of 22 carat gold. Their total weight is about 25 lbs, and they are the earliest known examples of the individual gold ice pail to survive. The use of the individual pail was a custom which developed in France with the desire to dine in more intimate surroundings, the pail placed on the table rather than a cooler on the floor. H. 26·7 cm (10·5 in) and 26·9 cm (10·6 in)

The great Duke died in 1722 and was survived by his widow for over twenty years.

In the course of their careers the Churchills amassed a vast fortune, leaving Sarah one of the richest women in Europe. She died on 18 October, 1744 at Marlborough House, at the advanced age of eighty-five. She had wearied of life and had announced 'I am going soon out of the world and am packing up'. Although she did not have the disposal of Blenheim or the settled estates (which went to Charles, the elder son of her second and favourite daughter Ann Spencer) she had a great deal of her own to bequeath including the considerable collection at Marlborough House and in her other houses at Wimbledon, Windsor and St Albans. Much of this passed to the sensitive younger son, John Spencer. Among the directions in her will is one referring to 'my 2 large gold flagons' which were to go to John Spencer. A list of 'Plate at Marlborough House November 14, 1744' made after Sarah's death refers also to '2 gold flaggons that are in the Iron Chest' and an inventory made at the same time by those administering her will and giving precise weights refers to 'Gold Plate: . . . 2 large

Flaggons with wrought handles' – 181 ounces 13 dwt and 183 ounces 13 dwt Troy which figures are identical to the weight of the pails now in the Museum.

So we do not yet know at which point in the Churchills' meteoric careers the ice pails were acquired for, as is common with gold plate of the period, they were not hallmarked and bear no date letter. Family tradition suggests that they were a gift from Queen Anne but this conflicts to some extent with the fact that stylistically they precede the period of the Churchills' greatest favour. An earlier reference than the will, a list of gold and silver plate signed by Sarah on 18 May 1712, has an entry referring to '2 very large Gold Ewers' which may or may not be the pails – there are no other details.

The entry in Sarah's will allied with the inventory weights is thus the first definite proof of their existence. Had they been silver the weight would have been decreased over the centuries by cleaning but, as solid gold, they remain much as they were in Sarah's day.

32

MRS DELANY'S FLOWER MOSAICS

In her seventies Mrs Delany began what she was to describe as a 'whim of my own fancy', her flower mosaics. The idea came to her as, sitting in her bedchamber she noticed the similarity of colour between a geranium and a piece of bright scarlet Chinese paper. With her scissors she cut out bright red petals, calyx, stalks and leaves in different shades of green. Her friend, the Duchess of Portland, came into the room when she had finished and, so accurate was the work, is said to have mistaken it for a real flower.

So began Mrs Delany's famous *hortus siccus*, a dry garden, composed not of dead plants and flowers but of myriads of pieces of paper, whose intricacy amazed her eighteenth-century contemporaries and still fascinates all who view the ten volumes of almost 1,000 lifesize plants and flowers in the Museum. They are a delight to the eye; close-up the detail is astounding – the light reflected at the edge of a horse-chestnut leaf is represented by a curving strip of paper a fraction of a centimetre in width: *Cactus grandiflorus*, the Melon Thistle has 190 parts, 399 spines protrude from a stem which in turn is composed of ten different shades of paper; white flowering accacia, *Mimosa latisliqua* has 543 leaves cut in different shades of green and 120 stamens in a single bloom. From a distance the hundreds of pieces merge and become one – a plant from the eighteenth-century countryside, the latest arrival at the Royal Botanic Gardens at Kew, a rarity from the greenhouses of the aristocracy. Sir Joshua Reynolds thought the *flora delanica* unrivalled in perfection of outline, delicacy of cutting, accuracy of shading and perspective, harmony and brilliancy of colours. The noted botanist Sir Joseph Banks declared they were the only representations of nature he had ever seen from which he could venture to describe botanically any plant without the least fear of committing an error.

Their creator, Mary Delany, was a well-

Rosa gallica var. Blush Rose. The detail is such that it includes an insect bite cut in the leaf. H. 174 mm (6.8 in)

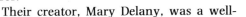

known eighteenth-century personality. A highly accomplished watercolourist and embroiderer she was not regarded as a great artist or a great beauty but her kindness and warmth won her the respect and affection of many notable people, among them George III and Queen Caroline, Handel, Swift, Burke, John Wesley, David Garrick, Lord Chesterfield and Hogarth.

She was born Mary Granville in 1700, a member of a well-connected family. Her father was associated with the Jacobite cause and when he fell from favour Mary although groomed for a life at Court was, at seventeen, forced to marry a rich sixty-year old Cornish landowner, Alexander Pendarves. She wrote unhappily of her wedding day:

I was married with great pomp. Never was woe drest out in gayer colours, and when I was led to the altar, I wished from my soul I had been led, as Iphigenia was, to be sacrificed.

and of her husband:

he was excessively fat, of a brown complexion, negligent in his dress, and took a vast quantity of snuff, which gave him a dirty look: his eyes were black, small, lively and sensible; he had an honest countenance but altogether a person rather disgusting than engaging.

Alexander died in 1724 after a life of gout, jealousy and heavy drinking leaving Mary not rich but comfortably off and in no hurry to re-marry. She now went about in society enjoying the pleasures of eighteenth-century London – masques, theatres, shopping in town – and country visits. In 1743 in early middle age she found married happiness with Dr Patrick Delany, a Protestant clergyman from Dublin. Mary was forty-three, her husband fifty-eight, but this time she ignored the wishes of her family who thought that she was marrying beneath her station.

Mary Delany enjoyed Ireland and the company of her new husband. They entertained frequently but she took particular pleasure in the upkeep of her gardens, especially at her house at Delville where grew 'honeysuckles, sweet briar, roses and jessamine ... violets, primroses and cowslips'. Encouraged by Dr Delany she occupied much of her time recreating her beloved flowers and plants in exquisite embroidery and delicate watercolours.

This happy period came to an end when Dr Delany died in 1768. His widow readjusted her life with the support of her friends and relatives and began to spend considerable time at the home of the Duchess of Portland, at

Bulstrode near Gerrards Cross in Buckinghamshire. As a child she had experimented with cut outs of paper and had later produced lively silhouettes and intricate birds. She had long had a serious interest in botany and at Bulstrode met some of the leading botanists of the day – Sir Joseph Banks, Daniel Solander of the British Museum, Philip Miller of the Chelsea Physic Garden, and Georg Ehret, one of the greatest botanical artists of all time. In about 1772 she began her flower collages and two years later these became a consuming hobby.

Her great-great-niece Lady Llanover wrote 'that part of the work which appears likely ever to remain a mystery is the way in which by the eye alone scissors could be directed to cut out the innumerable parts necessary to complete the outline and shading of every leaf, flower and stem so that they all hung together and fitted each other as if they had been produced instantaneously by the stroke of a

magic wand'. Equally intriguing is the question of the adhesive used – after two hundred years and much handling the tiny pieces of paper still adhere, undiscoloured, where they were placed by their creator. The paper came from a number of sources – from China and from paper stainers whose colours had run producing unusual tints; occasionally Mrs Delany would herself dye pieces to obtain the exact shade she required. Sometimes watercolour is used to indicate shading but mostly this was achieved by placing minute pieces layer upon layer.

Word of Mrs Delany's skill spread and in 1776 when she was staying with the Dowager Duchess of Portland, King George III and Queen Charlotte called and asked to see her flowers. This was the beginning of her friendship with the royal couple. The King later gave her a house at Windsor and three hundred pounds a year which the Queen is said to have brought over in her pocket book so as to avoid the attentions of the tax collector. Mrs Delany was now able with the King's blessing to include in her albums exotic plants from the Royal Botanic Gardens at Kew.

Mrs Delany wrote her farewell to her mosaics in 1782 when because of failing eyesight she was obliged to give up the intricate work:

The Time is come! I can no more
The Vegetable World explore;
No more with Rapture cull each Flower
That paints the Mead or twines the Bower;
No more with Admiration see
Its beauteous form and Symmetry;
No more attempt with Hope elate
Its lovely Hues to imitate.

She had completed almost one thousand flowers and plants. They were inserted in albums and labelled with botanical precision. Mrs Delany continued her comfortable and busy life amidst a warm circle of friends and relatives and died at the age of eighty-seven. She had been cared for in her old age by her great-niece Georgina Port. The *hortus siccus* passed to Georgina's daughter Augusta, Baroness Llanover who in 1897 presented this unique collection to the Museum.

Above. Carduus nutans, Musk or nodding Thistle, 'its leaves swirling like waves in a turbulent sea'. H. 208 mm (8.1 in)

Above left. Mary Delany (1700–88) by John Opie. 'A lady of singular ingenuity and politeness, and of unaffected piety'.

Left. Passeflora laurifolia (detail). 230 separate pieces of paper ranging from deep red to white have been used for the petals.

Left. Physalis. Winter Cherry,
one of the many pieces created
perhaps on a warm summer's
morning in 18th-century
Buckinghamshire or a winter's
day at St James's Place.
H.235 mm (9.2 in).

*Right. Æsculus hippocastanum,
Horse Chestnut.* 'I have bungled
out a horse chestnut blossom
that would make a fine figure
in a lady's cap' wrote Mrs
Delany at the age of 76. This
specimen is composed of
myriads of minute pieces of
coloured paper. H. 272 mm
(10.7 in)

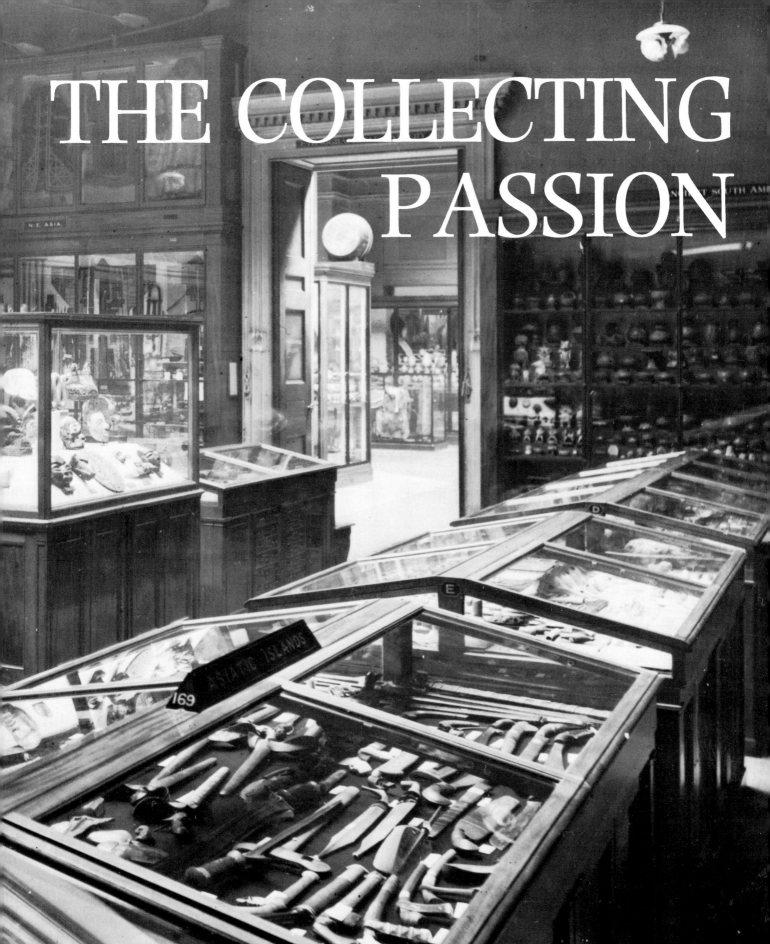

THE COLLECTING PASSION

33

SIR HANS SLOANE
Founder of
the British Museum

But what in oddness can be more sublime
Than S_____, the foremost toyman of his time?
His nice ambition lies in curious fancies,
His daughter's portion a rich shell enhances ...
How his eyes languish! how his thoughts adore
That painted coat which Joseph never wore!
He shows on holidays a sacred pin,
That touch'd the ruff that touch'd Queen Bess's chin

(Edward Young (1681–1765), *Satires*, IV, Love of Fame the Universal Passion)

'You will scarce guess how I employ my time', wrote the eighteenth-century author Horace Walpole and answered, 'chiefly at present in the guardianship of embryos and cockle-shells. Sir Hans Sloane is dead, and has made me one of the trustees to his museum ... He valued it at four score thousand; and so would anybody who loves hippopotamuses, sharks with one ear and spiders as big as geese!' For all Walpole's sarcastic remarks, he was participating in the foundation of the first national, secular and public museum in the world, which today numbers its collection in millions of objects and its priceless treasures in many thousands. Over two centuries ago the British Museum was founded to house the

Left. Sir Hans Sloane (1660–1753) from whose collections the Museum was founded. A terracotta model bust by J.M. Rysbrack, presented to the Museum by Sloane's daughters, for the statue recently in the Chelsea Physic Garden and now on loan to the Museum. At 23 Sloane was described as 'of medium height, hair very short, light chestnut, face rather long and grave marked with smallpox'. H. 68 cm (2 ft 2.25 in)

Right. Brass astrolabe with silver inlay 'constructed by the least of the students' Abd al-Ali son of Muhammed Rafi al Juzil and decorated by his brother Muhammed Baqir for the Safawid ruler Shah Sultan Husayn, dated 1712/13 AD. Perhaps the most beautiful astrolabe in the Museum. The instrument would have been made for the royal observatory. H. 53 cm (20·8 in)

collections of Sir Hans Sloane and many of his 'curious fancies' can still be seen today – among them a brass astrolabe made for Shah Sultan Husayn in 1712, a small wooden drum of Asante type thought by Sloane to be American Indian but now known to have been brought from Africa or made in Virginia by a seventeenth century African slave, a series of Chinese woodcuts their brilliant colours unfaded, an entire album of drawings by Albrecht Dürer as well as such items as Eskimo snowspectacles and Peruvian pottery.

What manner of man was the founder of the British Museum? The sitter for the bust by Rysbrack and the Museum's own full length portrait after Sir Godfrey Kneller has a quizzical but not unkindly expression, with a hint of the intense curiosity which drove him to collect so feverishly. The good 'bed-side manner' which commended him as physician to such patients as Queen Anne, George II, and the retired pirate Henry Morgan is apparent. He was a family man with two daughters, a son who died young, and four stepdaughters whose fortunes he scrupulously administered.

Sloane was born in County Down, Ireland in 1660 of Scots ancestry and in rather modest circumstances. By determination, ability and good fortune he became a royal physician and a very wealthy man. Another collector remarked of his career that it 'is an instance of the great power of industry which can advance a man to a considerable height in the world's esteem with moderate parts and learning . . .' His father was agent (or steward) for the Hamilton family, and it is probable that their patronage did much to give the young Sloane his start in the world.

He had acquired an interest in natural history as a boy and in 1679 left home for London to study medicine. He attended lectures in anatomy and physic and continued his study of botany which included visits to the Apothecaries Garden in Chelsea (which still exists today). At the age of twenty-three he extended his studies to France and took a degree in medicine at the University of Orange in the South. His great opportunity as a naturalist and physician came in 1687 when he was invited by the new Governor of Jamaica, the Duke of Albemarle, to accompany him and his family as personal physician. The party embarked in September and three months later arrived in Jamaica. Sloane's patient died the following autumn, having been of somewhat intemperate habits, accustomed to 'sitting up late and often being

promoted inoculation against smallpox and drinking chocolate mixed with milk.

Sloane's lucrative practice enabled him to indulge his great passion for natural science and collecting. Although as a scientist he is not considered to be in the first rank with such contemporaries as Sir Isaac Newton and Robert Boyle, yet he retained their friendship and respect and played an active part in scientific circles. He became a Fellow of the Royal Society in 1685, and in 1727 its President in succession to Newton.

He was a shrewd businessman. Although he was an inheritor of the tradition of the cabinet of curiosities he was also a product of the age of scientific enquiry. By the age of thirty-six he had already amassed a notable collection. In 1702 he had inherited the collection of his friend William Charleton (or Courten) of which John Evelyn the diarist wrote:

It consisted of miniatures, drawings, shells, insects, medals, natural things, animals …minerals, precious stones, vessels, curiosities in amber, Christal, agate, all being very perfect and rare in their kind, especially his books of birds, fish, flowers and shells, drawing and miniatures to the life'.

In 1710 he bought the collection of a wealthy London apothecary, John Petiver and in 1718 the herbarium of Leonard Plukenet. In an age of expanding exploration and as the fame of Sloane's collection grew, so travellers would look out for rare things to bring back to Bloomsbury. A grateful patient wrote:

Since you Dear Doctor, saved my life
To bless by turns and plague my wife …
According then to your command,
That I should search the Western land
For curious things of every kind,
And send you all that I could find: …
It is my wish, it is my Glory
To furnish your Nicknackatory

So large did the collection become that Sloane was obliged to take over the house next door. It was in Bloomsbury that in 1725 Benjamin Franklin called and sold him an asbestos purse and in 1740 the composer Handel is supposed, much to Sloane's disgust, to have placed a buttered muffin on one of his rare books.

In 1741, Sloane moved with his collections from Bloomsbury to a Manor House he had bought at Chelsea. (His connection with the borough is still commemorated in names such as Sloane Street and Square, Hans Place and Road). There he spent a comfortable old age although obliged to take to a wheelchair. Among his visitors were the Prince and

Soapstone figure of Guandi, Qing Dynasty, 17–18th c. AD. The God of War, a patron of the military and merchant classes, is the deified general Guan Yu (AD 160–219). H. 25 cm (9·9 in)

Above left. 'An Indian drum … from Virginia' (Sloane inventory). In fact of Asante origin, probably brought from Africa to North America or made in America by an Asante slave.

Left. Birds and bamboo in wind. From the Kaempfer collection. Kangxi period (1662–1722). 26.6 × 26.1 cm (10.5 × 10.2 in)

merry'. Sloane, however, put his time to good use, collecting some 800 species of plants and other specimens including a live snake.

Returning to England, where King William and Queen Mary now reigned Sloane set up a flourishing medical practice at his home in No. 3 Bloomsbury Place, (along the street from the present Museum). With Albemarle patronage he accumulated wealthy and aristocratic patients, although throughout his career he continued to allot time to treating the poor free of charge. Although Sloane adhered to some of what we now consider the horrifying medical treatments of his time (being particularly fond of using live millipedes, crabs' eyes and vipers fat) he had an interest in new techniques. He

Left. Bird on a lotus flower. Colour woodcut on paper with gauffrage. One of a selection of Chinese watercolours carefully preserved against the light, acquired by Sloane with the collection of Dr Engelbert Kaempfer in 1723–5 from a sale arranged with his widow and nephew. Kaempfer reached Japan in November 1690 and spent two years there, twice making the annual journey to the Shogun's court at Edo. 17th c. 28.7 × 36.4 cm (11.3 × 14.3 in)

Right. Study of Water Sky and Pine Trees by Albrecht Dürer (1471–1528) from the superlative album of Dürer drawings in Sloane's collection. Watercolour and bodycolour. 26.2 × 36.5 cm (10.3 × 14.3 in)

Princess of Wales (the parents of George III) who came in 1748. The royal couple were treated to a glittering display of Sir Hans's treasures – 'the verdant Emerald, the purple Amethyst, the golden topaz, the azure sapphire, the crimson garnet, the scarlet ruby, the brilliant diamond, the glowing opal'. From the collection of antiquities and ethnography were laid out 'precious and remarkable ornaments used in the habits of men, from Siberia to the Cape of Good Hope, from Japan to Peru', 'curious and venerable antiquities of Egypt, Greece, Hetruria, Rome, Britain and even America'.

Sloane died in January 1753 at Chelsea and was buried at Chelsea old church where the monument erected by his two daughters can be seen today. He left an amazing collection of some 80,000 objects (not including the plants in the herbarium), which included 1,125 'things relating to the customs of ancient times or antiquities', 32,000 coins and medals, 23,000 books, prints and manuscripts. In spite of initial hesitation by King George the collection was purchased for the nation.

What remains today of Sloane's 'nicknackatory'? He left a catalogue which is still in the Museum but this is less than helpful in identifying specimens which over two centuries have become separated from their labels. It is not known, for instance, what became of item No. 272 'A case made of bamboo lacquer'd in Japan wherein are five Chinese instruments of faether ear-pickers etc. for tickling the ears'. The greatest portion of the collection related to natural history. Some of this remains today in the British Museum (Natural History) in South Kensington but much because of its nature perished before the beginning of the nineteenth century.

The British Library retains a large collection of books and manuscripts, including Sloane's own papers which are of particular interest to students of the history of medicine. As previously mentioned, some items can still be identified in the Museum, among them a black leather album of Dürer drawings has now been broken up and remounted but is available in the Print Room together with a miscellany of drawings by other artists. There is a unique basket (probably Cherokee) from South Carolina, two finely woven Iroquois burden straps, a pair of snowshoes and a nest of thirty birchbark baskets from Hudsons Bay, a moose antler comb and a bird bone spoon from New England.

Right. 'A large Carolina basket made by the Indians of Splitt canes . . .' (Sloane inventory). This unique object is probably Cherokee from South Carolina and was made before 1753. L. 53.3 cm (21 in)

The preamble to his will gives a summary of his life and philosophy:

Whereas from my youth I have been a great observer and admirer of the wonderful power, wisdom and contrivance of the Almighty God appearing in the works of His creation, and having gathered together many things in my own travels and voyages . . . Now, desiring very much that these things, tending many ways to the confutation of atheism and its consequences, the use and improvement of physic and other arts and sciences, and benefit of mankind, may remain together and not be separated and that chiefly in and about the City of London, where I have acquired most of my estates, and where they may, by the great confluence of people, be of most use . . .

If Sloane's collection today pales by comparison with the later riches of the Museum, his unique contribution lies in persuading the nation to establish a Museum which was the first of its kind and which has been the model for many such institutions throughout the world.

34

THE RETIRING COLLECTOR
The Reverend Clayton Mordaunt Cracherode

'On Saturday morning early died at his home in Queen's Square, Westminster the Reverend Clayton Mordaunt Cracherode, MA, Student of Christ Church, one of the Trustees of the British Museum and Fellow of the Royal and Antiquary Societies' recorded *The Times* of 5 April 1799. The obituary in the *Gentleman's Magazine* ran to four pages and yet the subject was an extremely shy man who tried to avoid the public gaze. Cracherode's claim to fame was the choice collection, his life's work, which he bequeathed to the Museum. This consisted of a library of some 4500 printed books chosen for rarity and fine bindings, eight volumes containing 848 drawings and a number of prints, a cabinet of coins and medals, a fine collection of gems and a small but precious cabinet of minerals. The collection was built up from a fortune left by his father who on his death in 1773 left his son a very comfortable legacy of six hundred pounds a year in land and £100,000 invested in three per cents.

Cracherode was judged by his contemporaries to be something of an eccentric. He was a Londoner and in the eighteenth century his refusal to ride a horse had certain disadvantages. As an adult he never ventured farther from London than Clapham, indeed his farthest excursion at any time was to Oxford where he gained his degree. He never visited the parish of Binsey in Oxfordshire where he held a curacy, nor his Hertfordshire estate, celebrated for a famous chestnut tree which he contented himself with viewing in an etching.

For forty years Cracherode's routine never varied. Starting from his house in Queen

The 'rich, learned and most amiable' Clayton Mordaunt Cracherode (1730–99) who bequeathed an outstanding collection of books, drawings, coins and gems. A scholar with a talent for elegant Latin verse, he published nothing after the age of 18 but was one of the foremost collectors of his time.

Square (now Queen Anne's Gate) with its fine view of St James's Park, he would walk up the Strand to Mr Elmsly's the bookseller, then to the more noted shop of Mr Tom Payne at the Mews gate where in the parlour he would meet his literary friends. He called punctually every Saturday at Mudge the chronometer makers in Fleet Street to have his watch exactly regulated. He bought the best that money could acquire from dealers and from agents. Of his collecting policy a biographer quoted the maxim of John Selden:

The giving a dealer his price hath this advantage: – he that will do so shall have the refusal of whatsoever comes to the dealer's hand, and so by that means get many things which otherwise he never should have seen.

This pleasant life passed in literary conversation and good works, was marred by one great shadow. In purchasing the manor of Great Wymondley in Oxford his father had gained the privilege of handing the new sovereign the first cup with which he drank at his Coronation; his son therefore lived in

horror of King George II's death and of being forced into the limelight (a needless worry for the monarch outlived him by thirty years.)

A touching picture is painted of the final days of this 'rich, learned and most amiable' collector. Depressed by the rise of Napoleon his health broke down. Four days before his death he paid his regular visit to the Strand and 'seemed to take a last farewell of the Parlour at the Mews-gate'. He retained his collecting fever to the end. The last sight the bookseller had of him was his placing in one pocket a finely printed *Terence* and in the other a large paper *Cebes*, meanwhile giving a last longing look at a choice *Triveti Annales* and a beautifully bound *Pindar*. While he was on his deathbed his agent was still buying prints for him at Richardson's.

Cracherode was buried at Westminster Abbey with, as he had directed, 'as much privacy and as little expense as decently may be' and a small plain stone over his grave. His executors had one surprise: hidden away in a section of his library between the pages of the

An Indian Elephant by Rembrandt van Rijn (1606–69). Black chalk. One of four drawings of elephants probably all made in 1637. 17·7 × 25·5 cm (7 × 10·1 in)

Lake Nemi looking towards the Palazzo Dei Cesarini by John Robert Cozens (1752–99).
Watercolour over pencil. 37 × 53.4 cm (14.5 × 21 in)

books was a large sum of money in banknotes and an accidentally pressed secret spring revealed a hoard of four thousand guineas and some jewellery.

His collection formed with 'sound taste and excellent judgement' was bequeathed to 'that most excellent repository' the British Museum. It included twelve Rembrandt drawings, the Museum's first Raphael drawing, a number of landscapes by Claude Lorrain, a Dürer drawing of two flying angels of about 1518, and a selection of van Dycks. Amongst the Rubens drawings was an unusual drawing of trees reflected in water at sunset with an inscription in the artist's hand. Among the portraits of particular note is that of John Fisher, Bishop of Rochester, after Holbein. The coins, chiefly Roman, were remarkable for their rarity and fine condition. *Bibliotheca Cracherodiana* was inscribed over the room set aside for his library in Montagu House; a Cracherode Room exists today in Smirke's new building.

Selection from Cracherode's choice cabinet of coins: *Top.* Aureus of Trajan (AD 98–117), Mint of Rome (diam. 19 mm (0·7 in)). *Centre, left to right.* Aureus of Claudius I (AD 41–54), Mint of Rome (diam. 20 mm (0·8 in)); Decadrachm of Syracuse *c.*400 BC (diam. 35 mm (1·4 in)); Aureus of Carausius, usurper in Britain (AD 286–93), Mint of London (diam. 20 mm (0·8 in)). *Bottom.* Stater of King Lysimachus of Thrace (297–281 BC) (diam. 18 mm (0·8 in))

35

JOHN MALCOLM OF POLTALLOCH: Collector of Old Master Drawings

1. Irrespective of authorship, to collect only specimens of indisputable excellence as works of art.
2. To aim more particularly at the acquisition of authentic works of the *greatest* masters, and especially of drawings bearing the signatures of their respective authors.
3. In the case of less eminent masters to retain only exceptionally fine and well-preserved examples.
4. To select by preference works, the authenticity and relative importance of which were in a measure guaranteed by the fact of their having passed through celebrated collections of former times, as evidenced by the collectors' marks and written inscriptions upon them.

(Rules for the formulation of the Malcolm Collection, 1869).

One of the most beautiful objects in the Museum is Botticelli's *Abundance* or *Autumn*. This partly finished drawing of an ethereal young woman carrying an overflowing horn of plenty has often been reproduced but no reproduction can convey the sublime beauty and delicacy of the original. *Abundance* is but one of a collection of 970 drawings and engravings of the highest quality which came to the Museum in 1895 for the modest sum of £25,000 and which today, if they were to appear on the market, would be beyond price. At the time the Malcolm collection was acquired it was reputed to include some sixteen Leonardos, thirty Michelangelos, twenty-seven drawings by Raphael, eleven by the Carracci, twenty-two by Corregio, nine by Mantegna, nineteen Titians, twenty-six fine landscapes by Claude Lorrain, eleven Durers, and eighteen Rubens. Among the engravings all chosen for 'beauty of impression and condition' were examples of the German School from 1440–1540 and of the Italian from 1460–1520 with a few fine specimens from Rembrandt and van Dyck. This single purchase transformed the Museum's collection, especially in the Italian school, into one of the world's finest.

How did such a rich assemblage come together? It was amassed by a rather obscure collector, John Malcolm of Poltalloch in

Left. John Malcolm of Poltalloch (1805–93) whose collection of Old Master drawings transformed the Museum's holdings. The collection was sold for the modest price of £25,000 by his son John Wingfield Malcolm (1833–1902).

Head of a woman with an elaborate coiffure by Andrea del Verrocchio (1435–88). Perhaps a study for the head of the Madonna in an altarpiece at Pistoia of *c*.1475. Black chalk heightened with white bodycolour. 32.5 × 27.3 cm (12.8 × 10.7 in)

Left. A Philosopher by Michelangelo Buonarroti (1475–1564). Datable. *c.*1501–3. Pen and pale yellow-brown and grey-brown ink. 33.1 × 21.5 cm (13 × 8.5 in)

Opposite. Abundance or Autumn by Sandro Botticelli (1444/5–1510). Pen and brown ink and brown wash over black chalk, heightened with white bodycolour, on paper tinted pink. 31.7 × 25.3 cm (12.5 × 10 in)

Below, Landscape with Wooded Hills beside a River at Sunset attributed to Adam Elsheimer (1578–1610). Brush drawing in black and white bodycolour with touches of light violet-rose on brown prepared paper. 18.3 × 25.8 cm (7.2 × 10.1 in)

Argyllshire (1805–93) a Conservative MP for thirty years and a member of a Scottish family which could trace its ancestry back to the sixteenth-century 1st Laird, Donald McGillespie Vich O'Challum. The O'Challum line descended sideways and forwards from father to son to cousin to brother, the name changing en route to Malcolm. It included a second son who was the reputed father of the Marquis of Montcalm, leader of the French at Quebec and ancestor of the Malcolms of Pennsylvania. A brother-in-law was killed at Culloden but the family estates were safeguarded by the seventh and eighth lairds who signed resolutions supporting the Government during the Jacobite uprisings. The 10th and 11th lairds had estates in Jamaica and at the turn of the eighteenth century the Malcolms started to marry into prosperous English families.

John Malcolm was the fourteenth in the line. His collecting career seems to have begun in earnest about 1860 when he acquired a collection from John Charles Robinson

Bust of a Warrior in Profile by Leonardo da Vinci (1452–1519). In the style of Leonardo's master Verrocchio whose studio he entered about 1470 this may be intended to represent Darius since there is a resemblance to a copy of a Verrocchiesque profile-bust of Darius in Berlin. Metalpoint on cream-coloured prepared paper. 28.5 × 21 cm (11.2 × 8.3 in)

Robinson became Curator of the forerunner of the Victoria and Albert Museum in 1853. He and Franks worked in concert for their two institutions at the Bernal sale of 1855 which heralded a 'golden age of art collecting'. In one of the few accounts of how he made his collecting coups Robinson wrote:

Dealers in works of art in all the European countries were at this time comparatively humble and impecunious tradesmen. They seldom went far afield in their collecting expeditions and were contented with small profits and quick returns. [They were] Ignorant for the most part as to the historic and aesthetic value of the wares they dealt in, while fraudulent imitations of them, which have since become so universally rife, were comparatively infrequent and abnormal, and dangerous only to the merest tiro . . .

Every year he went abroad, government funds in hand or on call to 'tap these waters at their sources', to innumerable art auctions, dealers' gatherings, old family collections, convent and church treasuries often buying at 'rubbish prices'. Robinson loved the chase, calling it the most delightful of all pursuits and occupations, the collection of works of art in their original sources and habitations. In 1869 he quarrelled with the Director of the Victoria and Albert Museum, Sir Henry Cole, and resigned. He continued to build up his own collection and advise private collectors among them Malcolm and Queen Victoria's eldest daughter, Crown Princess Frederick of Prussia. He became Surveyor of the Queen's pictures from 1882–1901.

In 1893 John Malcolm died leaving his lands and works of art to his eldest son John Wingfield Malcolm (1833–1902). The son first considered handing over his father's collection to the Museum for nothing but decided that he could not afford to do this and offered it for the modest price of £25,000. A special grant was provided by the Treasury and this outstanding collection entered the Museum. Malcolm's sole condition in fixing the purchase price was that every item be marked as coming from the Malcolm collection. Today when the Museum mounts or lends an exhibition of Old Master Drawings more often than not this collectors' mark is to be seen, accompanied by the registration number 1895-9-15 . . . – a tribute to his remarkable generosity.

(1824–1913) an irascible, opinionated, handsome, brilliant polymath who was to guide Malcolm's taste and money. While Malcolm provided the cash Robinson was by far the better known figure. The counterpart of the Museum's A.W. Franks he was one of the young Victorians who turned from the cold and restrained art of Classical Greece and Rome to the richness of an idealised medieval Europe and the products of the Renaissance.

36

SIR AUGUSTUS WOLLASTON FRANKS
Victorian Polymath

Collecting is an hereditary disease, and I fear incurable
(The Apology of my life, A W Franks, undated ms, fol. 1).

There have been few members of the Museum staff who could write without exaggeration, as Franks did shortly before his retirement:

I think I may fairly say that I have created the department of which I am now Keeper, and at a very moderate cost to the country. When I was appointed to the Museum in 1851, the scanty collections into which the department has grown occupied a length of 154 feet of wall cases, and 3 or 4 table cases. The collections now occupy 2250 feet in length of wall cases, 90 table cases and 31 upright cases, to say nothing of the numerous objects placed over the cases or on walls.

There is a century between Franks and Sloane and yet both deserve to be remembered as founders of the British Museum. Sloane, the Cottons and Harleys left collections which were heavily weighted towards printed books, manuscripts and natural history. Others – Elgin, Townley, Salt, Layard, Rassam, to name but a few, laid the foundations of certain areas of the Museum's immense collections from the Ancient World. But to A.W. Franks must go much of the credit for establishing four of the Museum's present nine departments – Oriental Antiquities, Prehistoric & Romano-British Antiquities, Medieval and Later Antiquities and Ethnography. The range of topics on which he wrote and in which he collected seems amazing to today's specialists – topics as diverse as Indian sculpture, Japanese archaeology, Anglo-Saxon art, Himyaratic inscriptions, medals, bookplates, heraldry, megalithic monuments, monumental brasses, etc. In spite of this diversity his scholarship in some fields is still regarded with respect.

Rich and socially superior, he was not in

Augustus Wollaston Franks (1826–97) scholar and collector. Dame Joan Evans daughter of one of Franks's closest friends met him when she was still a child and describes him thus: 'He was . . . a grey dreamy person, with an unexpected dry humour and an incurable habit of addressing himself to his top waistcoat button'.

awe of the Museum's Trustees and was quite willing to risk their wrath to foster a pet project and to dip into his own pocket. He was at the centre of a web of collectors. He bought for himself and advised others, usually with an eye to the Museum's eventually acquiring their collections. From his friend Henry Christy, one of the pioneers of ethnography, came an immense collection of some 10,000 items. Another friend, Felix Slade, bequeathed a remarkable collection of glass. From Lady Charlotte Schreiber came fans and playing cards, from Octavius Morgan clocks and watches. There were many others. Franks himself made strategic donations which helped propel the Trustees in new directions. As early as 1855 for example he gave a collection of twenty-three pieces of majolica as bait to persuade them to acquire other specimens in the Bernal sale.

Two acquisitions, one a gift the other acquired by subscription, would alone have assured Franks a place in the Museum's history. One is the unique 'royal gold cup' of the sovereigns of France and England, the only such example of sumptuous gold plate to have survived from the Middle Ages. Made about 1380, the gold is richly enamelled in brilliant translucent colours. On the lid and bowl are scenes from the life of St Agnes. On the foot are the four symbols of the Evangelists. The cup was made in Paris, at the order of Jean, Duc de Berry and presented to the French King Charles V (1337–80) who was born on St Agnes Day. It passed to his son Charles VI (1368–1422) and in 1494 came into the possession of John of Lancaster, Duke of Bedford, third son of Henry IV. From him it passed to his nephew Henry VI and to later sovereigns of England until in 1604 James I gave it to the Constable of Castile to mark the conclusion of an Anglo-Spanish peace treaty. A Latin inscription on the stem in black enamel records its donation by the Constable to the nuns of Medina de Pomar in 1610. There the cup remained until the nineteenth century when it was acquired by a Baron Pichon who sold it to the dealers Wertheimer. Franks persuaded Wertheimer to part with it for its cost price to them of £8,000 (no mean sum in those days). He contemplated donating it to the Museum but, deciding to use his money for other gifts, arranged a private subscription amongst his wealthy friends. The cup returned to England in 1892.

Another unique object is the 'Franks Casket', given outright in 1867, having been rescued from use as a workbox by a French family in Auzun, Haute Loire. The casket is of whalebone and was probably made in Northumbria about 700 AD. The sides are inscribed with an old English text in runic characters. The scenes shown, not all identifiable, are a strange mixture of Northern mythology, classical legend and the Bible – the Adoration of the Magi, Wayland the Smith, the Sack of Jerusalem by Titus, a lost Old English legend concerning Egil. One side-panel is in the Bargello, Florence.

It may appear self-evident today that the national museum should collect national antiquities but this was not the case in the first

Above. The 'Franks Casket', whalebone, made in Northumbria *c.*700 AD. Bought by Franks and presented to the Museum in 1867. L. 22.9 cm (9 in)

Below. The Royal gold cup, detail from the inside of the bowl. Made in Paris, *c.*1380 for Jean, Duc de Berry and presented to King Charles V, it passed to the sovereigns of England and in 1604 was given to Spain. Franks and a group of friends acquired it for the Museum in 1892. The cup is decorated with scenes from the life and miracles of St Agnes, daughter of a wealthy Roman of the time of Constantine. The stem is Tudor and the inscription dates from 1610. H. 23.6 cm (9.2 in)

The Royal Gold Cup. Made in Paris *c.*1380 for Jean, Duc de Berry. H. 23.6 cm (9.2 in)

October 1850 Lord Prudhoe (now Duke of Northumberland) wrote complaining that there was no sign of his room and warning that 'this neglect ... will prevent other Collectors offering British antiquities to our National collection'. The Trustees at last appointed an Assistant to look after British material and in April 1851 Augustus Wollaston Franks joined the Museum and within a decade was to rise to the position of head of a new Department of British and Medieval Antiquities and Ethnography.

On his arrival Franks was twenty-five. He came from a family with influential connections – his cousin was the third Earl of Harewood – and possessed of a certain propensity for collecting. The family collectors included his maternal great grandfather Sir John Sebright, MP (hawks, fowl, prints), his mother (minerals and dried plants), his father (pictures), his maternal great grandfather (Irish and Welsh manuscripts and printed books). The family also appears to have successfully collected money – there were banking fortunes on both sides.

Franks was born in Geneva in 1826, and was brought up on the Continent, perhaps because his father Frederick had married successively two daughters of Sir John Sebright. At that time such marriages were legal if unchallenged but could be challenged at any time during the lifetime of both spouses therefore many such couples chose to live abroad. Franks was educated first at Eton (where he amused himself copying Egyptian hieroglyphs and cartouches) then at Trinity College, Cambridge where he devoted himself to a variety of interests including church architecture and archaeology, having decided that a good degree was not one of his priorities. When he came down from university Franks was first involved in the organisation of the 1850 medieval exhibition. His next choice was the British Museum although his family were not sure whether this was socially acceptable. Franks later recalled:

At that time it was thought probable that I should succeed to a very considerable estate and I very well remember the grave consultation as to whether it would not be *infra dig.* for me to take a post in the Museum ... A dear old East Anglian, who was one of my father's trustees, discovered that a Suffolk man (Mr Barnwell) had been employed at the Museum; so it was decided that I might accept the appointment.

On his death in 1897, after half a century with the Museum, his final gift was the 'Franks

half of the nineteenth century. The ancient Britons had a rather low reputation in the Victorian period, being regarded as benighted and lacking the civilising influence of the Romans.

There was, however, an increasingly influential antiquarian lobby determined to push the Museum into collecting British antiquities. Within the Museum the Keeper of Antiquities, Edward Hawkins, a numismatist, had some sympathy for the Ancient Britons since some at least did use coins. Lord Prudhoe gave the Museum a hoard of Iron Age bronzes found on his estate at Stanwick, Yorkshire in 1845 on condition that a 'British Room' was set aside for them. The Royal Commission of 1849–50 added its weight to the argument. In

Bequest'. It is difficult to imagine how one man, in full time employment, could have amassed so much especially when his lifetime's gifts are taken into account. The bequest included the Oxus treasure, a collection of silver plate, 3,300 finger rings of all ages and countries (including that of Æthelswith, sister of Alfred the Great), 150 drinking vessels (among them the notable glass tankard with silver mounts and the arms of the first Lord Burghley). A collection of 512 specimens of porcelain represented most of the factories of Europe and was added to an earlier gift of 1000 Chinese and 600 Japanese pieces. There were 1500 netsuke and 850 ojime (sword guards). As 'a sort of light supplement to ...other and graver antiquarian labours' Franks had acquired 80,000 bookplates – one of the largest and most comprehensive collections ever formed.

Franks is little remembered except in the Museum but if the visitor studies the labels in the galleries of the successors to his old Department his name continually appears. Like Wren his epitaph could be '*si monumentum requiris, circumspice*'.

Above left. 'Priest in Meditation' portrait of a devout Buddhist. Made in Japan *c.*1700 of wood, lacquer and pigment, it is one of Franks's many gifts in a field in which he pioneered scholarship and collecting. H. 41·5 cm (16·3 in)

Left. An Afro-Portuguese salt cellar made of ivory. Acquired by Franks in Brussels and presented in 1871. It was then attached by European brass mountings to part of a Yoruba Ivory armlet. 15th or 16th c. H. 12 cm (4.75 in)

37

BARON FERDINAND DE ROTHSCHILD AND THE WADDESDON BEQUEST

The great princes of Renaissance Europe vied with each other in the splendour of their artistic patronage. The cultivated prince would display the products of this patronage in a *schatzkammer*, a room full of richly decorated treasures where the ingenuity of Renaissance craftsmen was given free rein in precious metals, wood, enamels, seashells and jewels, so that the result dazzled the eye and proclaimed to the beholder the wealth of the patron. The Waddesdon Bequest, the gift of Baron Ferdinand de Rothschild, is a superb example of a Renaissance *schatzkammer* in miniature and it is from its now dispersed predecessors that many of its treasures are drawn.

The Bequest, which came to the Museum in 1898, is displayed in a separate gallery and the effect is of a sparkling riot of colour, brilliance and luxury. Baroque pearls, garnets, emeralds, rubies, diamonds, contrast with green, black, white and lilac enamels. The objects are made of gold and silver, of multicoloured minerals – honey coloured and variegated green, white and red agate, dark green jade, grey chalcedony, cloudy yellow and red jasper, blue lapis lazuli, bloodstone, brown onyx, translucent rock crystal – and include natural oddities, such as ostrich eggs and nautilus shells. Scenes from classical mythology compete with those from the Bible – Judith and Holofernes, the Rape of Helen and the Choice of Paris. Huntsmen and their hounds mingle with peasants carrying baskets. There is a fantastic menagerie of lizards and locusts, unicorns and chimerae, bears and monkeys, dragons and sea monsters. Real and mythical individuals are depicted – Moses and Neptune, Diane de Poitiers and Helen of Troy.

The craftsmanship is amazing. Consider the painstaking detail of the two-handled vase of

honey-coloured agate dating from Roman times, to which has been added a wealth of decoration – gold and silver mounts, heads of Pan and acanthus leaves, satyrs in opaque white with outstretched arms, a knob of ruby grapes their leaves enamelled in translucent green. A border of blue and gold strap work is dotted with white surrounds; scroll work of white enamel on black enamel is relieved with gold foliage, enamelled studs consisting of pearls in white on richly decorated rosettes with cloisons of ruby enamel with between them a drapery of blue.

The greatest collections are those which bear the imprint of the taste and enthusiasm of a single individual who bought not as an impersonal investment but for his or her own pleasure. The creator of the Waddesdon Bequest was Baron Ferdinand de Rothschild, member of the immensely rich banking family

Baron Ferdinand de Rothschild MP (1839–98) in his sitting room at Waddesdon Manor, with his dog Poupon.

which had its origins in Frankfurt. He belonged to the Austrian branch, was born in Paris in 1839, a great-grandson of the bank's founder Mayer Amschel. As a child he delighted in handling his father's collection of works of art. He had little interest in the family banking business and in 1860 he moved to England. He became a British subject and in 1865 fell in love with and married Evelina, the daughter of Baron Lionel de Rothschild of the English branch of the family. Baron Ferdinand's happiness lasted only eighteen months. His wife was injured in a railway accident and died while giving birth to a stillborn son; her husband survived her for over thirty years but never remarried. He turned to charitable and public work and in 1874 embarked on a lifetime project – the construction and furnishing of a fine house at Waddesdon in Buckinghamshire.

Waddesdon Manor is now owned by the National Trust and is open to the public. While out hunting Baron Ferdinand had been entranced by the views from the summit of the hill on which it stands and so, when the death of his father provided him with sufficient

Miniature Flemish altar piece of boxwood dated 1511, carved with scenes from the Life and Passion of Christ. H. 25·1 cm (9·9 in)

Far left. One of the finest pieces of the Waddesdon Bequest, the gold enamelled reliquary of the Holy Thorn made in Paris *c.*1405–10 for Jean, Duc de Berry. The reliquary was made to contain a thorn from Christ's Crown of Thorns taken from that brought from Constantinople to Paris by King Louis IX. The thorn is set in a sapphire behind a window of rock crystal. H. 30.5 cm (12 in)

Left. The Lyte Jewel. A gift in 1610 from James I (whose portrait by Nicholas Hilliard is shown) to Thomas Lyte who had traced the king's pedigree back to the mythical Brut Gold, enamelled, set with 29 diamonds. H. 6.2 cm (2.4 in)

Below. The Aspremont-Lynden ewer, silver gilt, made in Antwerp 1544–5. H. 34·3 cm (13·5 in)

Below right. The Ste Valérie Chasse. A champlevé enamelled reliquary casket manufactured at Limoges *c.*1170 which depicts the martyrdom of Saint Valérie, a Christian convert on the orders of her fiancé a Roman proconsul. H. 29·2 cm (11·5 in)

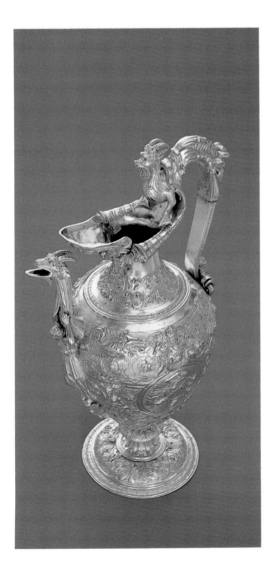

means, he purchased the land and engaged a French architect and a French landscape gardener. The hilltop was levelled, mature trees planted in the park and the ornate French-style building began to arise. He had begun collecting *objets d'art* when a young man but now he had a focus for his enthusiasm. In 1880 he was at last able to move into the 'Bachelors' Wing' and three years later there was a grand house-warming.

At Waddesdon Baron Ferdinand and his sister, Miss Alice, entertained extensively. He found time for public service as well as collecting; he was elected Member of Parliament for Aylesbury in 1885 and in 1896 became a Trustee of the Museum. Many of the objects now in the Museum were purchased rather late in Baron Ferdinand's life although the nucleus of the collection belonged to his father Baron Anselm.

In 1898 Baron Ferdinand died suddenly on his fifty-ninth birthday. He bequeathed, as his sister wrote, 'to the nation he loved so well' a small but choice part of his total collection which had been kept in the New Smoking Room of the Bachelors' Wing at Waddesdon. The Bequest consisted of almost three hundred items and was conditional on its being permanently displayed in the Museum in a separate room to be known as the Waddesdon Bequest room.

While most of these beautiful objects date from the Renaissance there are, in the tradition of the *schatzkammer*, a number of older pieces. The oldest items are four Hellenistic bronze medallions of unknown origin and use found in a tomb in the province of Trebizond. A legacy of the Middle Ages is a *champlevé* enamelled reliquary (probably manufactured in France at Limoges in the decade 1170–80) which depicts the martydrom of Saint Valérie. From outside Europe comes a fourteenth-century enamelled glass Mosque lamp from Syria. Perhaps the most magnificent object in the Bequest, the centrepiece of the Waddesdon Room, is the gold enamelled Reliquary of the Holy Thorn made in France for the Duc de Berry, between 1405 and 1410.

Each object is of the highest quality and it is not possible to do full justice to the splendour of the Bequest. The collection of German and Netherlandish silver plate is, for example, the finest to be seen in England. Amongst the

Drinking glass with the stem blown to form a hunchback, made of cristallo and trimmed with blue glass, Venice *c.*1600. H. 30·5 cm (12 in)

choice pieces from the renowned glass manufacturers of Venice is a splendid and unusual opaque turquoise blue cup, made to imitate the original stone which contrasts with a clear 'crystallo' cup ornamented with blobs of aubergine and red glass. The amazing microscopic boxwood carvings have a particular fascination: a miniature altarpiece dated 1511, for example, compresses a crowded crucifixion scene into a minute space. There are nine pieces of Italian maiolica and brilliant, almost luminous French enamels, painted and fired on copper. Pride of place amongst the arms and armour goes to the shield of iron hammered in relief signed by Giorgio Ghisi 1554, damascened with gold and partly plated with silver, elaborately decorated with scenes from the Iliad and ancient mythology. The jewellery includes finger rings and heavy pendants, hat medallions and hair ornaments glittering with precious stones. The best known is the 'Lyte Jewel' – a gift from James I to Thomas Lyte who traced the King's pedigree back to the mythical Brut, the founder of the British Kingdom.

Although perhaps somewhat ornate for modern taste the Waddesdon Bequest is nevertheless a breathtaking spectacle. Each piece repays close individual inspection and inspires awe at the skill of the known and unknown craftsmen who worked not only in peace but in times of war and famine, plague and pestilence, without the tools and power sources we take for granted today. In the words of an early catalogue, Baron Ferdinand's gift to the nation 'furnishes a monument of the patriotism and liberality of its former owner that will give wholesome pleasure to many thousands to whom he can have been little more than a name'.

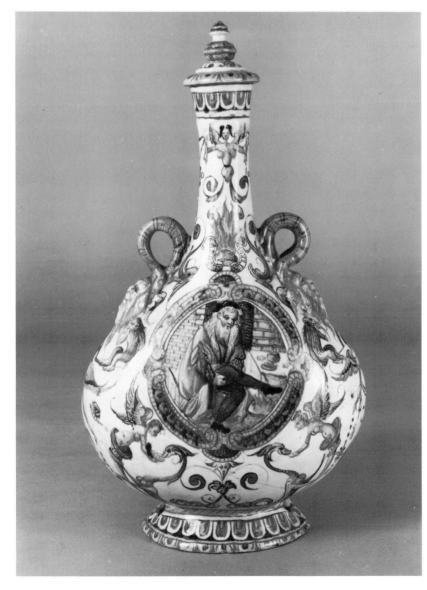

Above. Waddesdon Manor, Buckinghamshire, where Baron Ferdinand de Rothschild displayed the collection in his New Smoking Room. The house is set on the top of a hill with fine views through wooded parkland.

Left. Italian maiolica bottle painted with the device and motto used by the Duke of Ferrara on the occasion of his marriage to Margarita Gonzaga, probably made in Urbino 1579. H. 39·4 cm (15·5 in)

THE DEPARTMENTS OF THE BRITISH MUSEUM AND THEIR COLLECTIONS

The objects described in the earlier sections of this book represent a tiny fraction of the vast holdings of the Museum and give only some indication of its immense range from both the ancient and the modern worlds. The collections are today divided administratively between nine curatorial departments – Egyptian, Greek and Roman, Medieval and Later, Oriental, Prehistoric and Romano-British and Western Asiatic Antiquities plus Coins and Medals, Prints and Drawings and Ethnography. Some further indication of the extent of the Museum's collections is given in the following pages.

COINS AND MEDALS

The first coins to reach the Museum came in the Sloane and Cotton numismatic cabinets in 1753. The Museum now has nearly five hundred thousand coins of all periods and places from the seventh century to the present day. It is one of the three largest collections in the world, the most representative of world coinage as a whole and has a high proportion of significant rarities.There are also some 40,000 medals of all kinds, including awards and decorations. The Museum is now building a national collection of banknotes and paper money. There is in addition a fine collection of some 46,000 tokens, jettons, weights and badges.

Left. Gold medal struck to commemorate the defeat of the Spanish Armada in 1588 (obverse) showing Queen Elizabeth I in all her finery. It is thought to have been designed by the miniature painter Nicholas Hilliard. 61 × 54 mm (2·4 × 2·1 in). The medal collection ranges in date from such early examples as Pisanello's bronze medal of the Byzantine Emperor John VIII Palaeologus (made in 1438–9) and Quentin Matsys' portrait of Erasmus dated 1519 to contemporary medals of abstract design.

The Armada Medal (rev.). A bay tree flourishing on an island, uninjured by lightning, wind and rain with the legend NON IPSA PERICVLA TANGVNT (not even dangers affect it).

Above right. José Guadalupe Posada (1852–1913), medallist Ronald Searle. Bronze. diam. 6.7 cm (2.6 in).

Below right. Ignacy Jan Paderewski (1860–1941), medallist Vladislav Müldner Nieckowski. diam. 12.8 cm (5 in).

Left. Entrance Hall of the old Museum in Montagu House, George Scharf the Elder, August 1845. Roubiliac's statue of Shakespeare is on the right. The Museum had at this time an extensive collection of classical and Egyptian antiquities as well as books, manuscripts, natural history, coins and medals and prints and drawings. It had not yet begun systematically to collect British material and ethnography.

One of the earliest coins in the world, a 6th c. BC stater of Sardes made of electrum (a natural gold-silver alloy). The Museum's extensive collection of classical coins comprises some 90,000 specimens from the Greek world and 140,000 from Rome and Byzantium.

Gold noble of Edward III (reigned 1327–77) worth 80 pennies. The noble was introduced in 1346. The king is shown armed in a ship carrying a shield charged with the arms of England which includes the lilies of France. Diam. 35 mm (1.4 in). There are around 48,000 British coins in the collection, ranging from the earliest coins imported from northern France in the 1st c. BC. their design derived from the gold stater of Philip II of Macedon (351–338 BC), and the collection covers the whole history of British coinage to issues currently in circulation. Other European groups include over 5,000 coins of Celtic origin and 72,000 from medieval and modern Europe.

Moghul gold coin of Jahangir (1605–27). The Museum has an extensive non-European collection including some 60,000 coins from the Middle East and South Asia and about 24,000 from the Far East together with a miscellany of other medieval and modern coins from outside Europe.

The second earliest recorded note issue in Europe – a Swedish banknote of 1663. Before 1979 the Museum had only 4,000 notes, few of them outstanding. There are now about 21,000 specimens (including the new Isle of Man plastic pound note), the acquisition of material from the Marquess of Bute collection in 1984 making the Museum's holdings one of the world's leading collections in this field.

The Waterloo Medal by Benedetto Pistrucci (1784–1855) with portraits of the victors over Napoleon – the Prince Regent (George IV), Francis II of Austria. Alexander I of Russia and Frederick William III of Prussia. An electrotype, the medal was never struck. Diam. 13.3 cm (5.2 in).

EGYPTIAN ANTIQUITIES

Since Sir Hans Sloane bequeathed some 150 Egyptian objects (small figures of gods, amulets, scarabs and shabti figures) in 1753, the collection has grown over the centuries to some 70,000 items, illustrating every aspect of the ancient civilisation focused around the Valley of the River Nile from the 5th millennium BC down to the medieval Christian (Coptic) culture around the 10th century AD. The first major objects to arrive were those ceded to the Crown by the French in 1801 after the defeat of Napoleon's Egyptian expedition. They included the Rosetta Stone and the great sarcophagus of Nectanebo which had been used for some centuries as a public bath in Alexandria. The nucleus of the collection of monumental sculptures came in the 1820s much of it acquired by Henry Salt, British Consul-General in Cairo, through the agency of Giovanni Belzoni. From the end of the 19th century the emphasis in acquisition shifted to well-documented objects from excavations; fieldwork remains the principal source today. (Generally the scope of this Department's collection diminishes with the entry of the Arabs into Egypt in 641 AD, Islamic material being the province of Oriental Antiquities).

Painting from the Tomb of Nebamun. Thebes, *c.*1400 BC. showing fowling in the marshes. The hunter is accompanied by his wife and daughter and a striped ginger cat as retriever. H. 82 cm (2 ft 8 in) For the historical period beginning *c.*3000 BC the Museum's collections of sculptures, paintings and objects of all kinds and many materials richly illustrate the achievements of the Egyptians in art, craftsmanship and industry.

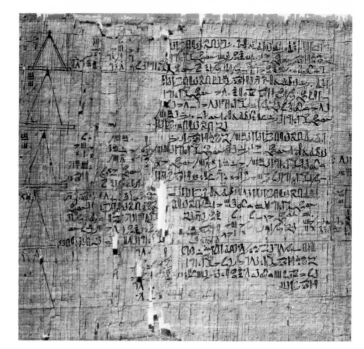

Section of the Rhind mathematical papyrus, Hyksos period, *c.*1575 BC, from the Ramesseum. Thebes. The text includes methods of measuring the area of a square, a circle, a triangle and determining the slope of pyramids. This version was copied from a papyrus written in an earlier period, perhaps the late Middle Kingdom (*c.*1850 BC). H. 34 cm (1 ft 1 in). The Museum's collection of papyri is the best in the world and contains examples of most categories of ancient document.

Left. Unfinished limestone statue of an unnamed nobleman and his wife late 18th Dynasty *c.*1340 BC. The Museum has an outstanding collection of royal sculpture and private pieces such as this. H. 1.3 m (4 ft 3 in)

Below. The 'Hunters' Palette' from the Predynastic period *c.*3500 BC. Men with feathers in their hair and wearing kilts to which are attached animals' tails are shown armed for hunting. The circular cavity at the top of this slate palette was used for grinding eye paint. L. 66.6 cm (2 ft 2 in). The Museum's collections from this period include a good selection of excavated material from key sites.

GREEK AND ROMAN ANTIQUITIES

The Museum possesses one of the finest collections of Greek and Roman antiquities in the world, covering almost every aspect of Greek and Roman art. The objects range in date from the Bronze Age civilisations of the Cyclades and Crete beginning c. 3000 BC down to the late Roman Empire. The collection is particularly rich in monumental sculpture from the Eastern Mediterranean especially of the Classical and Hellenistic periods.

Portrait of Antistius Sarculo and of his wife and former slave, Antistia Plutia. Anstistius Sarculo had served as master of the Alban College of Salian priests, an order of well-born Romans who celebrated the opening and the closure of the military campaign season with ritual dances and songs. The marble relief was set up to their deserving patrons by Rufus and Anthus, two freedmen of the family. Made in Rome, about 30–10 BC, this is one example of the Museum's splendid collection of Greek and Roman portraits. H. 64.7 cm (2 ft 1.5 in)

The so-called 'Master of the Animals', a nature-god whose Cretan name is not known, holding two water birds. The pendant is from the mysterious Aegina Treasure, found on the island of Aegina but probably originally from a rich Cretan tomb. It was made in Crete c. 1600 BC, the period of the Minoan civilisation's greatest prosperity. H. 6 cm (2·4 in)

Terracotta head from Tamassos, Cyprus, 660–600 BC. H. 36 cm (14·1 in). The Museum has an outstanding Cypriot collection, ranging from the Early Bronze Age to the Roman Empire, much acquired from excavations the Museum undertook there between 1894 and 1896.

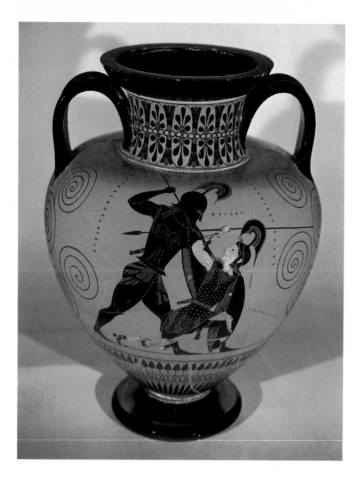

Above. Achilles slaying the Amazon queen Penthesilea at Troy. According to a late legend the hero falls in love with his adversary in the act of killing her. Blackfigured neck amphora (storage jar) signed by the vase-painter and potter Exekias. Made in Athens *c.*540 BC and found at Vulci, Italy. H. 41·2 cm (16·2 in). The collection of Greek vases, founded on the immense collection made by Sir William Hamilton in South Italy and purchased in 1772, is one of the largest and most comprehensive in the world.

Above right. Bronze parade mask, Roman 2nd c. AD, found on the face of a skeleton in a tomb at Nola. The mask is that of a woman. Parade masks were used for cavalry displays and it has been suggested that female masks were worn by soldiers representing Amazons. H. 24·9 cm (9·8 in)

Right. Apollo stringing a bow. Hellenistic copy of a lost original of *c.*200 BC. From a bronze hoard found at Paramythia North-Western Greece in 1792 and bequeathed by Richard Payne-Knight. H. 23.08 cm (9.87 in)

MEDIEVAL AND LATER ANTIQUITIES

In this Department is to be found a vast and heterogeneous collection of the post-classical art and archaeology of Europe – ivories, silver, glass, ceramics, jewellery, engraved gems, icons, archaeological material, tiles, rings, seal dies and matrices, metalwork, enamels and much more. Other Christian and Jewish cultures of this period outside Europe are included for example Byzantium, Coptic Egypt, Cyprus, Syria, Asia Minor, Russia, Goa. The Museum does not however attempt to make comprehensive collections in every medium: for instance furniture, medieval sculpture, European folk life, arms and armour, manuscripts, paintings, printed books and pamphlets, modern technology are collected by other national institutions.

Left. Gothic ivory showing the Madonna and Child trampling the devil in the form of a dragon (Revelations 12), made in Paris *c.*1320–30. The leaning pose of the two figures is dictated by the shape of the tusk. One of the Museum's important collection of English and Continental ivories. H. 33.2 cm (13 in)

Far left. Gilt crucifix figure of the dead Christ. Possibly made in the county of Anjou *c.*1100. 27·2 cm (10·75 in)

Below. An English gittern (and detail). One of the few major musical instruments of the Middle Ages to have survived, it was made *c.*1290–1330 and the style of carving is paralleled in manuscripts of this period. In 1578 it was in the possession of either Queen Elizabeth I or her favourite Robert Dudley, Earl of Leicester, and it bears the royal arms and Leicester's badge. At some point it was remodelled into a violin. L. 70 cm (27·6 in)

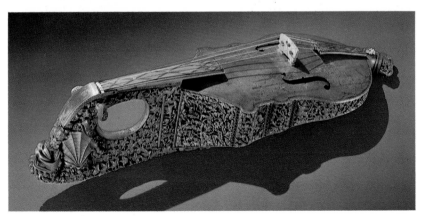

Above. Life size stoneware bust of Prince Rupert (1619–82) wearing the 'collar' and 'mantle' of the Garter. Nephew of Charles I who fought for the Royalist cause during the Civil War. After the Restoration he took part in the founding of the Hudsons Bay Company. Modelled by an unidentified sculptor, made at John Dwight's pottery at Fulham *c*.1675.

Above left. The Museum has one of the finest collections of silver plate of all periods in existence. This example of a cup and cover is from the 1969 Wilding Bequest of 30 superb pieces of Huguenot silver. It is hallmarked London 1702 and bears the maker's mark Louis Cuny (*fl.* 1702–33) who is known to have escaped to England from religious persecution in France by 1697. This is probably the earliest marked piece by this maker to have survived. H. 24·1 cm (9·5 in)

Left. Oak clock with black stencilled decoration, mother-of-pearl face and oblong mirror made in England in 1919 and designed by Charles Rennie Mackintosh (1868–1928). One of an increasing range of examples of 20th-century decorative art. H. 37 cm (14.5 in). The Department is also responsible for a horological collection of some 3,000 items – one of the finest in the world.

ORIENTAL ANTIQUITIES

The serious study of Eastern art and antiquities only started in the West in the nineteenth century and the Department of Oriental Antiquities, founded in 1933, benefited greatly from the activities of the pioneer collectors. The Department now deals with the cultures of the whole of Asia from the Neolithic period to the twentieth century (with the exception of the ancient civilisations of the Near East and Persia before the founding of the Islamic religion in AD 622 which are the province of other departments). Its vast geographical span thus includes the Middle East, Iran, and North Africa from the Arab Conquest, Afghanistan, Russian and Chinese Central Asia, Siberia, Mongolia, China, Japan, Korea, the Philippines, the Indian sub-continent, Sri Lanka and South East Asia. Unlike the Department of Ethnography (which collects in the same geographical area) it has tended to concentrate on urban as opposed to traditional rural societies. It has particularly outstanding collections of ancient Chinese bronzes, Chinese and Japanese decorative arts in all materials, oriental painting and graphic illustration, Indian, South-East Asian, Central Asian and Tibetan religious art, Islamic metalwork, ceramics and woodwork.

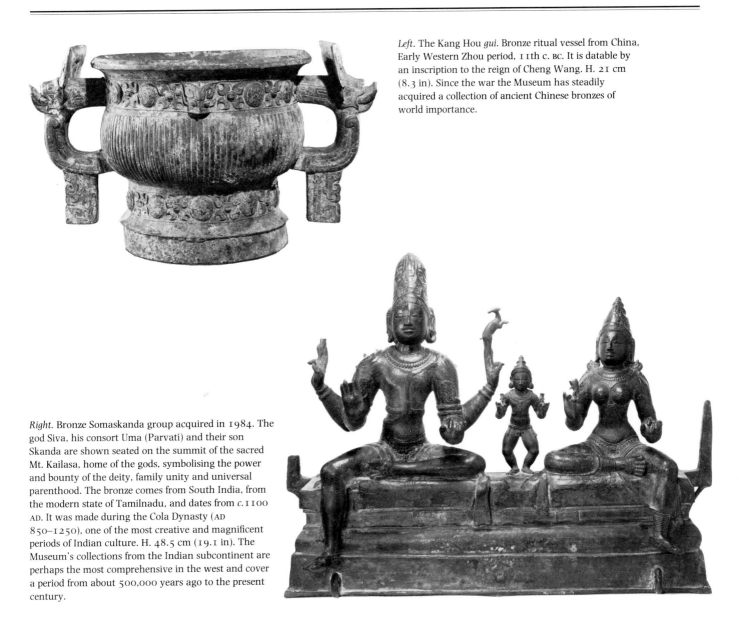

Left. The Kang Hou *gui*. Bronze ritual vessel from China, Early Western Zhou period, 11th c. BC. It is datable by an inscription to the reign of Cheng Wang. H. 21 cm (8.3 in). Since the war the Museum has steadily acquired a collection of ancient Chinese bronzes of world importance.

Right. Bronze Somaskanda group acquired in 1984. The god Siva, his consort Uma (Parvati) and their son Skanda are shown seated on the summit of the sacred Mt. Kailasa, home of the gods, symbolising the power and bounty of the deity, family unity and universal parenthood. The bronze comes from South India, from the modern state of Tamilnadu, and dates from *c.* 1100 AD. It was made during the Cola Dynasty (AD 850–1250), one of the most creative and magnificent periods of Indian culture. H. 48.5 cm (19.1 in). The Museum's collections from the Indian subcontinent are perhaps the most comprehensive in the west and cover a period from about 500,000 years ago to the present century.

Right. Possibly the most famous of all Chinese paintings is the handscroll 'The Admonitions of the Instructress to the Palace Ladies' (*Nü Shi Zhen*) attributed to Gu Kaizhi (344–405? AD). It is painted in ink and colours, mostly vermilion, on silk and consists of a sequence of 9 scenes preceded by short moralising inscriptions from a 3rd c. text by Zhang Hua. The scroll is considered to be a Tang (618–907 AD) copy which closely follows the style of the 4th-c. original. H. 24·9 cm (9·8 in)

Sculpture from the great Buddhist Stupa at Amaravati. Deccan, India. They date largely from the 2nd and 3rd c. AD but some may be earlier. *Top right.* Queen Māyā's Dream. *Left.* The interpretation of the Dream. *Bottom right.* The birth of Siddharta. *Left.* The child presented to the clan Rishi. H. 160 cm (5 ft 3 in)

Above. Cat Licking its Paw. A hanging scroll in ink and colours on paper from Japan by Katsukawa Shunshō (1726–92 AD). In recent years the Museum has strengthened its holdings of Japanese pictorial art especially from the 19th and 20th centuries. This delightful painting comes from the collection of Ralph Harari (d.1968).

PREHISTORIC AND ROMANO-BRITISH ANTIQUITIES

The scientific study of prehistory is of recent origin, the word being coined in the 19th century when man's great antiquity was first recognised. Although the Museum has had prehistoric material for many years, serious collecting only started in the last century and this Department as a separate section was founded only in 1969. The earliest objects in the Museum's collections date from man's first appearance more than two million years ago – crude basalt and quartzite choppers and chopping tools from the Olduvai Gorge, Tanzania. The Department has literally millions of objects from the Paleolithic and Mesolithic periods throughout the world, from the Neolithic, Bronze Age and Iron Age in Europe. It also holds the Museum's collection of material from Roman Britain, one of the finest collections of Roman provincial material in the world.

Above. Two swimming reindeer delicately carved on the point of a mammoth tusk *c.*10,500 BC. Found in 1866 in a rock shelter 25 feet above the river Aveyron at the base of a cliff called Montastruc, Bruniquel in South-West France. (L. 20·7 cm (8·1 in).) The Quaternary collection (spanning the Old and Middle Stone Ages – 2½ million years to about 5,000 years ago) is one of the finest of its kind in the world with especially important collections from France, Africa, the Near East and the Far East.

Left. One of a pair (and detail) of the finest examples of Early Celtic (La Tène) art in existence. A pair of wine flagons inlaid with coral (now faded to white) from Basse Yutz, Lorraine, France, manufactured *c.*400 BC. The handles are in the form of a dog or wolf standing with forepaws on the rim, a duck sails along a river of wine out of the spout. The collection includes many other outstanding examples of Celtic art from Britain and the Continent. H. 39 cm (15·5 in)

Right. Head of a cult statue of Mercury found during excavations at West Hill, Uley, Gloucestershire in 1979 on the site of a late Romano-British temple. It was probably carved from local limestone in the 2nd half of the 2nd c. AD. The Museum has long been active in collecting excavated material. H. 28·6 cm (11·3 in)

Below. Finely worked flint tools made in Scandinavia 4,000 years ago. Polished gouge from Denmark. Neolithic. L. 16.1 cm (6.3 in); sickle from Viborg, Jutland. L. 19.6 cm (7.7 in) and dagger from Denmark. L. 24.4 cm (9.6 in). Both late Neolithic 2400–1600 BC.

PRINTS & DRAWINGS

For combination of quality with breadth of coverage, the Museum has one of the best overall collections of western prints and drawings in the world, numbering between two and a half and three million items (of which some 100,000 are drawings). The collection ranges in date from the fourteenth century to the present day. It is strongest in works of artists born before the middle of the nineteenth century but gaps in the collection are being filled where possible.

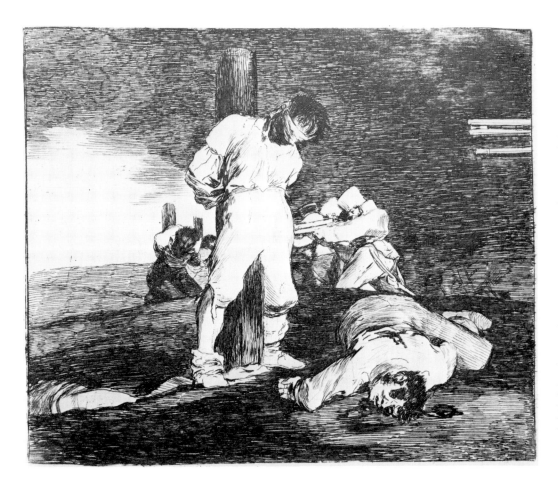

Left. Francisco Goya (1746–1828) *And there's no help for it* (*The Disasters of War* Plate 15). From a series of prints illustrating the Spanish struggle against Napoleon Bonaparte between 1808 and 1812. The series of woodcuts, engravings and etchings from their beginnings in the early 15th c. is as representative as any in existence and includes almost complete series of the engravings and etchings of, amongst others, Schongauer, Dürer, Lucas van Leyden, Rembrandt and Goya. Besides the major series of artists' prints there are series of prints of documentary interest – portrait, historical, satirical, topographical and reproductive prints after paintings, sculpture and drawings.

Below. A unique pack of 52 French humanist playing cards published in Paris 1544. H. 10 cm (3.9 in). Among the other miscellanea are fans, tradesman's cards and bookplates.

J.M.W. Turner (1775–1851) *Prudhoe Castle*, a watercolour prepared for
Charles Heath's series of Picturesque Views in England and Wales. 29·2 × 40·8 cm
(11·4 × 16 in). Although the Turner Bequest of some 20,000 drawings which was
temporarily housed in the Museum since 1931, is now to be transferred to the Tate
Gallery, the Museum still retains a fine collection of Turner's watercolours made for
exhibition and sale and an unsurpassed collection of engravings by and after him.
The representation of the English school is the largest section of the Museum's
collection of drawings.

Right. Claude Lorrain (1600–82) *Landscape with Pine Trees.* 32·2 × 21·6 cm
(12·6 × 8·5 in). The Museum has over 300 drawings by this artist in addition to the
Liber Veritatis, the artist's record of his works, the most comprehensive collection in
the world. Other artists particularly well represented are Michelangelo, Raphael,
Dürer, Rubens, Rembrandt and Watteau. The collection represents almost all the
chief draughtsmen of the western tradition by examples of their work significant on
grounds of aesthetic quality and art-historical importance.

WESTERN ASIATIC ANTIQUITIES

This Department's collections are drawn from the ancient peoples of virtually all those lands, east of Egypt and west of Pakistan, where Semitic, Turkish and Indo-European languages are now spoken. Thus they portray the art and life of such peoples as the Sumerians, Babylonians and Assyrians from what is now Iraq; the ancient Persians, including the Achaemenians, Parthians and Sassanians; the Urartians and the Hittites, who extended from Turkey into North Syria; other peoples of Syria and Ancient Palestine including the Hebrews, and the Phoenicians with their colonies as far afield as Carthage and all the states of the Arabian peninsula; from the earliest agricultural settlements *c.*8000 BC until the advent of Islam in the 7th century AD.

The Siege of Lachish. A series of bas reliefs from the palace of Sennacherib (704–681 BC) at Nineveh showing his attack on the city of Lachish in Palestine in 701 BC, the fall of the city and the bloody fate of the inhabitants. The Museum's collections of Assyrian reliefs is unparalleled.

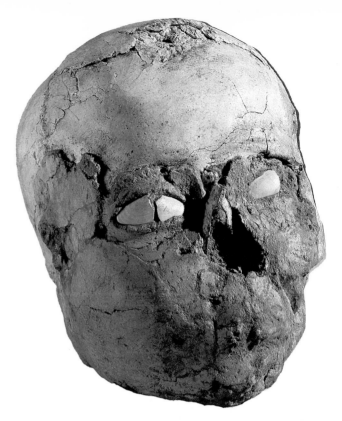

Above. Alabaster face from a funeral stele, South Arabia. *c.*3rd–2nd c. BC. H. 18·2 cm (7·1 in). These ancient kingdoms owed their prosperity to the trade in aromatic gums, frankincense and myrrh.

Below. The Flood Tablet. A clay tablet written in cuneiform script in the 7th c. BC and relating part of *The Epic of Gilgamesh* a story 1,000 years older. It tells how the gods determine to send a flood to destroy the earth and how a man, Utanapishtim, is ordered to build a boat into which he takes birds and beasts of all kinds. Part was discovered by Layard during his excavations of the library of the Assyrian King Ashurbanipal at Nineveh and its significance realised by George Smith in 1872. In 1873 Smith visited the site and found a further piece. The Museum's collection of some 150,000 cuneiform tablets with its nucleus in the 20,000 tablets from the royal library and archives of the Assyrian kings discovered at Nineveh mainly in 1849, 1854 and 1873–9, is the largest in the world. H. 15·5 m (6·1 in)

Above. The Jericho skull. One of a number dating from 7000–6000 BC found by Dame Kathleen Kenyon during excavations at Jericho in 1953. A human skull has been taken as the base with features modelled in plaster and the eyes of bivalve shells. The strength of this Department's collections has its origins in material acquired by 19th and 20th-c. archaeological expeditions sponsored by the Museum to sites such as Nimrud, Nineveh, Carchemish and Ur. H. 20·3 cm (7·9 in)

Below. Sassanian silver bowl. King Shapur II (AD 309–79) hunting stags. 4th c. AD Diam. 18 cm (7 in). The Sassanian dynasty was founded in 224 AD by Ardashir who successfully led a revolt against the Parthian king from his native province, Persis, in the heartland of Iran. Weakened by the internal strife it fell in 642 AD.

ETHNOGRAPHY

At the Museum of Mankind in Burlington Gardens (behind Piccadilly) and in a storehouse in East London is the Museum's immense anthropological collection of about a third of a million objects. This is the finest of its kind in the world and represents many aspects of the art and life of the indigenous peoples of Africa, Australia and the Pacific Islands, North and South America and parts of Asia and Europe. With the exception of the Cook collection and the Mixtec-Aztec turquoise mosaics this book has dealt almost exclusively with the collections at the main Museum in Bloomsbury, largely because it is difficult to do justice to both in a single volume. Ancient as well as recent and contemporary cultures are represented at the Museum of Mankind and much of the material is of particular interest since it was made prior to extensive European contact. Today the Department's main collecting focus is an emergency programme to acquire properly documented material on the life, production techniques and technologies of societies which are fast disappearing. The Departmental library, now combined with that previously belonging to the Royal Anthropological Institute is one of the largest in the world in this area.

Guatemalan textile (detail) from a collection acquired in 1981. Most of the pieces were woven in the 20th century on the traditional Maya back-strap loom and coloured with natural dyestuffs. In some cases the designs are Maya as well as Spanish symbols. For example the cross may represent the four corners of a maize field, the double-headed eagle a Mayan deity.

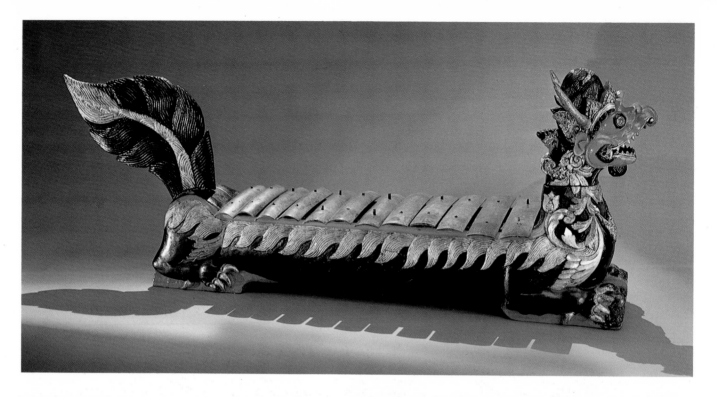

Above left. A saron demong (instrument with metal keys) from the 'Raffles Gamelan' a complete band of musical instruments from Java collected by Sir Thomas Stamford Raffles (1761–1826). The Raffles collection also includes intricately pierced and painted shadow puppets and theatrical masks. L. 100 cm (39.5 in)

Far left. Benin bronze figure of a hunter, an antelope slung over his shoulders.

Left. Asante umbrella top in the form of five *sankofa* birds, made of wood covered with gold foil. The king and major chiefs made extensive use of local gold and imported silver for their regalia. The first Asante objects to enter the collections came from T.E. Bowditch's mission to Ashanti in 1817.

Above. Lintel from a Mayan building at Yaxchilan, Mexico. This ancient civilisation flourished in South-Eastern Mexico, Yucatan, Guatemala and Belize. AD 600–800. H. 24.8 cm (9.7 in). The ceremonial sites of monumental stone architecture were abandoned and engulfed by tropical forest long before the coming of the Spaniards in the 16th c. The most important collections in the Museum were made by A.P. Maudslay between 1881 and 1894.

THE BRITISH MUSEUM

The Museum was founded on 7 June 1753 when King George II gave his assent to the first British Museum Act which, with relatively minor changes, was to guide the institution through its first two centuries. 'Whereas Sir Hans Sloane of Chelsea in the County of Middlesex, Baronet, having, through the Course of many Years, with great Labour and Expense, gathered together whatever could be procured, either in our own or Foreign Countries, that was rare and curious . . .' began the Act. Sir Hans Sloane (1660–1753) was one of the most noted collectors of his day, with a particular penchant for natural history. Not wishing to see his beloved collection dispersed (it amounted at his death to some 79,575 objects excluding the library and the plants in the herbarium) he bequeathed it on two months' option to various bodies in return for the payment of £20,000 to his two daughters. The terms of his will were to be overseen by a group of twenty-seven trustees.

First among the potential recipients was King George II for the nation. The King being rather indifferent, but the nation, or at least some of the trustees headed by the Speaker of the House of Commons, more enthusiastic, the decision was taken by Parliament to acquire Sloane's collection at no cost to the public purse by holding a lottery to raise the purchase price and buy a suitable repository. A new group of trustees headed, *ex officio*, by the Archbishop of Canterbury, the Lord Chan-

cellor and the Speaker of the House of Commons, was appointed by the Act; the lottery produced £95,194. 8s. 2d. and the new museum was in business. Two other founding collections were acquired. One was the library of manuscripts collected by the 'judicious and excellent antiquary' Sir Robert Bruce Cotton (1571–1631) and his descendants Sir Thomas (1594–1662) and Sir John (1621–1701) which had been given to the nation in 1700 and which included the magnificently illustrated eighth-century Lindisfarne Gospels, the manuscript of Beowulf and two of the four extant copies of Magna Carta. There was also, for £10,000, the Harleian collection of manuscripts which had been put together by the shrewd and unscrupulous Robert Harley, 1st Earl of Oxford (1661–1724) and his son Edward (1689–1741) the latter having gone through his wife's fortune of £400,000 in the process. (The Harleian library of printed books, prints and pamphlets had unfortunately been auctioned off). In 1756 George II donated the Royal Library of the kings and queens of England and with it came the privilege of copyright deposit (today vested in the British Library).

The Trustees purchased for £10,250 a fine but decaying mansion in semi-rural Bloomsbury – Montagu House, on the site of which the present Museum is still located. The seven acre site, once known as Bakers Field, had been sold to the Rt Hon. Ralph Montagu by the

The Encampment in the Museum Gardens, 5 August 1780, showing troops temporarily stationed there to suppress the violent Gordon Riots. The gardens which contained exotic plants had been opened to the public in 1757.

Print Room, Montagu House, etching by George Cruikshank, 1828. John Thomas Smith, the Keeper, stands on the left eulogising a print which is in a portfolio before six connoisseurs, who pay great attention, while a lady is quietly turning over the leaves of a book of prints opposite.

Bedford family in 1675 and it was Montagu's house which was the Museum's first home. The Trustees appointed staff and organised the collections into three Departments (Printed Books, Manuscripts and that *omnium gatherum* Natural & Artificial Productions). In 1757 they opened their fine gardens which stretched northwards behind the house and which were filled with exotic flora as an adjunct to the botanical collections and on 15 January 1759 the Trustees opened their doors to the public, the 'studious and curious' they were directed by the Act to admit. (The Act did not oblige the Trustees to permit a leisurely tour and early visitors appear to have been conducted at speed through the building in strictly controlled groups.)

In the early years the library and natural history collections rather overshadowed the rest but gradually the antiquities collections began to expand from Sloane's nucleus. The first mummy arrived in 1756 with other Egyptian antiquities bequeathed by Colonel William Lethieullier. From the three Pacific voyages made by Captain Cook between 1767 and 1779 came artefacts made by craftsmen as yet unaffected by European contact. In 1772 the Museum purchased Sir William Hamilton's incomparable collection of Greek vases, its first classical antiquities of any consequence. In 1799 the Reverend Clayton Mordaunt Cracherode bequeathed a choice library, a cabinet of coins, medals and gems, and an important series of original drawings. In 1802 George III presented the collection of Egyptian antiquities made by Napoleon's scientific expedition, among them the Rosetta stone.

All this was too much for cramped Montagu House – the floors were quite unsuited to such objects even had there been room. The Trustees' thoughts turned to the erection of a new building. Work started on a new gallery for the Egyptian collection in 1804, plans were revised to cope with a further acquisition, the Townley collection of classical sculpture. The new 'Townley Gallery', erected to the North-west of Montagu House in Palladian style, to the design of the Trustees' architect George Saunders (c.1762–1839) was opened by Queen Charlotte in 1808. Once the rebuilding started it never stopped and indeed appears to have gone on more or less continually until the present day.

With the application of more rigorous academic standards the Museum, always concerned with scientific enquiry, was now becoming even less of a cabinet of curiosities. The importance of the antiquities collections (the 'cuckoo in the nest' previously an appendix of natural history) was at last recognised by the establishment of a Department of Antiquities in 1807. In 1808 a Keeper of Prints and Drawings was attached to this Department, appointed in the aftermath of an unsavoury series of thefts by a gentleman who had insinuated himself into the good graces of the Keeper of Printed Books (in whose department this collection was then housed) by judicious gifts of fish and peas.

Montagu House was again bursting at the seams – the Centaurs, Lapiths, Greeks and Amazons from the Temple of Apollo at Bassae had arrived in 1815, Lord Elgin's collection was purchased by the government and presented to the Museum in 1816. Robert (later Sir Robert) Smirke (1781–1867) who designed Covent Garden Theatre and the Royal Mint was appointed to the Office of Works in 1815 and so became the Trustees' architect. He was first commissioned to design a temporary building for the Elgin collection. The Trustees first considered constructing two wings northwards but as their collection grew so their plans became more ambitious. Impetus was given to this expansion when in 1823 George IV presented his father's magnificent library of 62,250 volumes and 19,000 unbound tracts with the condition that it be kept distinct from the rest of the collection. Parliament voted £40,000 for a suitable repository. Smirke envisaged a grand quadrangular building in neo-classical style and his design was approved by the Trustees in 1823. Unfortunately government funds could only be made available in fits and starts so the great design was almost thirty years in the building. Smirke planned an austere classical edifice; by the time it was completed the style had gone out of favour and the interiors were a riot of Victorian colour. Work on the east wing began in 1823 and was completed in 1827.

In the illustration (handwritten annotations):

11.

lower diam. of Column 3f.
diam. of Base 7f.2½?.
total height of Column 43½

New Building of
British Mus
Jan
9 Ser

'2 and 300 masons with their labourers are now employed many of them working upon blocks of stone each from 5 to 10 tons weight' (Robert Smirke 1844). Shaping the Portland stone columns for the Colonnade. George Scharf the Elder c.1845.

This was the King's Library, one of the noblest rooms in London. The western and northern sections were erected in piecemeal fashion. A departure from the quadrangular scheme was the new Elgin Room completed parallel to the west wing. Eventually by 1847 the new entrance hall had opened and both the Townley Gallery and virtually all of Montagu House had gone, only the red brick foundations of the latter remaining below the great bulk of Smirke's 'tall, long, severe pigeon-haunted colonnade'. On Easter Monday 1837 the Museum had opened on its first public holiday and some 24,000 visitors turned up with consequent stress on the floors. Visitors of decent appearance had been permitted to wander unescorted since 1810, henceforth the Museum was assured of a popular clientele.

Yet again the new building was hardly completed when Layard's Assyrian discoveries came crowding in, the first colossal bull and lion arriving in 1849. The Library too expanded in the mid-nineteenth century as the copyright laws were strictly enforced. In 1846 Robert Smirke was succeeded as Trustees' architect by his younger brother Sydney (1798–1877). Sydney, with the Principal Librarian Antonio Panizzi (1797–1879) in 1852 produced a scheme for a domed Reading Room to fill Robert's quadrangle. Work started in 1854 and the room was opened in 1857 'a temple of marvellous dimensions, rich in blue, white and gold', the future haunt of such notables as Karl Marx, Thomas Hardy, G.B. Shaw, Rudyard Kipling and V.I. Lenin (alias Jacob Richter).

In 1824 the Museum had received the Payne Knight Bequest of books, bronzes, coins and drawings (including one of the finest Claude Lorrain collections in existence) which further enriched the Department of Antiquities. In 1842 came the Lycian marbles, the tombs and other memorials of the Kings of Lycia (among them the Nereid monument) which had been discovered at Xanthos by Charles Fellows. The sculptures from the Mausoleum of Halicarnassus excavated by C.T. Newton arrived in 1856–7. With its concentration on classical and Biblical antiquities the name 'British' Museum was still in one respect a misnomer for little attempt had been made to collect national antiquities and certain trustees and staff nursed the hope that they and ethnography could be found a home elsewhere. Such was the neglect that by 1850 all the antiquities of ancient Britain and Gaul

Reception of the remains of the Tomb of Maussollos from Halicarnassus in 1857.

'Ceremony of removing a piece of Sculpture', Randolph Caldecott (1846–86). The bearded figure in the top hat is Sir Charles Newton, Keeper of Greek and Roman Antiquities, 1861–85 'not strictly speaking a popular chief; his manner was severe and autocratic . . . but . . . he was universally respected'.

could be collected in four cases in one room with a mere thirteen more cases for later British and Medieval antiquities. However a strong lobby, supported by the Royal Commission of 1849–50 was determined to change this. The donation of a collection of antiquities from Stanwick by Lord Prudhoe with the condition that a room be set aside for British material and the subsequent appointment of Augustus Wollaston Franks in 1851 were to lead to a transformation which took advantage of new developments in European archaeology triggered off by Danish, French and English research.

Prints and Drawings had been a separate department since 1836. In 1860 the resignation of the eighty-year-old Keeper of Antiquities Edward Hawkins provided an opportune moment for the Trustees to break up his unwieldy department which embraced, *inter alia*, a bewildering combination of coins, ethnography, Egyptian mummies, Greek marbles and Assyrian bulls. The new division reflected the Victorians' sense of priorities: Greek and Roman Antiquities, Coins and Medals and, the *omnium gatherum* on this occasion, 'Oriental Antiquities' which in spite of its name included a sub-department of British and Medieval Antiquities (now becoming a focus of serious study and collection), Ethnography (still despised, specimens being accepted by the Museum but never deliberately purchased), Egyptian and Assyrian antiquities (which became a separate department in 1886). British and Medieval with Ethnography became independent under Franks in 1866. Franks laid the basis of the Chinese and Japanese collections and ensured that the Museum would be the first in Europe to admit the east as a suitable field for archaeological and art historical research. He was also responsible for the acquisition of the Christy collection of some 10,000 items of prehistory and ethnography.

The western galleries were being built up

The Print Room in the White Wing before its transfer to the King Edward VII building in the 1920s. In the foreground is the poet Laurence Binyon (1869–1943), later Keeper of the Department 1932–33. This room is now the Medieval Gallery.

piecemeal, often by roofing over suitable spaces (in one area the outer drainpipes of Smirke's original building still exist, behind the plaster, now buried deep inside the Museum). The Front Hall was extended northwards in 1877 to take the Lycian sculptures. In the 1880s came the first major break in the Museum's collections: the removal of the natural history specimens to South Kensington. 'Out with weazles, ferrets, skunks; Elephants, come, pack your trunks' had *Punch* earlier declared, 'Here, in future, folks shall scan; Nothing but the works of Man'.

Scientific archaeology was developing; the Museum financed excavations in the 1860s to Cyrenaica, Sardis, Rhodes and Halicarnassus. John Turtle Wood excavated at Ephesus between 1863 and 1875 uncovering the successive temples of Diana. The Museum was active in Mesopotamia, Asia Minor, Cyprus and Egypt. Yet more space for such material was provided by the completion in 1884 to the designs of Sir John Taylor (1833–1912) of a wing to the east of the main building. This was financed from the bequest of one William White who had died as long ago as 1823, his widow's life interest expiring only in 1879.

In 1895 the Trustees purchased from the Bedford Estate the freeholds of all the surrounding buildings. Although there were grandiose plans for expansion drawn up by John James Burnet (1859–1938), only the northern scheme materialised with the erection of the King Edward VII galleries on which work started in 1906. These were opened in

1914, financed by the Treasury and a bequest from Vincent Stuckey Lean, a barrister and expert on proverbs of all nations. After the War the Trustees decided to request the government Department of Scientific and Industrial Research to report on the condition of objects which had been in storage for safe keeping and offer assistance in restoration and preservation. A laboratory was sanctioned as a short term experiment in 1922. Its work was so successful that it was made permanent and taken over by the Trustees in 1931 and is now the oldest such laboratory in continuous existence in the world.

After the First World War excavations resumed in the Middle East, most spectacularly at Ur. In the 1930s funds were provided by Sir Joseph Duveen (1869–1939) for the erection of a worthy home for the sculptures of the Parthenon to be designed by John Russell Pope. The building was completed in 1938 but its opening was delayed by the outbreak of the Second World War. Planning for the evacuation of the nation's art treasures had been completed long before 1939 and towards the end of August the order to move was given. All easily movable material of first importance, including the whole collection of coins and medals, had gone in a few days. The removal of heavier items took longer. Although the building was badly damaged by incendiaries in 1941 the antiquities collections were safe.

Rebuilding and reinstalling the dispersed collections took up much of the Museum's resources in the postwar years and, in line with advances in scholarship, there was some

Objects being moved to safety in an Underground railway tunnel following the outbreak of war.

Aerial view of the Museum site. The surrounding buildings were purchased by the Trustees from the Bedford Estate in 1895.

further rearrangement of the Departments. Ethnography, at last recognised as a proper discipline, became fully independent in 1946. The Egyptian collections separated from those of Western Asia in 1955. In 1969 the old 'British and Medieval' department split in two to form Prehistoric and Romano-British and Medieval and Later Antiquities. In 1970 the ethnography collection moved to a temporary home at the Museum of Mankind in Burlington Gardens off Piccadilly.

In 1963 a new British Museum Act came into force, replacing that of 1753 and succeeding provisions. The Board of Trustees was slimmed down from fifty-one to twenty-five. The Sovereign continues to appoint one Trustee, fifteen are provided by the Prime Minister, five elected by the Board and one each is nominated by the British Academy, Royal Academy, Royal Society and Society of Antiquaries.

The second major upheaval in the Museum's history came in 1973 when the library departments (Printed Books, Manuscripts and Oriental Manuscripts & Printed Books) split off to form part of a new body, – the British Library. Parts continue in the Museum building, as sitting tenants, but the intention is that they will be gone to a purpose-built library near St Pancras station around the turn of the century. Today therefore the Museum consists almost entirely of the successors of the old Department of Antiquities.

The second half of the twentieth century has seen a major expansion in the Museum's public services – the establishment of education and design sections and of a publishing company. The latest major addition to the building is Colin St-John Wilson's 'New Wing' formally opened in 1980. The Egyptian Sculpture Gallery was redesigned with the assistance of funds from private benefactors, including the sculptor Henry Moore, and opened in 1981. The Wolfson Galleries of Classical Sculpture and Inscriptions were completed in 1985.

Since its foundation the Museum has witnessed ten reigns (numbering among these sovereigns generous benefactors and four Trustees). It has survived more or less unscathed numerous wars, revolutions and civil insurrections. After two hundred and thirty years it is still perhaps the greatest museum in the world.

Bibliography

TREASURE

1. Treasure Trove

I.M. STEAD
Celtic Art
British Museum Publications 1985

EDWARD BESLY and ROGER BLAND
The Cunetio Treasure, Roman Coinage of the Third Century AD
British Museum Publications, 1983

CATHERINE JOHNS and TIMOTHY POTTER
The Thetford Treasure: Roman Jewellery and Silver
British Museum Publications, 1983

K.S. PAINTER
The Mildenhall Treasure: Roman Silver from East Anglia
British Museum Publications, 1977

K.S. PAINTER
The Water Newton Early Christian Silver
British Museum Publications, 1977

GEORGE HILL
Treasure Trove in Law and Practice from the earliest time to the present day
Clarendon Press, 1936

CHARLES R. BEARD
The Romance of Treasure Trove
Marston, 1933

2. The Treasure of the River Oxus

B.A. LITVINSKIY and T.R. PICHIKIYAN
'The Temple of the Oxus', *Journal of the Royal Asiatic Society*, 2, 1981, pp. 133–67

R.D. BARNETT
'The Art of Bactria and the Treasure of the Oxus', *Iranica Antiqua*, VIII, 1968, pp. 34–53

O.M. DALTON
The Treasure of the Oxus, 3rd edn
British Museum Publications, 1964

A.R. BELLINGER
'The Coins from the Treasure of the Oxus', *ANS Museum Notes*, X, 1962, pp. 51–67

A. CUNNINGHAM
'Relics from Ancient Persia in Gold, Silver and Copper'
Journal of the Asiatic Society of Bengal, 1881, pp. 151–86; 1883 pp. 64–7, 258–60

3. Turquoise Mosaics from the Aztec Empire

H.B. NICHOLSON with ELOISE QUINOÑES
Art of Aztec Mexico: Treasures of Tenochtitlan
Washington D.C., 1983

ESTHER PASZTORY
Aztec Art
New York, 1983

ELIZABETH CARMICHAEL
Turquoise Mosaics from Mexico
British Museum Publications, 1970

BERNAL DIAZ DEL CASTILLO
The Discovery and Conquest of Mexico, (from an original manuscript)
Farrar, Straus and Giroux, 1956

MARSHALL H. SAVILLE
Turquois Mosaic Art in Ancient Mexico
Museum of the American Indian, Heye Foundation, 1922

EDWARD B. TYLOR
Anahuac: or Mexico and the Mexicans, Ancient and Modern
Longman, Green, Longman & Roberts, 1861

BURIED CIVILISATIONS

4. Amelia Edwards and the Egypt Exploration Society

T.G.H. JAMES (ed.)
Excavating in Egypt, The Egypt Exploration Society 1882–1982
British Museum Publications, 1982

AMELIA B. EDWARDS
A Thousand Miles up the Nile
Longmans, 1877 (reprinted by Century Publishing with an introduction by Quentin Crewe, 1982)

5. Excavations at Nimrud

JULIAN READE
Assyrian Sculpture
British Museum Publications, 1983

SETON LLOYD
Foundations in the Dust: The Story of Mesopotamian Exploration
Thames & Hudson, revised edn 1980

MAX MALLOWAN
The Nimrud Ivories
British Museum Publications, 1978

MAX MALLOWAN
Nimrud and its Remains
Collins, (2 vols), 1966

R.D. BARNETT
Assyrian Palace Reliefs in the British Museum
British Museum Publications, 1970

R.D. BARNETT
'Lady Layard's Jewellery'
Archaeology in the Levant, (eds P.R.S. Moorey and P.J. Parr)

AUSTEN HENRY LAYARD
A Popular Account of Discoveries at Nineveh (abridged by him from his larger work)
John Murray, 1851

6. The Rosetta Stone and the Decipherment of Hieroglyphs

CAROL ANDREWS
The Rosetta Stone
British Museum Publications, 1981

7. The Fourth-Century Hinton St Mary Mosaic Pavement

T.W. POTTER
Roman Britain
British Museum Publications, 1983

DAVID S. NEAL
Roman Mosaics in Britain
Britannia Monograph series no. 1 Society for the Promotion of Roman Studies, 1981

K.S. PAINTER
'The Roman Site at Hinton St Mary, Dorset' and C.C. TAYLOR
'The Later History of the Roman Site at Hinton St Mary, Dorset'
British Museum Quarterly, XXXII, 1967

J.M.C. TOYNBEE
'A New Roman Mosaic Pavement found in Dorset'
Journal of Roman Studies, LXIV, 1964, pp. 7–14

SCULPTURE

8. The Bust of Ramesses the Great and Giovanni Belzoni

T.G.H. JAMES and W.V. DAVIES
Egyptian Sculpture
British Museum Publications, 1983

STANLEY MAYES
The Great Belzoni
Putnam, 1959

COLIN CLAIR
Giovanni Belzoni: Strong Man Egyptologist
Oldbourne, 1957

G. BELZONI
Narrative of the Operations and Recent Discoveries within the Pyramids, Temples, Tombs, and Excavations in Egypt and Nubia; and of a Journey to the Coast of the Red Sea, in search of the Ancient Berenice; and another to the Oasis of Jupiter Ammon
John Murray, 1820

9. The Lion Hunt of Ashurbanipal

JULIAN READE
Assyrian Sculpture
British Museum Publications, 1983

R.D. BARNETT
Assyrian Palace Reliefs in the British Museum
British Museum Publications, 1970

10. The Townley Collection of Classical Sculpture

B.F. COOK
'The Townley Marbles in Westminster and Bloomsbury'
BM Yearbook, 2, Collectors and Collections, pp. 34–78
British Museum Publications, 1977

B.F. COOK
The Townley Marbles
British Museum Publications, 1985

11. 'Hindoo' Stuart and the Bridge Collection of Indian Sculpture

JORG FISCH
'Charles Stuart: a solitary Vindicator of Hinduism'
Journal of the Royal Asiatic Society, June 1985

RAMAPRASAD CHANDA
Medieval Indian Sculpture in the British Museum
Kegan Paul, 1936

Obituary, *Gentleman's Magazine*, Nov. 1828, pp. 606–7 (reprinted from *The Indian Gazette*)

12. The Bodhisattva Tara

J. VAN LOHUIZEN DE LEEUW
Sri Lanka, Ancient Arts
Commonwealth Institute Exhibition, London, 1981

SENARAT PARANAVITANA
Art of the Ancient Sinhalese
Colombo, 1971

VINCENT A. SMITH
A History of Fine Art in India and Ceylon
Oxford, 1911

13. Hoa-Haka-Nana-Ia ('Breaking Waves'): A Statue from Easter Island

THOR HEYERDAHL, *Aku-Aku*
The Secret of Easter Island
George Allen & Unwin, 1958
The voyage of Captain Don Felipe Gonzalez in the Ship of the Line San Lorenzo, with the Frigate Santa Rosalia in company to Easter Island in 1770–1. Preceded by an Extract from Mynheer Jacob Roggeveen's Official Log of his discovery of and visit to Easter Island in 1722. Transcribed, translated and edited by Bolton Glanville Corney, *Hakluyt Society*, 1908

14. The 'Roubiliac Shakespeare' and the actor David Garrick

HELEN R. SMITH
David Garrick 1717–1779, A brief Account
British Library, 1979

HUGH TAIT
'Garrick, Shakespeare and Wilkes'
British Museum Quarterly, XXIV, 1961, pp. 100–7

KATHERINE A. ESDAILE
The Life and Works of Louis François Roubiliac
Oxford University Press, 1928

VOYAGES OF DISCOVERY

15. Captain James Cook

J.C.H. KING
Artificial Curiosities from the North West Coast of America: Native American Artefacts in the British Museum collected on the Third Voyage of Captain James Cook and acquired through Sir Joseph Banks
British Museum Publications, 1981

HUGH COBBE (ed.)
Cook's Voyages and the Peoples of the Pacific
British Museum Publications, 1979

T.C. MITCHELL (ed.)
'Captain Cook and the South Pacific'
BM Yearbook 3, 1979

J.C. BEAGLEHOLE
The Life of Captain James Cook
Black, 1974

B.A.L. CRANSTONE and J.H. GOWERS
'The Tahitian Mourner's Dress: A Discovery and a Description'
British Museum Quarterly, XXXII, 1967–8, pp. 138–44

J.C. BEAGLEHOLE (ed.)
'The Journals of Captain James Cook on his voyages of discovery'
Hakluyt Society, 3 vols, 1955–69

TEMPLES AND TOMBS

16. Death in Egypt

R.O. FAULKNER
The Ancient Egyptian Book of the Dead, (ed. Carol Andrews)
British Museum Publications, 1985

CAROL ANDREWS
Egyptian Mummies
British Museum Publications, 1984

MORRIS BIERBRIER
The Tomb-Builders of the Pharaohs
British Museum Publications, 1982

A.J.S. SPENCER
Death in Ancient Egypt
Penguin, 1982

W.R. DAWSON and P.H.K. GRAY
Catalogue of Egyptian Antiquities in the British Museum I: Mummies and human remains
British Museum Publications, 1968

17. The Discovery of the Royal Cemetery at Ur

LEONARD WOOLLEY
Ur 'of the Chaldees': The final account, Excavations at Ur, revised and updated by P.R.S. Moorey
Herbert Press, 1982

MAX MALLOWAN
Mallowan's Memoirs
Collins, 1977

T.C. MITCHELL
Sumerian Art Illustrated by objects from Ur and Al-'Ubaid
British Museum Publications, 1969

LEONARD WOOLLEY
Ur of the Chaldees: A record of seven years of Excavation
Penguin, revised 1950
Catalogue published in 10 volumes between 1927 and 1976; *Texts* in 8 volumes 1928–74 by The British Museum and the University of Pennsylvania

18. Canon Greenwell and the 'Folkton Drums'

I.H. LONGWORTH
Prehistoric Britain
British Museum Publications, 1985

I.A. KINNES and I.H. LONGWORTH
Catalogue of the Greenwell Collection
British Museum Publications, 1986.

J.C. HODGSON
'Memoir of the Rev. William Greenwell, DCl, FRS, FSA, A Vice-President'
Archaeologia Aeliana, Society of Antiquaries of Newcastle upon Tyne, 3rd series, 15, 1918

WILLIAM GREENWELL
'Recent Researches in Barrows in Yorkshire, Wiltshire, Berkshire, etc'
Archaeologia 52, 1890

19. The Rillaton Gold Cup

C.F.C. HAWKES
'The Rillaton Gold Cup . . . Note Addressed to HRH The Prince of Wales'
Antiquity, LVII, July 1983, pp. 124–6

R.A. SMITH
'The Rillaton Gold Cup'
British Museum Quarterly, XI, 1936–7

EDWARD SMIRKE
'Some Account of the Discovery of a Gold Cup in a Barrow in Cornwall, AD 1837
The Archaeological Journal, XXIV, 1867, pp. 189–202

20. The Mausoleum at Halicarnassus: One of the Seven Wonders of the Ancient World

SIMON HORNBLOWER
Mausolus
Oxford University Press, 1982

G.B. WAYWELL
The Free-Standing Sculptures of the Mausoleum at Halicarnassus in the British Museum: A Catalogue
British Museum Publications, 1978

C.T. NEWTON
Travels & Discoveries in the Levant
Day and Son, 1865

C.T. NEWTON
A History of Discoveries at Halicarnassus, Cnidus and Branchidae, 1862

21. Lord Elgin and the Sculptures of the Parthenon

B.F. COOK
The Elgin Marbles
British Museum Publications, 1984

WILLIAM ST CLAIR
Lord Elgin and the Marbles
Oxford University Press, 1967 (revised 1983)

SUSAN WOODFORD
The Parthenon
Cambridge University Press, 1981
'Report of the Select Committee appointed to inquire into the expediency of purchasing the Collection mentioned in the Earl of Elgin's Petition to the House, etc.' *Parliamentary Papers*, 1816, III, p. 49

22. The Monument of Julius Classicianus, Procurator of Britain

PETER MARSDEN
Roman London
Thames and Hudson, 1980

F. COTTRILL
'A Bastion of the Town Wall of London, and the Sepulchral Monument of the Procurator Julius Classicianus'
Antiquaries Journal, XVI, 1936, pp. 1–7

C.F.C. HAWKES
'The Sepulchral Monument of Julius Classicianus'
British Museum Quarterly, X, no. 2, 1935, pp. 53–5

23. The Sutton Hoo Ship Burial

RUPERT BRUCE-MITFORD
The Sutton Hoo Ship Burial:
vol. I *Excavations, Background, the Ship, Dating and Inventory*, 1975
vol. II *Arms, Armour and Regalia*, 1978
vol. III *Late Roman and Byzantine silver, hanging bowls, drinking vessels, cauldron and other*

containers, textiles, the lyre, pottery bottle and
other items, (ed. Angela Care Evans), 1983

KATHERINE EAST
A King's Treasure: The Sutton Hoo Ship Burial
Kestrel Books, 1982 (for children)

RUPERT BRUCE-MITFORD
The Sutton Hoo Ship Burial, A Handbook, 3rd edn
British Museum Publications, 1979

POTTERY AND PORCELAIN

24. The Godman Collection of Islamic Pottery

MICHAEL ROGERS
'The Godman Bequest of Islamic Pottery'
Apollo, July 1984

OLIVER HOARE
'The Godman Collection'
Christie's Review of the Year, 1983, pp. 390–4

ARTHUR LANE
Later Islamic Pottery: Persia, Syria, Egypt, Turkey
Faber and Faber, 1957

ARTHUR LANE
*Early Islamic Pottery: Mesopotamia, Egypt and
Persia*
Faber and Faber, 1954

THOMAS DEGREY
Frederick Du Cane Godman, an appreciation, 1919

FREDERICK DU CANE GODMAN
*The Godman Collection of Oriental and Spanish
Pottery and Glass 1865–1900*
Printed for private circulation, 1901

25. The Addis Gift of Chinese Porcelain

JESSICA RAWSON
Chinese Ornament: The Lotus and the Dragon
British Museum Publications, 1984

NIGEL WOOD
'Chinese Porcelain'
Ceramic Review, 89, 1984

JESSICA RAWSON
'A Gift for Ceramics'
TLS, 24 June, 1983

J.M. ADDIS
Chinese Porcelain from the Addis Collection
British Museum Publications, 1979

26. The 'Cleopatra' Vases from Chelsea

J.V.G. MALLET
'The Site of the Chelsea Porcelain Factory'
English Ceramic Circle Transactions
9, part 1, 1973

R.J. CHARLESTON (ed.)
English Porcelain 1745–1850
Ernest Benn, 1965

J.V.G. MALLET
'Two Documented Chelsea Gold-Anchor Vases'
Victoria & Albert Museum Bulletin
1, no. 1, 1965 (the Foundling and Chesterfield
pair)

THE ART OF THE CRAFTSMAN

27. The Portland Vase

AILEEN DAWSON
Masterpieces of Wedgwood in the British Museum
British Museum Publications, 1984

D.L. HAYNES
The Portland Vase
British Museum Publications, 1975

BRIAN FOTHERGILL
Sir William Hamilton: Envoy Extraordinary
Faber and Faber, 1969

28. The Hull Grundy Gift of Jewellery

CHARLOTTE GERE, JUDY RUDOE, HUGH TAIT (ed.)
TIMOTHY WILSON
*The Art of the Jeweller: A Catalogue of the Hull
Grundy Gift to the British Museum: Jewellery,
Engraved Gems and Goldsmith's Work* (2 vols)
British Museum Publications, 1984

VIVIENNE BECKER
'Profile: Anne Hull Grundy'
Art and Auction
November, 1982

HUGH TAIT and CHARLOTTE GERE
*The Jeweller's Art: An Introduction to the Hull
Grundy Gift to the British Museum*
British Museum Publications, 1978

29. The Twelfth-Century Lewis Chessmen

MICHAEL TAYLOR
The Lewis Chessmen
British Museum Publications, 1978

DONALD M. LIDDELL
Chessmen
Harrap, 1938

FREDERIC MADDEN
'Historical Remarks on the Introduction of
Chess into Europe and on the ancient
Chessmen discovered in the Isle of Lewis'
Archaeologia XXIV, 1832, pp. 203–91

30. Clocks and Watches

HUGH TAIT
Clocks and Watches
British Museum Publications, 1983

31. The Marlborough Gold Ice Pails

VIRGINIA COWLES
The Great Marlborough and his Duchess
Weidenfeld and Nicolson, 1983

HUGH TAIT
'The Gold Ice Pails of the Marlboroughs'
National Art-Collections Fund Review, 1983, pp.
84–5

DAVID BRONTË GREEN
Sarah Duchess of Marlborough
Collins, 1967

WINSTON S. CHURCHILL
Marlborough: His Life and Times
Harrap, 2 vols, 1947 (first published in 4 vols
in 1933 to 1938)

32. Mrs Delany's Flower Mosaics

RUTH HAYDEN
Mrs Delany: her life and her flowers
British Museum Publications, 1980

GEORGE PASTON
*Mrs Delany, (Mary Granville), A Memoir
1700–88*
Grant Richards, 1900

AUGUSTA HALL (Baroness Llanover) (ed.)
*The Autobiography and Correspondence of Mary
Granville, Mrs Delany*
6 vols, Richard Bentley, 1st series, 1861; 2nd
series 1862

THE COLLECTING PASSION

33. Sir Hans Sloane: Founder of the British Museum

H.J. BRAUNHOLTZ
Sir Hans Sloane and Ethnography
Trustees of the British Museum, 1970

E. ST JOHN BROOKS
Sir Hans Sloane: The Great Collector and his Circle
Batchworth Press, 1954
British Museum Quarterly, XVIII, no. 1
Trustees of the British Museum, 1953

34. The Retiring Collector: The Reverend Clayton Mordaunt Cracherode

Obituary, *Gentleman's Magazine*, April 1977, pp.
354–6

35. John Malcolm of Poltalloch: Collector of Old Master Drawings

J.C. ROBINSON
'Our Public Art Museums: A Retrospect'
The Nineteenth Century Review, December 1897,
pp. 940–64

J.C. ROBINSON
*Descriptive Catalogue of Drawings by the Old
Masters, forming the collection of John Malcolm of
Poltalloch, Esq.*
1st edn 1868, 2nd edn 1876, privately printed

36. Sir Augustus Wollaston Franks: Victorian Polymath

DAVID M. WILSON
*The Forgotten Collector: Augustus Wollaston
Franks of the British Museum*
Thames & Hudson, 1984 (16th Walter
Neurath Memorial Lecture)

37. Baron Ferdinand de Rothschild and the Waddesdon Bequest

HUGH TAIT
The Waddesdon Bequest
British Museum Publications, 1981

MRS JAMES DE ROTHSCHILD
The Rothschilds at Waddesdon Manor
Collins, 1979

THE MUSEUM AND ITS HISTORY

The British Museum, Report of the Trustees
Trustees of the British Museum/British
Museum Publications, published triennially
since 1966, most recent 1981–4

The British Museum and its Collections
British Museum Publications, 1982

MARJORIE CAYGILL
The Story of the British Museum
British Museum Publications, 1981

A.E. GUNTHER
*The Founders of Science at the British Museum,
1753–1900*
Halesworth Press, 1980

EDWARD MILLER
That Noble Cabinet: A History of the British Museum
Deutsch, 1973

J. MORDAUNT CROOK
The British Museum: a case-study in architectural politics
Allen Lane, 1972

FRANK FRANCIS (ed.)
Treasures of the British Museum
Thames & Hudson, 1971

EDWARD EDWARDS
Lives of the Founders of the British Museum with its chief Augmentors and other Benefactors 1750–1870
Trubner & Co., reprinted by Burt Franklin, 1969

The British Museum Quarterly, XVIII, nos 1–4
Trustees of the British Museum, 1953 (bicentenary edition)

ARUNDELL ESDAILE
The British Museum Library
Allen and Unwin, 1946

ROBERT COWTAN
Memories of the British Museum
Bentley, 1872

JOHN and ANDREW VAN RYMSDYK
Museum Britannicum
I. Moore, 1778

Captions to part-title illustrations

Illustration pages 14–15. Part of the Cuerdale hoard found in a bank of the River Ribble in Lancashire in 1840. Probably abandoned by a Viking army around 903 AD, it is the largest Viking silver hoard yet found in Britain or Scandinavia and consisted of over 7,000 coins, $725\frac{1}{2}$ ounces of silver ingots and $103\frac{1}{2}$ ounces of silver ornaments. When laid out after its discovery it covered an entire room. Part was presented to the Museum by Queen Victoria.

Illustration pages 36–37. 'The drums and shrill pipes of the Kurdish musicians increased the din and confusion . . . (the women's) ear-piercing *tahlehl*, added to the enthusiasm of the men . . . Away went the bull . . . (Layard). Layard and Rassam directing the lowering on to rollers of the winged bull from the North-West Palace at Nimrud. 18 March 1847. Large scale Assyrian excavation began in the 1840s with spectacular discoveries such as this colossal gateway figure.

Illustration pages 56–57 A Section of the Townley gallery. (Left) A reclining naiad or water nymph, probably 2nd c. AD. (Right) The 'Townley Venus', proconnesian marble, 1st or 2nd c. AD, adapted from a lost Greek original of the 4th c. BC, found at Ostia in 1775.

Illustration pages 88–89. The death of Captain Cook in Kealakekua Bay, Hawaii, February 1779. Cook made three momentous voyages of discovery starting in 1768, his ships ranging from Antarctica to Alaska. In 1774 his journal recorded the spirit which animated many explorers: 'I whose ambition leads me not only father than any other man has been before me, but as far as I think it possible for man to go'. Engraving after a drawing by John Webber.

Illustration pages 98–99. The Parthenon from the east in 1765 showing a mosque inside the building and the surrounding houses which cluttered the Acropolis. Unfinished watercolour by William Pars.

Illustration pages 136–37. A contrasting selection from the Museum's collection of pottery and porcelain (not to scale). (*Left-Right*) Wedgwood creamware plate *c.*1760–75 (diam. 25 cm (9.8 in)). A blue jasper ware vase and cover presented to the Museum by Josiah Wedgwood 1786, known as the 'Pegasus Vase' (H. 46 cm (18.1 in)). Creamware plate from the 'service with the green frog' made for the Empress Catherine the Great of Russia 1773–4, (diam. 24.9 cm (9.8 in)). Black figured amphora by the potter Andokides made in Athens 530–520 BC, the painting attributed to Psiax (H. 39.5 cm (15.5 in)).

Illustration pages 150–51. A 'garden' of jewellery from the Hull Grundy Gift.

Illustration pages 180–1. The Museum's ethnographical galleries towards the end of the 19th c. – 'for purposes of studious research to work out problems of ancient art none of them are superfluous' (Trustees' report, 1885)

Illustration pages 226–7. The Museum's first home – Montagu House in Bloomsbury purchased 1754. Originally designed by Robert Hooke (1635–1703) for the Rt Hon. Ralph Montagu on the lines of a French nobleman's hotel, it was gutted by fire in 1686 but rebuilt on almost identical lines. The house was demolished in the 1840s when the Smirke building was erected.

Photographic acknowledgements

Unless otherwise indicated below, the colour photographs in this book were taken by Lee Boltin, © British Museum Publications and Lee Boltin 1985, and the black-and-white illustrations were provided by the British Museum Photographic Service, © The Trustees of the British Museum 1985. We offer them our warmest thanks. In addition kind permission has been granted by the following individuals and institutions to reproduce their photographs.

Aerofilms Ltd p.233 bottom; Lee Boltin pp.26 bottom, 31, 33, 50, 72 top, 93 bottom, 115, 119, 124 centre, 125, 225; British Library pp.92, 93; British Museum pp.14–15, 90, 100–1, 104, 131, 134, 142, 150–1, 170 left, 171, 175, 178, 179, 186, 187 top, 190, 194, 195, 198 bottom, 199, 202, 206, 209, 212 top left, 216 top and right, 217 bottom, 220; The Dean and Chapter of Durham Cathedral p.113; Egypt Exploration Society pp.40, 41; Robert Harding Picture Library p.83; Illustrated London News Picture Library p.111; Lord Lambton and the Trustees of the Lambton Picture Settlement (photo National Portrait Gallery) p.85; Dugald Malcolm p.192; National Army Museum (photo Barnes & Webster Ltd) p.78; National Maritime Museum p.82; National Portrait Gallery pp.59, 84, 176; Scottish Tourist Board p.165; Alan Sorrell p.128; National Trust Waddesdon Manor pp.201, 205; Towneley Hall Art Gallery and Museums, Burnley Borough Council p.71; Gordon Tregear p.141; Universal Pictorial Press and Agency Ltd p.144; Viscount Wimborne p.44; Woolf-Greenham Collection (photo Barrie Aughton Studio) p.116.

Index